THIRD WAVE FEMINISM AND TELEVISION

READING CONTEMPORARY TELEVISION

SERIES EDITORS: KIM AKASS AND JANET McCABE

The *Reading Contemporary Television* series aims to offer a varied, intellectually groundbreaking and often polemical response to what is happening in television today. This series is distinct in that it sets out to immediately comment upon the TV *zeitgeist* while providing an intellectual and creative platform for thinking differently and ingeniously writing about contemporary television culture. The books in the series seek to establish a critical space where new voices are heard and fresh perspectives offered. Innovation is encouraged and intellectual curiosity demanded.

PUBLISHED AND FORTHCOMING

THIRD WAVE FEMINISM AND TELEVISION

JANE PUTS IT IN A BOX

EDITED BY MERRI LISA JOHNSON

I.B. TAURIS

LONDON · NEW YORK

Published in 2007 by
I.B.Tauris & Co. Ltd
6 Salem Rd, London W2 4BU
175 Fifth Avenue, New York NY 10010
www.ibtauris.com

In the United States and Canada distributed by Palgrave Macmillan,
a division of St. Martin's Press, 175 Fifth Avenue, New York, NY 10010

ISBN   978 1 84511 245 5 (Hb)
ISBN   978 1 84511 246 2 (Pb)

A full CIP record for this book is available from the British Library
A full CIP record for this book is available from the Library of Congress
Library of Congress catalog card: available

Typeset in Monotype Garamond by illuminati, Grosmont,
www.illuminatibooks.co.uk
Printed and bound in Great Britain by
TJ International Ltd, Padstow, Cornwall

CONTENTS

ACKNOWLEDGEMENTS

The seeds of this collection were planted in the process of editing a special issue of *The Scholar and Feminist Online*, so my gratitude goes first to the Barnard Center for Research on Women and the work that Deborah Siegel, Janet Jakobsen, and David Hopson put into that issue, as well as to Janet McCabe and Kim Akass, who contributed essays to the issue and solicited the current book manuscript for their new series, Reading Contemporary Television, at I.B. Tauris, based on that issue. Second, the library assistance of Margaret Fain, Allison Faix, and Sharon Tully literally made this book possible, so I offer them my sincerest thanks. For her editorial assistance and secretarial skills, Leigh Hendrix merits serious gratitude as well. I would also like to thank the Faculty Welfare and Development Committee at Coastal Carolina University for funding a research grant that allowed me a summer of intensive work (and a nice book budget, to boot). Finally, I am grateful to each of the contributors for producing new work in the field of feminist television criticism and for working collaboratively with such vigor towards a third wave feminist media theory.

FOREWORD

RHONDA HAMMER

AND DOUGLAS KELLNER

The studies in *Third Wave Feminism and Television* break new ground in TV criticism and take on a panorama of television phenomena that have been generally avoided, or barely touched upon, by mainstream television studies. Their focus is on a number of innovative television programs that go beyond the norms and conventions of standard network fare. Series engaged range from the edgier programs aired on HBO like *The Sopranos*, *Oz*, and *Six Feet Under* and Showtime's *The L Word* and *Queer as Folk* to network series like *Buffy the Vampire Slayer* and the reality-TV show *The Bachelor*.

Neither wholly embracing nor rejecting the pleasure of viewing these programs, the studies assembled here problematize categories like "the audience" and "pleasure," as well as gender, sexuality, and TV criticism itself. As Merri Lisa Johnson notes in the Introduction to the book, from the beginning much feminist TV criticism rejected wholesale disavowal of television as a "bad object," yet deployed the tools of feminist theory and criticism to engage television as requiring critical engagement. Taking up recent developments in feminist theory, queer theory, and postmodern cultural studies, the contributors to *Third Wave Feminism and Television* step over the stalemated dichotomies of "positive" and "negative" gender role models in media studies, searching for a more complex voice for feminist television studies.

In this collection, third wave feminism meets television head-on, and the results expand TV criticism as well as feminist theory. "Third wave" feminism is a term that has been used by a number of women, as well as popular media, to describe contemporary versions of feminisms that evolved over the past decades. Some have associated this term with young feminists who were influenced by the legacies of feminism's second wave, but did not feel fully accounted for by it. Yet the term is highly contested and has been employed to describe a number of diverse feminist and anti-feminist theories and practices. On the whole, the Third Wave approach to television studies employed in the writings of *Third Wave Feminism and Television* embodies the apt definition of Leslie Heywood and Jennifer Drake in *Third Wave Agenda*. As they explain it: "Third wave feminists often take cultural production and sexual politics as key sites of struggle, seeking to use desire and pleasure as well as anger to fuel struggles for justice" (4).

The TV series engaged in this book themselves explored novel terrain in depicting gender, sex, violence, and the realities of contemporary life. They have persistently "queered" television by featuring single mothers, lesbians, gay men, and sexually conflicted individuals. The essays collected here seduce and sexualize established TV studies by bringing in topics, theoretical perspectives, and voices usually outside the realm of mainstream academic discourse. The result is a set of original and provocative essays that challenge cultural studies to seriously engage popular TV shows too often trivialized as guilty pleasures and set aside.

In the Introduction, editor Merri Lisa Johnson contextualizes the contributions within a number of controversial debates in feminist media and television studies. She identifies the classic Laura Mulvey article on "Visual Pleasures and Narrative Cinema" as provoking long-standing arguments on the role of "pleasure" in women's viewing and decodings of media, particularly film. One school of feminist thought criticizes the "pleasures" gained by patriarchal media texts, while many third wave feminists reflect upon, describe, and analyze their pleasures in TV viewing, interrogating the texts and culture that produce the pleasures – as do the contributors to *Third Wave Feminism and Television*.

Regardless of one's position in relation to what Johnson describes as the "pleasure wars," pleasure is an apt metaphor for the joys for both the writers and readers of these articles. Each chapter provides an exciting examination of some of the most popular and multidimensional television series from the mid-1990s to the present. Indeed, the significance of such landmark recent popular culture programs as *The Sopranos, The L Word, OZ, Buffy the Vampire Slayer, Queer as Folk, The Bachelor*, and *Six Feet Under* is further established by the cogent observations and close readings put forward by the essays in this collection, as well as their long-term popularity on television, cable, reruns and rental/sales of videotapes and extensive DVD productions.

The readings assembled in the collection exemplify cultural studies scholar Stuart Hall's theory of "encoding/decoding" and his analysis of "negotiated readings," an interpretive practice by which critical audiences of media texts negotiate for new meanings between the "encoding" of media messages in the text and the "decoding" of various audiences. We were struck by some of the complex negotiated readings of episodes of the programs that take on standard interpretations of the series and also read against the grain and provide original insights.

Such close reading is facilitated by new media technologies that helped make these negotiations possible and have revolutionized TV studies, making detailed scrutiny of formal and thematic dimensions of various episodes and series possible. Indeed, with VCRs, TiVo, DVDs, DVR, and computers, we ourselves have closely followed most of these series and looked at others to see what the buzz was about and what our students were writing papers on. Since few studies have treated the new wave of U.S. television series to such meticulous diagnostic analysis, these essays fill a specific void in contemporary media criticism, in some cases offering interpretations that challenged our own viewings and perspectives. While the focus of the articles is gender- and sex-centric, class, race, the law, ideology critique, and questions of power are also on view here.

The intimate knowledge of the writers with subcultures and sexual proclivities outside of the mainstream provide a pleasurable survey for those in the mainstream (the "het set") to come to terms with new practices, modes of representation, and ways of talking about culture. The studies also enable those searching for alternatives in media culture and life to see their pleasures and proclivities taken up in very serious yet always entertaining and illuminating ways.

Third Wave Feminism and Television thus expands our view of what is on television today and going on in our culture, as well as providing new ways of talking about television. It legitimates the daring of TV producers who believed that there was an audience that was open, hip, sophisticated, and intelligent enough to view and celebrate series like *The Sopranos, OZ, Six Feet Under, The L Word,* and *Queer as Folk.* The studies collected here show that the current generation of TV critics is willing and eager to take on controversial topics, to put their own experiences and voices on line and into text, and that television studies has a varied and promising future.

REFERENCES

Hall, Stuart. "Encoding and Decoding." *Media and Cultural Studies: Key Works.* Ed. Douglas Kellner and Meenakshi Gigi Durham. Malden, MA: Blackwell, 2001. 163–173.

Heywood, Leslie, and Jennifer Drake, eds. *Third Wave Agenda: Being Feminist, Doing Feminism.* Minneapolis: University of Minnesota Press, 1997.

It Got So Bad Jane Had to Put It in a Bucket

Jane is tired of death.
She's tired of others thinking it
aloud, what we lose we
lose she says as she cleans a carrot in the kitchen bright
with industry, we lose things and so
on. She
roams through her house, aware

death is out there on the road
photographing busboys and cousins and
danger accelerates into a curve.
The hospital flickers on the hill, the night stops

and turns away from the Jolly
Pirate All-Nite Donut Shoppe where women
wipe the circles left from cups bitter until
the counters wink and glitter like

a lounge-singer's neck. Next
he had a heart attack, the obit photo
blurred his face it could have been
a picture of his frowning heart, bemused
as we are by unexpected violence far away.

His albums sold a bunch, and Jane
listens for a sign: frog-in-the-throat, taut
vocal chord, a tongue coated with grease
that slips from *kiss* to *miss*, vibrato
vibrato…

     Jane plays a lick
and tables death. Mirror, Mirror, Jane
is ugly in her house. Ugly hips, ugly
elbow, ugly spleen-face. She
is very like her selfs and like her deaths, though
not exactly. Perhaps outside the house,
she is becoming.

                              Cathy Eisenhower

INTRODUCTION

LADIES LOVE YOUR BOX:
THE RHETORIC OF PLEASURE AND DANGER
IN FEMINIST TELEVISION STUDIES

MERRI LISA JOHNSON

In a 2003 promotion for a new show on Comedy Central, comedian Wanda Sykes offered a characteristically pointed observation about the "reality romance" genre of television. Commenting on the wildly popular *Joe Millionaire* as its season finale neared, Sykes announced the show ought to be called *Bitches Love Money*.

She cocked her head and asked, "Are all the feminists in a coma?"

Watching television alone in my apartment, I looked back and forth at the imaginary people seated to my left and right. *Is she talking to me?* A sharp sound burst from between my lips, something between a laugh and a squawk. *Ba!* The television addresses my feminist commitments once again.

Yes, again.

I had been enjoying a secretly feminist relationship with my television for many years. I started watching *The Sopranos* and *Six Feet Under* around the spring of 2001, during that uniquely painful part of the academic career between getting my Ph.D. and securing a tenure-track position. Florence Dore sings a country song about spending all her money on wine and three-dollar stamps, an ode to the despair of the academic job search. I hummed along to her CD as I dialed the number to the cable company and requested that they close my account. Having just read bell hooks's *Class Matters*, I thought of this budgeting decision as a gesture of "solidarity with the poor." I determined not to rent another movie until I had read every book I owned. In her own gesture of solidarity with the poor, my aunt Cheryl started lending me tapes of these HBO original series. I could not believe my eyes: Brenda's ambivalence towards marriage on *Six Feet Under* – her insistence on getting a proposal from Nate mixed with her diatribes against romance and monogamy – dramatized the very debates in feminism over the marriage mystique about which I had recently been writing. Tony Soprano's anxiety complex – his fears of being undone by psychiatry and cunnilingus, combined with cold gangster justice – illustrated the mottled surface of masculinity theorized in all the hot books on gender performativity.

I was being hailed as a feminist – by my television!

Cut off from the feminist connections of graduate school and back in my hometown for a temporary teaching post, I cherished the time spent with these characters as they grappled with feminist-influenced conflicts over gender, sex, desire, and power. The measure of what constitutes a "feminist enough" character or series – a common gauge in feminist television and film studies – depends significantly on the viewer's particular situation. Hardly amounting to a radical revolution in sexual politics, these shows nevertheless filled a void of feminist conversation in a life unfolding far away from art theaters and research universities.

Conservative cultural pundits frequently decry the entry of white middle-class women into the workforce, post-sexual revolution, by announcing with despair that we now have a generation of Americans raised by television. Television is, according to their logic, doing something bad to the children it raises: teaching them violence and promiscuity, shortening attention spans and lowering shock thresholds.

Conservatives are not alone in dismissing the television as "idiot box." For progressive pundits, media culture is not progressive enough. Where are the positive images of women and people of color?, many critics want to know. Or maybe the images are *too* positive: the Cosbyfication of racial imagery speciously erasing the poverty and urban despair of many African-American families, or the choicesoisie of liberal feminism ignoring the pressures on and implications of women's choices, masking a "new traditionalism" as television shows from *thirtysomething* to *Sex and the City* reposition women inside the home as if such a return marked the apex of feminist social transformation.[1]

As riddled with stereotypes as media culture admittedly is, television can also provide rare insight into alternative ways of living in the world. The small screen paradoxically provides a broader horizon. For rural adolescents, television can be the sole window into big-city subjects like homosexuality, singlehood-by-choice, multiculturalism, and, I'm not kidding, existentialism – my philosophy minor may well have stemmed from a certain episode of *Family Ties* in which Alex's little sister, Jennifer, reads Kierkegaard at the kitchen table. Television extended my sight line beyond the living room walls and the Appalachian Mountains that surrounded them. It provided additional frames of intelligibility to supplement what I learned from church, family, and region. I begged babysitters to let me stay up and watch *Diff'rent Strokes* and *Facts of Life*. Born with a temperament that naturally resonated with the idea that "it takes different strokes to move the world," I grew elated at stories of cross-racial adoption and cut my political teeth on the Drummonds's persistent struggle to blend their family harmoniously despite remaining racial biases within the dominant culture. I can still remember dancing in front of the television while the theme music played, hopping from floor to blue stool to couch and then floor again before the first scene began. I felt overwhelmed, filled to bursting with this new world of birds and bees and high-rise buildings. I listened closely as Ann Romano pronounced her status as divorcee on *One Day at a Time* with a reminder to her superintendent – "It's *Ms.* Romano" – the feminist marker reverberating between her teeth with an instructive buzz.

As a single woman supporting myself, I think back fondly to these images and still watch television with an eye towards its feminist content. There is, of course, a Marxist-inflected analysis to be made of the fact that I turn to television to mitigate the "on the treadmill quality" of my life (Bordo 59). The use of television as "indispensable to the reconstitution of the labour-power of the wage-earner" (Althusser 87) would seem, from this angle, to be an instance in which leisure is not "free time" but rather a holding pattern for the worker as she recharges for another day in the academic salt mines.

In such an analysis, the television screen functions as opiate and anodyne, diversion and cheap date.

Ironies abound.

In my first book, *Jane Sexes It Up: True Confessions of Feminist Desire*, I scrutinized the guilty pleasures of romance with great urgency. Eventually those pleasures dried up, and I saw them as deep-seated illusions; in Marxist terms, they constitute a fantasy structure designed "to mystify the social contradictions and material conditions of women's exploitation in patriarchal capitalism" (Ebert 9). Now I spend the evening with my television instead, experiencing this "primetime panacea" (Pender, "Kicking Ass" 167) as a space free from the hassles of romantic negotiations: what to watch, whether to watch, where to set the volume (familiar codes for control in many relationships). Like Miranda on HBO's *Sex and the City*, I have traded Steve-o for TiVO. Taking in the television as "feminist comfort food" (Pender, "Kicking Ass" 166), I am fully cognizant of replacing one opiate of the masses (romance) with another (media culture). Fully cognizant, too, of the irony of using television to get away from work and then writing an academic book about it. Within this imbrication of lures and illusions, I am once again asserting what might be perceived as a problematic desire.

Wanting to watch television anyhow.

Wanting to watch television, for instance, as stress relief, a small gesture of control over my time and mind. In one sadly mismatched romantic relationship, I closed myself into my bedroom each evening after dinner to watch television; the activity created a magical space around me, a box that protected me from the intrusions of fraught conversation. In this role, the television functioned to enlarge the available space in which I could rest, despite the problematic context of a bad relationship and the economic and emotional limits that kept me from moving out sooner. This minor improvement in my situation calls to mind John Fiske's work on "[t]he politics of popular culture," which he argues "is progressive, not radical":

It is concerned with the day-to-day negotiations of unequal power relations in such structures as the family, the immediate work environment, and the classroom. Its progressiveness is concerned with redistributing power within these structures toward the disempowered; it attempts to enlarge the space within which bottom-up power has to operate. It does not, as does radicalism, try to change the system that distributes that power in the first place. (*Understanding Popular Culture* 56)

Television was my escape route from these "day-to-day negotiations." Once I became ready for more radical change, I moved out – and took the TV with me.

In the introduction to *Feminist Television Criticism: A Reader*, Charlotte Brunsdon, Julie D'Acci, and Lynn Spigel assert a positive relationship between feminism and television, noting a progression in feminist cultural studies away from simplistic dismissals of popular culture:

> Since the 1970s, feminists have become increasingly interested in television as something more than a bad object, something that offers a series of lures and pleasures, however limited its repertoire of female roles. For its part, over the last twenty-five years, television too has engaged with the themes and tropes of feminism. ... Indeed, much of the current entertainment output of television features strong women, single mothers, and female friends and lovers – that is, female types who are integral to feminist critique and culture. (1)

With its focus on "the contradictions and reciprocities of the relationships between feminism and television," *Feminist Television Criticism* defines the field in terms of dialogue and possibility, yet the phrase "since the 1970s" gestures discreetly to a history of feminist film theory that continues to trouble feminist critics. The reception of "television as something more than a bad object" is an opening in the conversation I want to pick up and run with, but something drags at my heels.

Those "lures and pleasures" recall an unresolved debate in feminism over the politics of pleasure: the problem of bad pleasures lurking and lulling women into false consciousness, complicity with patriarchy, masochistic submission. "[O]ne of the crucial concerns of feminist film theory," writes Jane Gaines in "Women and Representation: Can We Enjoy Alternative Pleasure?," "intersects with a burning issue in women's movement politics – correct pleasure" (86). It is not entirely clear what correct pleasure is, but its opposite in feminist discourse is masochistic pleasure. In "Pleasure under Patriarchy," Catherine MacKinnon concludes: "Masochism insures that pleasure in violation defines women's sexuality, so women lust after self-annihilation" (42). This statement, echoed in the work of Sandra Lee Bartky, Andrea Dworkin, and other separatist feminists, casts women's desire in a suspect light – what becomes, in feminist television studies, the lurid glow of the television screen – and wanting to watch television appears, in this framework, to be merely another outlet of women's lust for self-annihilation. This distrust of female (and feminist) desire joins feminist film theory and feminist theories of sexuality at the hip.

In a series of debates, or "sex wars," originating at the Barnard Scholar and Feminist conference in 1982, feminists fought doggedly over the problem of women licking the boot of patriarchy.[2] Porn, sex work, intercourse, butch/femme role play – these were key sites of struggle between separatists and sex radicals. Separatists wrote angrily against women who participated in these male-identified practices. Sex radicals responded with matching fury at the perceived insult and prescriptivism, scoffing at the notion of "politically correct sex," a vision of mutuality often pictured as two women lying side by side, matching each other's rhythms stroke for stroke. Freedom, agency, power, and pleasure were put under the microscope to be examined for the faint line between socially constructed desire (what feminists should disavow) and reconstructed sexuality (a state feminists allegedly should achieve – our behaviors, fantasies, and longings lining up smoothly with our political ideals).

These debates had already occurred in feminist film studies several years earlier, constituting what we might think of as the *pleasure wars*, a philosophical debate reaching back to Plato and Aristotle, and drawing on rich tributaries from Marxist and Freudian criticism. Laura Mulvey's heavily cited thesis on the abolition of pleasure in the cinema, "Visual Pleasure and Narrative Cinema," mirrors separatist treatises in the sex wars. She is the Ti-Grace Atkinson, the Andrea Dworkin, the Catherine MacKinnon of film theory. Mulvey writes, in exhilarating manifesto style,

> It is said that analysing pleasure, or beauty, destroys it. That is the
> intention of this article. The satisfaction and reinforcement of the

ego that represent the high point of film history hitherto must be attacked. Not in favour of a reconstructed new pleasure, which cannot exist in the abstract, nor of intellectual unpleasure, but to make way for a total negation of the ease and plenitude of the narrative fiction film. The alternative is the thrill that comes from leaving the past behind without simply rejecting it, transcending outworn or oppressive forms, and daring to break with normal pleasurable expectations in order to conceive a new language of desire. (8)

After being criticized for neglecting the female spectator, Mulvey more directly addresses the question of "whether the female spectator is carried along, as it were, by the scruff of the text, or whether her pleasure can be more deep-rooted and complex" ("Afterthoughts," 29). Of the latter, she is doubtful:

[I]t is always possible that the female spectator may find herself so out of key with the pleasure on offer … that the spell of fascination is broken. On the other hand, she may not. She may find herself secretly, unconsciously almost, enjoying the freedom of action and control over the diegetic world that identification with a hero provides. It is *this* female spectator that I want to consider here. (29)

As a result of this focus, the name "Mulvey" has come to serve as shorthand for totalizing disavowals of visual pleasure in cinema. Her attack on satisfaction consistently rankles the third wave feminist media critics in *Third Wave Feminism and Television*.

Yet Mulvey's call "for a total negation of the ease and plenitude of the narrative fiction film" and her invitation "to break with normal pleasurable expectations in order to conceive a new language of desire" tempt my latent revolutionary leanings. Film *does* warrant feminist intervention. "Normal" pleasure often requires serious "troubling." I find I want to take her dare. In analyzing contemporary televisual pleasures, I can't leave the radical feminist psychology of Laura Mulvey entirely behind. Her condemnation of cinematic pleasure calls for a hard look at my own truant thumb resting on the remote control. Marxist critique, too, crowds me on couch. I settle in for a pleasant evening of television viewing – fleece blanket, hot chocolate, HBO on Demand – and in the exhalation of rest and leisure, Terry Eagleton's words catch in my throat: "pleasurable conduct is the true index of successful social hegemony, self-delight the very mark of social submission" (21). Just when the television show starts to feel really good, when it holds my attention and dramatizes the very feminist debates that compel me, am I to understand that this moment is the measure of my submission to the status quo? That I am sufficiently entertained, lulled into false contentedness? I am not only "caught looking," I am *caught liking*. "The pleasures of the aesthetic are in this sense masochistic," Eagleton reasons, and "the delight that matters is our free complicity with what subjects us, so that we can [in Althusserian terms] 'work all by ourselves'" (25). From this angle, the feminist subject matter of television is precisely the pleasure quotient that guarantees third wave feminists' participation in an otherwise patriarchal media culture. We lean in towards the complex images on the screen – masochistic mobsters, sadistic vampire slayers, network harem fantasies, lesbian tutor texts – and we are goners.

The pleasures of reading Eagleton and Mulvey are, it seems to me, at least as masochistic as the pleasures against which they warn us in aesthetic and cinematic products, in that both theorists require us to trash the delight that doubles as complicity.

All pleasure is masochistic?, third wavers ask with raised eyebrows. Destroy our *own* pleasure? we query. Put our*selves* back into a pre-orgasmic, pre-Kinsey relationship to pleasure?

Tall order.

As the call for collective anticlimax comes down from above, I am torn between pleasures: the pleasure of petulantly resisting the call (I'll watch what I want to watch) and the pleasure of performing feminist self-restraint (corseted in theory, sitting in a straight-backed chair, facing away from the screen in flawless self-abnegation). It is difficult to imagine wanting to hold all pleasure at arm's length like a good social critic. Laura Mulvey, my critical dominatrix, cracks the whip of feminist consciousness and I submit on certain gray afternoons to her strict guidance.

I'd like to make much of Brunsdon's above-cited "more than," but I can't rest easy in it, for, in exceeding its status as bad object, television does not negate its bad-objectness. The lures and pleasures and limited female roles blur into a single image on the screen.

How to tell them apart?

Many taxonomies of the female spectator have appeared in feminist film studies, toying with the gender and sexuality of watching. She is, in most accounts, giving something up, in thrall to the flickering images of patriarchy. Picture her down on her knees, redefining her pleasure in terms of the available subject position of subordination, very much like the female spectator in Daphne Gottlieb's poem "Her Submissive Streak," a title that harkens back to Mulvey's theory of narrative pleasure as masochistic for women. The female persona goes down on her boyfriend in a leather barcalounger, her back to the television screen, a figure of subservience and self-denial. Her chaps and whips and corset have been stored in the closet so that she can take on the more traditional, less playful version of feminine submission: the role of wife. "It's like that sometimes,/ I guess," ponders the poem's narrator, who mourns this transformation from the kinkiness of "youthful/ foolishness" to the truly perverse rationalizations of nonreciprocal sexuality:

> She's right. It's kinky,
>   the way he doesn't look away
>
> from the TV,
>   as her head bobs
>
> in his lap
>   like a fisherman's float
>
> on a nature program,
>   hectic
>
> with the pace
>   his breath sets.
>
> His crotch swells
>   under her mouth's
>
> prowess. He's such
>   a sweetheart
>
> he waits
>   until the
>
> commercials
>   to come.

In this image, male pleasure takes precedence over female pleasure. He enjoys a preponderance of stimuli, "with one of his hands wrapped around a remote,/ the other, a bottle of beer," not to mention the agreeable girl bobbing hectically in his lap. The closest she comes to pleasure is the sweetness of his timing, which really has nothing to do with her since she's not watching the program anyway. This "submissive streak" – taking pleasure in his nonchalance, "the way he doesn't look away/ from the TV" – affirms male sexual dominance and works as a metaphor of the female spectator, who may also be seen as contorting herself to frame her relationship to mass media as sweet or kinky or otherwise pleasurable.

I bring this image into play here to hold open, in quintessential third wave feminist form, my own "paradox of spectatorship" – the conflicted identity of the feminist fangirl.[3] "The difficulty," as Mary Ann Doane suggests, "is to hold on, simultaneously, to the notion that there are constraints [on spectatorship] and to the notion that there are gaps, outlets, blind spots, excesses in the image – to keep both in tension" (41). Even as I wax lyrical about the feminist-friendly content of much contemporary television, I want to keep in mind the horror of the media, to remember that sluts die first, as another of Gottlieb's poems reminds us, to recall the blowjobs in the glow of late-night television – call up all the ways that women's pleasures in popular culture are undeniably intertwined with our learned submission to existing power structures and limited female imagery. I feel compelled to find some way to acknowledge the submissive streak in the feminist spectator without redrawing her as always or utterly masochistic. I have to ask, for instance, if the woman in this poem would be any better off sitting in the leather barcalounger watching television; to ask whether watching television is in some sense, frankly, like sucking the dick of patriarchy.

In *Outlaw Culture*, bell hooks writes about the need to transform the structure of our desire as women in patriarchy and to "actively construct radically new ways to think and feel as desiring subjects" (112–13). Her assessment of heterosexual women's residual attachment to conventional masculinist erotic desire could be productively applied to the feminist viewer of television culture. In enjoying certain television series, we must, in hooks's words, ask ourselves if we are drawn the "usual 'dick thing'" of media culture, as self-defeating fans of problematic female characters, consumers of violent plots and conservative romantic imagery. Do we need, as feminist viewers, to come up with radically new ways to watch television as desiring subjects? Or is there something kinky about liking television, something worth preserving? What does it mean to like television, or to like men, or to like sex, once feminists have mounted crippling critiques of these sexist cultural segments? What does it mean to experience feminism as a forbidding voice, marking must-see-TV as the concentration camp orgasm of media culture? Feminist film theory, in wrestling with television as lure and pleasure, may well have fallen into the same pattern Amber Hollibaugh noted with dismay in the feminist sex wars: "Our collective fear of the dangers of [television] has forced us into a position where we have created a theory from the body of damage done to us" (486).[4]

One might usefully recast feminist attraction to television imagery in the same terms Ellen Willis once used to describe women's pleasure in rock music: "This was not masochism but expediency" (170). In other words, we take what we need from the available culture, sieve out the rest. This "negotiated reading" is not, as some third wave feminists have argued, an instance of turning away from the hard work of personal and cultural transformation. It is, rather, an acknowledgement that incremental shifts in power may be the most we can hope for, and that the kinds of pleasure available to women in the current media culture include the pleasures of oppositional reading as well as the pleasures of seeing feminist concepts dramatized on television. The least compelling pleasure on hand is, however, "the wry pleasure of recognizing patriarchy up to its tricks yet again" (Fiske, "British Cultural Studies," 266).

In a recent round-table discussion of film feminisms in *Signs*, Linda Williams explains her reluctance to participate in terms of "the burdens of what feels like orthodox feminist position taking" in the field (1264). Williams, well known for her unorthodox feminist analysis of porn, argues against "the paradigms of seventies feminist film theory" with their "singular and perhaps too clearly identifiable patriarchal villain" (1270–71). In her resistance to "a moralizing feminism" and simultaneous rejection of the "postfeminist" label (1271), Williams paves the way for a third wave feminist television studies, and, like her, the contributors to *Third Wave Feminism and Television* move "toward a more relaxed understanding of gendered fun" (1266–7). The need for this more relaxed feminist stance arises directly from the tight grinding of teeth and clamp of jaws at work in much feminist cultural studies, the fret and sweat of feminist anxiety.

Reading ideological critiques of various films and television shows provides an excellent exercise in seeing through the structures of sexism and racism and can therefore be incredibly useful in the feminist classroom. Returning to this sort of work, like a musician practicing her scales, refreshes and renews the key principles and commitments of feminist critique, and I take genuine intellectual pleasure in reading the best practitioners of these critiques: the thrilling triple threat of bell hooks, Susan Bordo, and Tania Modleski. There is pleasure to be had in being put through the feminist paces in Modleski's essays on postfeminist film; take, for instance, her analysis of *Gorillas in the Mist* as a problematic instance of postfeminist ideology in which a strong female lead is softened in predictable ways and killed off in the end. Dian Fossey (played by Sigourney Weaver), as Modleski demonstrates, is presented as a tenacious underdog with whom audience members sympathize in the face of insurmountable obstacles to progressive environmentalist research and policy formation. Then Fossey's feminism – her self-sufficiency, her radical ideals – is neutralized by the film as its narrative structure "takes it all back." The story of what can happen to a woman when she goes off on her own and takes matters into her own hands, the cautionary tale most of us know all too well, lingers and obscures the progressive energies the story almost galvanizes.[5]

True enough, but the problem with the analytical formula of *Feminism without Women* is that it boils every text down to its patriarchal capitalist white supremacist skeleton as if revealing something new. This structure is why the text works so well for students, but for the feminist scholar it may feel rote after a while. I begin reading Modleski's "thuses" in the muffled lilt of Charlie Brown's teacher: "Thus the black man [in *Clara's Heart*] comes to serve as the white male's oedipal scapegoat, and the black woman is positioned, as in so many popular representations (like Spielberg's *The Color Purple*) as sexual victim" (131). That generalization-as-aside ("as in so many popular representations") can feel wearying. In describing the misogynist implications of the Tom Hanks film *Big* (directed by Penny Marshall), Modleski concludes, "Thus once again we see woman presiding over her own marginalization, participating in a nostalgia

for a time in which human relationships are felt to have been relatively uncomplicated, although the cost of this simplicity is her own
repression" (98–9). The forced march through a landscape marked by
sexism is the "once again" which third wave feminists avoid in *Third
Wave Feminism and Television* as we seek a rhetorical strategy designed
to liberate other kinds of meanings from media texts. Our redirection
does not constitute a turning away from the skepticism and critique
Modleski encourages, but a thoroughgoing acceptance of skepticism
and critique as the givens of our approach, joined with a desire to
go beyond them, into some as-yet-unformed level of discourse,
drawing on the intersectionality of black feminism, the subversive
identifications of queer theory, and a post-sexual revolution longing
to locate unexpected conclusions in feminist media theory.

For example, to return to Wanda Sykes's joke about *Joe Millionaire*,
the implied feminist critique behind renaming the show *Bitches Love
Money* is based on a reading of the show as sexist because it reproduces stereotypes of conniving gold-diggers, and because it deploys
the motifs of romance – red roses, special meals, lingering gazes,
unexpected gifts – in the service of a conservative backlash against
women's independence of feminist critiques of "wifework" under
patriarchy. This is the set of associations beneath my own groan at
the popularity of reality romance. But to say the show is sexist is
like saying the sky is blue.

Yeah, it's sexist.

And?

All the feminists are not in a coma, but our alertness does not
predispose us to a particular stance on reality romance or anything
else on television.

Perhaps I am revealing a self-incriminating postmodern blasé
mood, the "nothing shocking" of grunge lyrics circulating in my
subconscious – a common characteristic of Generation X – but
the pervasiveness of racism and sexism, their presence "in so many
popular representations," is both a cause of dismay and, basically,
business as usual in this Reagan-era redux of the second term of
George W. Bush. "[T]hird wavers," Helene Shugart asserts, "are in
no doubt about the significance of sexism and the consequent role
of feminism." At the intersection of third wave and Gen X, Shugart
traces an awareness of sexism as a commonplace fact of life. There

is nothing shocking here. No new intellectual turns. We already know, as Susan Gubar notes in "What Ails Feminist Criticism," that "racism, classism, sexism, and homophobia reign supreme," and our hearts rise up at her call for "more mirthful scholarly lexicons" (891).[6] There is still work to be done in the direction of raising consciousness and instilling critical media literacy, but for those of who already get it, we want to know, *what else is there to say?* What is the most useful work for feminist media critics nowadays? Is it still about revealing the internalized racism of sit-coms on UPN? Or tracing new permutations of the marriage plot on the fall line-up of the WB? Flipping through these by-now formulaic feminist analyses, I look up from the book in my lap and wonder, *what else is on?*

Both sides of the pleasure/danger debate reside in the analyses of third wave feminist media critics. This is our inheritance, even as we experience mixed feelings over the rhetoric of "pleasure" and "danger." This dichotomy continues to fragment women's studies, operating as another fracture (in addition to generation), splitting peers from peers and generating cross-generational alliances. *Perhaps the pleasure/danger divide is what was always at stake,* masked by the diversionary rhetoric of generations and waves.[7]

Many third wave feminists emphasize "danger," seeing only the always-already-ness of patriarchal capitalist white supremacist media manipulation and commodification. Cristina Lucia Stasia's essay on female action heroes, for instance, foregrounds the danger of being "seduced by images": "My concern is that these new female action heroes provide images of an equality that has not been achieved, and that they mitigate their viewers' interests in exploring inequalities. It is easy to be seduced by images of strong women fighting, but these images capitalise on a basic belief in feminism evacuated of any consciousness of why girls still *need* to 'kick ass'" (181–2). This language of seduction replays the terms of debate in the feminist sex wars, reaching all the way back to the social purity doctrines of nineteenth-century feminism, positing media culture as a threatening man and the female spectator as vulnerable maiden. We might call this group *separatist feminist media critics* because they ultimately encourage women to turn off the television, give pop culture the cold shoulder. Consider Rebecca Munford's critique of Girlie culture,

"Wake Up and Smell the Lipgloss," in which the media are presented as an "insidious form of indoctrination" (142) and the focus is deliberately shifted from the agency and playfulness of Girlie to its "dangerous paradoxes" (147), "[t]he dangers of colonisation and recirculation" (148), the "risks" and "problem[s]" of Riot Grrrl (149). This language departs significantly from the earlier (and I would argue definitive) characterization of Girlie by Jennifer Baumgardner and Amy Richards in *Manifesta: Young Women, Feminism, and the Future* as "girls in their twenties or thirties who are reacting to an antifeminine, antijoy emphasis that they perceive as the legacy of Second Wave seriousness" (80). These two attitudes towards Girlie culture can be mapped neatly on to the pleasure/danger divide in feminism.

Susannah Mintz's treatment of feminism and television in her essay "In a Word, *Baywatch*," likewise focuses on danger with a bland totalizing formula we might call the "stating the obvious" moments in feminist media criticism, redirecting a phrase she uses to describe Lieutenant Van Buren's role on *Law and Order*. Like "Debbie Downer" on recent seasons of *Saturday Night Live*, this feminist voice interrupts us mid-hilarity to set the record straight:

> While the preponderance of women represented as smart and capable is meant to prove TV's 'feminist' leanings, marking its transcendence of the sexism that drove *Charlie's Angels* or *Three's Company*, television nonetheless demonstrates the way in which misogyny can go underground, asserting its force through less visible – and therefore more difficult to combat – avenues. This makes television an enormously effective tool with which to sustain patriarchal ideology. (59)

Jane Gaines asserts provocatively that the priority of sexual correctness in film practice and gaze theory "offer[s] feminists a rather tight-lipped satisfaction" (87), an image that captures well the limited pleasures produced by this focus on danger in third wave feminist television studies.

Other third wave feminists more strongly identify with the "pleasure" side. These media critics – who have not had much air time to date – import sex radical theories into television studies, valuing fantasy as a space of free play, advocating acceptance of our darker drives, and indulging in fascination with imagery that queers gender, decenters heterosexuality, and valorizes the erotic. We might call this group *sex radical media critics* or *visual pleasure libertarians* because of their positive attitudes towards viewer agency and productive pleasures. They conduct negotiated readings, rife with creative identifications between viewer and text, often motivated by a sense of the text as polymorphously perverse, offering sites of pleasure all over the textual body. The third wave feminist media theory in *Third Wave Feminism and Television* belongs almost solely to this side, engaging with what may seem to be politically incorrect television – the "should-not-be-looked-at-ness" delineated by positive-images criticism.[8]

The essays in *Third Wave Feminism and Television* thus counter the trend in feminist television studies of reading for the wry pleasures of catching patriarchy at its old tricks once again. As is the case in feminist sexuality studies, there is not enough work being done to articulate what we like about television, what it does for us, what we do with it – while always taking note of where it falls short – as well as where we do. Certain television series perhaps require what Patrocinio Schweickart calls "a dual hermeneutic: a negative hermeneutic that discloses their complicity with patriarchal ideology, and a positive hermeneutic that recuperates the utopian moment – the authentic kernel – from which they draw a significant portion of their emotional power" (619). Schweickart seeks to complicate the "resisting reader" of feminist literary criticism, and in the same spirit I would like to complicate the resisting viewer of film theory, asking, with Schweickart, "Where does the text get its power to draw us into its designs? Why do some (not all) demonstrably sexist texts remain appealing even after they have been subjected to thorough feminist critique?" (618). In television studies, as in literary criticism, "The usual answer – that the power of male texts is the power of the false consciousness into which women as well as men have been socialized – oversimplifies the problem" (618). The viewer's "authentic liberatory aspirations" (619) must be taken into account. Here I would agree with Tania Modleski in *The Women Who Knew Too Much: Hitchcock and Feminist Theory* that "the female spectator need not occupy either of the two viewing places typically assigned her in feminist film theory: the place of the female masochist, identifying with the passive female character, or the place of the 'transvestite,' identifying with the active male hero"

(25). Modleski resists the "denial of pleasure to the female specta-tor," reminding us that "other pleasures remain possible," including the pleasure of "analysis itself, in understanding how the joke works even when it works against women" (27). In this view, watching television after work is not merely the cultural trap of alleviating the on-the-treadmill quality of life under patriarchal capitalism. It can be a genuinely feminist activity that allows women to pause and reflect on their own fears, anxieties, and desires mid-revolution.

Although the presence of our own pleasure in television culture often provides the "opaque moment" through which we enter a discussion of various series, the contributors to *Third Wave Femi-nism and Television* refrain from participating in the either/or of the pleasure/danger debate, or what Patricia Pender calls the "Good Buffy/Bad Buffy" model of feminist television studies. Like Pender, we strive "to rethink the terms of the debate staged around [various characters's genders] by questioning the logic of the transgression/ containment model":

> The model of feminist agency usually employed to analyze *Buffy* dictates that Buffy is "good" if she transgresses dominant stereo-types, "bad" if she is contained in cultural cliché. Yet the binary logic itself works to restrict a range of possible viewing positions and to contain *Buffy*'s political potential. ("I'm Buffy," 38)

Instead, Pender advocates a less totalizing analysis, one that focuses on how the particular images of femininity on this show articulate with the ambiguous sexual politics of parody. The kinds of questions Pender poses model the intricately textual and contextual approaches to pop culture for which *Third Wave Feminism and Television* creates a forum in third wave feminism:

> How, for instance, does the exaggerated or cartoonish representa-tion of Buffy's femininity mediate its 'earnestness'? Does Buffy's femininity in fact *require* amelioration? And how does an under-standing of her 'over-the-top girliness' as 'necessary' to her makeup challenge the very political judgments that are frequently made about her character? (38)

Another good example of this sort of work appears in Kristyn Gorton's recent analysis of the *Ally McBeal* phenomenon in which women across America became avid Ally fans and feminists raised the frantic question, *What does this mean?*, fearing the implantation of more anorexic logic in our young girls, scoffing in horror at the micro-miniskirts this lawyer donned for court in every episode. The show itself raised the questions, What is the relationship of Ally McBeal to feminism, to young women, and to cultural debates over gender and power, in response to the infamous *Time* magazine cover that featured Ally as the face of a problematic new (post)feminism? (apologies all around – I may vomit if I hear about that cover one more time). Gorton moves instructively from the question, "Should women enjoy a character like Ally McBeal with all her snivelling, whining and man problems?" to "Or maybe we should ask *why* women enjoy a character like Ally McBeal?" (160). Her answer may be applicable to a wide range of images of women on television: "programmes such as *Ally McBeal* become pleasurable insofar as they offer play with some of the conflicting inheritances of feminism: desire for both independence and companionship" (161). Gorton draws on the work of Ien Ang, whose theory of the melodramatic imagination acknowledges the cultural work of primetime television in assisting women in working out their feelings of insecurity that cannot be divulged in the florescent light of the workday. "[I]t can be argued that Ally, as a character," explains Gorton, "allows women to explore their feelings of anxiety about their position within a male-dominated workplace, about being thirty-something and about marriage and children" (161). Far from a reactionary text or backlash against feminism, *Ally McBeal* points up the remaining conflicts in women's lives in this period of troubled entitlement. "Some women enjoy Ally's fantasies, in part, because the demands of the second wave have *not* yet been met," says Gorton, and furthermore, "while *Ally McBeal*'s success has generally been read within the academy as a representation of the triumph of postfeminism, the contention here is that it demonstrates the continuing salience of the demands of second wave feminism to modern women" (162).

Gorton's work coincides with key tenets of postfeminist television criticism as delineated by Amanda Lotz, and of this list I will highlight one in particular as central to the project of *Third Wave Feminism and Television*: critical attention to "the way situations illustrating the contemporary struggles faced by women and feminists are raised and examined within series" (116). One important element that connects all the chapters is the dialogical reading of televisual texts in light of feminist theory and of feminist theory in light of certain televisual texts; that is to say, each contributor offers a close reading of a specific series, invoking feminism as a frame of reference, and in addition to this familiar practice, the contributors explore a less familiar approach in cultural studies as they read the televisual text not merely as the object but as the source of theory.[9] Reading television as theory opens up the possibility of granting media culture a more important role in contemporary conversations about gender and sexuality; each show is a performance of theory, a dramatization of its insights and impasses. Television is, as Linda Williams once said of pornography and Colin McArthur of gangster films, one of the ways our culture talks to itself about itself.[10]

The shortcomings of "primetime feminism," as Bonnie J. Dow articulates them – "a white, middle-class, heterosexual bias, an assumption that a 'seize the power' mindset and more vigorous individualism will solve all women's problems, and a conflation of feminist *identity* with feminist *politics*" (207) – give reason for serious pause. Dow cautions, "we need to appreciate media for what it can do in giving us images of strong women; yet, at the same time, we need to maintain a very keen sense of the limitations of media logic" (214). This balance between appreciation and skepticism, or pleasure and danger, shapes each of the following essays. The progressive moves of these shows are all, we concede, intercut with moments of containment, flashes of stereotypes, plot crutches, and predictable jokes, yet they constitute a significant and sustained effort at writing outside the box of essentialism (the idea that femininity and masculinity are natural inborn identities) and beyond the walls of identity politics (the idea that our identity categories are rigid, stable, and directly related to our political orientation). For this reason, the following essays focus on the conversations made possible by various series without feeling the need to subordinate this positive approach to an obligatory deprecation of television culture. This collection of third wave feminist media theory does not therefore ask, Is the show *feminist* or not?, or Is it feminist *enough*?, but rather takes for granted that all the shows on television today contain a mixture of feminist, postfeminist, antifeminist, and pseudofeminist motifs.

We sort through these competing energies to ask more precise contextual questions:

- Why is this show popular right now?
- What specific desires and fears are being addressed by it?
- What material concerns in women's lives are being sublimated, resolved, mystified, alleviated in this fantasy?
- How do these shows reflect and participate in the unresolved feminist sex wars?
- In what ways does it respond to, contest, misinterpret, or translate feminist concerns about romance, marriage, family, desire, sexuality, and money?
- How are women (contestants, viewers, feminists) *using* it?

In response to anticipated criticisms of *Third Wave Feminism and Television*, let me be clear about the politics of this third wave feminist media theory: the contributors are in no way interested in uncritically embracing television; we are under no illusions that television or any other media outlet in contemporary culture is primarily feminist in content or intention; we are not diametrically opposed to the insights of second wave feminist film theory regarding pleasure, false consciousness, and the female spectator. For these reasons, "postfeminist" (rehabilitations notwithstanding) probably does not apply to us. As third wave feminist media critics, we recognize that pop culture is a ubiquitous part of our lives. It is therefore necessary to address it, to develop a reading practice that attends to its contradictions in content, in its role in our lives, and in its attitudes towards feminism.

Once again, the poetry of Daphne Gottlieb provides a set of images through which to conceptualize this theoretical move in feminist television studies. Her most recent book of poems explores the concept of the "final girl" in horror films, creatively interacting with Carol Clover's work in *Men, Women, and Chainsaws*. Clover's analysis of splatter films posits the heroine as a transgendered figure, a masculinized girl with whom male and female spectators can both identify. Gottlieb expands this figure into a wide context of American culture, imagining a range of situations in which girls face horrific social conditions in the media and in real life, from Mary Rowlandson, whose captivity narrative is a staple of colonial American literature, to Patty Hearst, kidnapped in 1974 and becoming infamous for identifying with her kidnappers and developing Stockholm Syndrome. In "Final Girl II: The Frame," Gottlieb writes a sort of handbook for heroines of horror films:

> You are here because you are in danger
> and you are in danger because you are here.
> You've got a bad case
> of the captivity narrative.

I imagine this "bad case of the captivity narrative" as one way of explaining women's pleasures in popular culture. Yet the poem ends with an image of survival:

> The story runs all the way
> to daybreak, when you can be a girl
> again and everything will be returned home.
> Until then, everything
> is electric projection
> and we are
> your captive audience.

There is a throat-ripping harshness to Gottlieb's "tits and scream" poems, but even in this angry voice, the feminist spectator can imagine her way into a more powerful position. In "Gone to Static," she is not the one on her knees sucking off some guy holding a remote control in one hand and a beer in the other, but the one facing the television and calling up the images she desires:

> the whisky is open
> the vcr is on.
> I'm running
> the film backwards
> and one by one
> you come back to me.

Rather than watching the women walk one by one into the slaughter-house of film history, in *Third Wave Feminism and Television* we are calling them back to us, pausing at the line break between "I'm running" – the flight response, the fear, the urge to turn off the television – and "I'm *running the film* backwards" – an image of control and desire (like running the fuck) and the rewriting of history, a "writing beyond the ending" that transforms the arc of these captivity narratives so that all the girls come back to us. Post-horror, post-static, post-frame – where "everything/ is electric projection" – we might consider the feminist spectator as a sort of "final girl" and feminist television studies as a space of camaraderie and survival: "it's just you and me/ and the bourbon and movie/ flickering together."

Ultimately, *Third Wave Feminism and Television* is about liking television without being duped by it, adopting a differential consciousness that allows us to move around inside our responses, between what we like and what we critique, balancing on the shifting grounds between hegemony and agency in which every text is "an inevitable site of ideological struggle" (Fiske, "British Cultural Studies," 259) and every reading is "interested in the latent possibility of alternative viewpoints erupting" within the text (White 163). The third wave feminist media theory fostered here accommodates both the joyful, playful exuberance women feel when we see feminist influences in contemporary television, and the incendiary refusals and revisions women make in the face of the media as captivity narrative. The discontinuity readers might feel in moving from the *liking* parts of each chapter to the *disliking* parts is precisely the point of third wave feminist media theory: the pleasure and danger of women's relationships to television have yet to be reconciled.

In the meantime – against all the anxieties that lead third wave feminist media critics to "mak[e] speech about [televisual] pleasure taboo" and to experience television as the new "great guilty secret among feminists," and because, as Carole Vance has forcefully argued in another context, "Feminists are easily intimidated by the charge that their own pleasure is selfish" (7) – I offer this slightly modified version of Germaine Greer's famous exhortation as a brief respite from ruthless self-scrutiny:

Ladies.
Love your box.

NOTES

1. Elspeth Probyn describes several television shows from the late 1980s that participate in "a sort of 'vulgarization' of feminist discourses" (127). Probyn focuses on *thirtysomething* as "a post-feminist vision of the home to which

women have 'freely' chosen to return" (128), arguing that this "new age of 'choiceoisie' (130) obscures the politics of particular choices (134). Beth Montemurro revisits the rhetoric of choice in *Sex and the City*, arguing that the position of liberal feminism is indicted by the show, as one character insists that leaving career for husband and family is her feminist-guaranteed choice, and the other three main characters variously question and condemn her. Jhally and Lewis addressed a parallel problem with *The Cosby Show*: "Black viewers are thus caught in a trap because the escape route from TV stereotypes comes with a set of ideologically loaded conditions. To look good, to look 'positive,' means accepting a value system in which upper middle class status is a sign of superiority. This is more than crude materialism; for a group that has been largely excluded from these higher socioeconomic echelons, it is cultural and political suicide" (122).

2. While many feminists have problematized the term "sex wars" as reductive and sensationalistic, it remains the most familiar and recognizable way to reference these debates and is used throughout *Third Wave Feminism and Television*. To avoid the unwieldiness of excessive quotation marks, this note should function as a knowing wink at our readers throughout the book any time the phrase "sex wars" appears.

3. I take the phrase "paradoxes of spectatorship" from an article by Judith Mayne, in which she argues persuasively that "one of the problems in spectatorship studies is the desire to categorize texts *and* readings/responses as either conservative or radical, as celebratory of the dominant order or critical of it" (172). By exploring the spectator position of the "feminist fangirl," I avoid this reductive choice and draw on the "both/and" thinking attributed by Adela Licona to third wave feminism.

4. The original text reads: "Our collective fear of the dangers of sexuality has forced us into a position where we have created a theory from the body of damage done to us" (227). The ease with which "sexuality" can be replaced by "television" in many key statements from the sex wars underscores the continuity of the pleasure/danger divide across these two fields of feminist debate.

5. The passage from Modleski asserts that the film *Gorillas in the Mist* "seems to respect the notion of a woman sacrificing the opportunity for a husband and family in order to pursue a career, a career that, indeed, involves her living the sort of adventurous and dangerous life usually reserved for men in popular films and that also accords her the kind of single-minded dedication to a cause typically attributed to the male scientific investigator. But the film *takes it all back*, as it were, by 'deprofessionalizing' Fossey, neglecting to mention her growth as a scientist who in the course of her research in the mountains of Rwanda earned a Ph.D. from Harvard. The film further subverts its apparently liberal attitude to women's independence by suggesting that Dian is merely channeling and sublimating … her sexual desires and maternal instincts into her cause" (122, my stress).

6. In her 1998 essay "What Ails Feminism," Susan Gubar asserts that many feminists "make obeisance to the necessity of considering (without subordinating) race, class, gender, sexuality, and nation in litanies that often translate into depressingly knee-jerk essays rejecting out-of-hand the speculations

of a given literary or theoretical work simply because it neglects to discuss *x* (fill in the blank – bisexual Anglo Pakistani mothers; the heterosexual, working-class, Jews-for-Jesus community of Nashville, and so forth). Too often, each text becomes grist for a mill that proves the same intellectually vapid – though politically appalling – point that racism, classism, sexism, and homophobia reign supreme" (891).

7. A significant pattern is emerging in discourse on third wave feminism in which women who are chronologically third wave are renouncing the wave model as a diversion and distortion. Lisa Maria Hogeland, in "Against Generational Thinking; or, Some Things That 'Third Wave' Feminism Isn't," writes, "There is, I argue, nothing specifically generational about any of these feminisms; they are political stances with particular histories in the movement. They may be differently nuanced for women of various age groups, historical experiences, and geographical or institutional locations – but these differences in nuance do not add up to generational difference, not least because the nuances themselves are so uneven. The effect of using claims of generational difference is to reify ageism in the movement – on both sides of a putative generational divide" (np). Her argument "that generational thinking pushes emotional buttons" strikes me as convincing. Lisa Jervis, the co-founder and publisher of *Bitch: Feminist Responses to Pop Culture*, pronounces "The End of Feminism's Third Wave," making the particularly relevant argument that "third wave" and "second wave" are labels that mask ideological disagreements, especially pertaining to "the issues motivating both sides of the '80s sex wars" (np). She concludes: "I want to see these internal disagreements continue. I want to see as much wrangling over them as ever. But I want them articulated accurately. And that means recognizing the generational divide for what it is – an illusion." Despite these disavowals, it is still useful to invoke "third wave" in certain contexts. For instance, Deborah L. Siegel notes the emergence of "third wave" as "a response to what one might call the cultural dominance of 'postfeminism,'" and in this case denotes "a stance of political resistance to popular pronouncements of a moratorium on feminism and feminists." Ultimately, third wave feminism is driven by the voices marginalized by hegemonic second wave feminism; up to now, that marginalization has primarily been presented in terms of race, giving rise to U.S. Third World feminism, but the sex radical voices of the second wave were equally marginalized, and it is their persistent battle for pleasure without penalties that I see as the third wave work carried forward by *Third Wave Feminism and Television*.

8. I take this term from Ellis Hanson, who outlines the problematic models of feminist and gay film criticism and offers queer film theory as a possible unsettling of these models.

9. The idea of reading television as theory was included in the call for papers and therefore shaped the submissions significantly; I am indebted for this idea to the work of Jane Gallop in *Living with His Camera*. She writes: "The book for the third chapter – Kathryn Harrison's *Exposure* – is not a text of theory but a novel. I find it nonetheless to be a substantial contribution to understanding photography, and so I read it as theory.... The view of photography and the photographer in this novel is very much in keeping

with Sontag's view, but as a novel it allows us to explore the personal, familial, and psychological dimensions of photography that Sontag's essay only gestures toward" (14).

10. Invoking Fredric Jameson's work on medieval romance and Colin McArthur's work on gangster film as her models, Williams writes, "We can therefore ask of the current hard-core genre, What problems does it seek to solve? What is it 'talking to itself' about?" (*Hard Core* 129).

REFERENCES

Althusser, Louis. *Lenin and Philosophy and Other Essays*. Trans. Ben Brewster. New York: Monthly Review Press, 2001.

Ang, Ien. "Melodramatic Identifications: Television Fiction and Women's Fantasy." In *Feminist Television Criticism: A Reader*. Ed. Charlotte Brunsdon, Julie D'Acci, and Lynn Spigel. Oxford: Clarendon Press, 1997. 155–66.

Baumgardner, Jennifer, and Amy Richards. *Manifesta: Young Women, Feminism, and the Future*. New York: Farrar, Straus & Giroux, 2000.

Bordo, Susan. *Twilight Zones: The Hidden Life of Cultural Images from Plato to O.J.* Berkeley: University of California Press, 1997.

Brunsdon, Charlotte, Julie D'Acci, and Lynn Spigel, eds. *Feminist Television Criticism: A Reader*. Oxford: Clarendon Press, 1997.

Doane, Mary Ann. *Femmes Fatales*. New York: Routledge, 1991.

Dow, Bonnie J. *Prime-time Feminism: Television, Media Culture, and the Women's Movement since 1970*. Philadelphia: University of Pennsylvania Press, 1996.

Eagleton, Terry. "The Ideology of the Aesthetic." In *The Politics of Pleasure: Aesthetics and Cultural Theory*. Ed. Stephen Regan. Buckingham: Open University Press, 1992. 17–31.

Ebert, Teresa. *Ludic Feminism and After: Postmodernism, Desire, and Labor in Late Capitalism*. Ann Arbor: University of Michigan Press, 1996.

Fiske, John. *Understanding Popular Culture*. London: Routledge, 1989.

———. "British Cultural Studies." In *Channels of Discourse: Television and Contemporary Criticism*. Ed. Robert C. Allen. Chapel Hill: University of North Carolina Press, 1987. 254–89.

Gaines, Jane. "Women and Representation: Can We Enjoy Alternative Pleasure?" *Issues in Feminist Film Criticism*. Ed. Patricia Erens. Bloomington: Indiana University Press, 1990. 79–92.

Gallop, Jane. *Living with His Camera*. Durham NC: Duke University Press, 2003.

Gillis, Stacy, Gillian Howe, and Rebecca Munsford, eds. *Third Wave Feminism: A Critical Exploration*. New York: Palgrave, 2004.

Gorton, Kristyn. "(Un)fashionable Feminists: The Media and *Ally McBeal*." In Gillis, Howe, and Munsford, 154–63.

Gottlieb, Daphne. *Why Things Burn*. New York: Soft Skull, 2001.

———. *Final Girl*. New York: Soft Skull, 2003.

Greer, Germaine. "Lady Love Your Cunt." *The Madwoman's Underclothes: Essays and Other Occasional Writings*. New York: Atlantic Monthly, 1986. Orig. *Suck*, 1971.

Gubar, Susan. "What Ails Feminist Criticism?" *Critical Inquiry* 24 (1998): 878–902.

Hanson, Ellis. *Out Takes: Essays on Queer Theory and Film.* Durham NC: Duke University Press, 1999.

Heywood, Leslie and Jennifer Drake, eds. *Third Wave Agenda: Being Feminist, Doing Feminism.* Minneapolis: University of Minnesota Press, 1997.

Hogeland, Lisa Maria. "Against Generational Thinking; or, Some Things that 'Third Wave' Feminism Isn't." *Women's Studies in Communication* 24, no. 1 (2001): Infotrac.

Hollibaugh, Amber. "Desire for the Future: Radical Hope in Passion and Pleasure." In *Pleasure and Danger: Exploring Female Sexuality.* Ed. Carole S. Vance. London: Pandora, 1989. 401–10.

Jeffreys, Sheila. "How Orgasm Politics Has Hijacked the Women's Movement." *On the Issues.* www.echonyc.com/~onissues/s96orgasm.html (accessed 1 August 1999).

Jervis, Lisa. "The End of Feminism's Third Wave." *Ms. Magazine.* Winter 2004. www.msmagazine.com/winter2004/thirdwave.asp (accessed 3 January 2004)

Jhally, Sut and Justin Lewis. *Enlightened Racism: The Cosby Show, Audiences, and the Myth of the American Dream.* Boulder CO: Westview Press, 1992.

Johnson, Merri Lisa, ed. *Jane Sexes It Up: True Confessions of Feminist Desire.* New York: Four Walls Eight Windows, 2002.

Licona, Aleda C. "(B)orderlands Rhetorics and Representations: The Transformative Potential of Feminist Third-Space Scholarship and Zines." *NWSA Journal* 17, no. 2 (2005): 104–29.

Lotz, Amanda. "Postfeminist Television Criticism: Rehabilitating Critical Terms and Identifying Postfeminist Attitudes." *Feminist Media Studies* 1, no. 1 (2001): 105–21.

MacKinnon, Catherine A. "Pleasure under Patriarchy." In *Sexuality and Gender.* Ed. Christine L. Williams and Arlene Stein. Malden, MA: Blackwell, 2002. 33–43. Orig. 1989.

Mayne, Judith. "Paradoxes of Spectatorship." In *Viewing Positions: Ways of Seeing Film.* Ed. Linda Williams. New Brunswick: Rutgers University Press, 1995. 155–83.

Mintz, Susannah B. "In a Word, *Baywatch.*" In *Catching a Wave: Reclaiming Feminism for the 21st Century.* Ed. Rory Dicker and Alison Piepmeier. Boston: Northeastern University Press, 2003. 57–80.

Modleski, Tania. *Feminism without Women: Culture and Criticism in a "Postfeminist" Age.* New York: Routledge, 1991.

———. *The Women Who Knew Too Much: Hitchcock and Feminist Theory.* New York: Methuen, 1988.

Montemurro, Beth. "Charlotte Chooses Her Choice: Liberal Feminism on *Sex and the City.*" *The Scholar and Feminist Online* 3, no. 1 (2004) www.barnard. edu/sfoline/hbo/montemurro_01.htm.

Mulvey, Laura. "Visual Pleasure and Narrative Cinema." *Screen* 16, no. 3 (1975): 6–18.

———. "Afterthoughts on 'Visual Pleasure and Narrative Cinema' inspired by King Vidor's *Duel in the Sun* (1946)." In *Visual and Other Pleasures.* Bloomington: Indiana University Press, 1989.

Munford, Rebecca. "'Wake Up and Smell the Lipgloss': Gender, Generation and the (A)politics of Girl Power." In *Third Wave Feminism: A Critical Exploration.* Ed. Stacy Gillis, Gillian Howe, and Rebecca Munsford. New York: Palgrave, 2004. 142–53.

Pender, Patricia. "'I'm Buffy and You're... History': The Postmodern Politics of *Buffy.*" In *Fighting the Forces: What's at Stake in "Buffy the Vampire Slayer."* Ed. Rhonda V. Wilcox and David Lavery. Lanham: Rowman & Littlefield, 2002. 35–44.

———. "'Kicking Ass Is Comfort Food': Buffy as Third Wave Feminist Icon." In *Third Wave Feminism: A Critical Exploration.* Ed. Stacy Gillis, Gillian Howe, and Rebecca Munsford. New York: Palgrave, 2004. 164–74.

Probyn, Elspeth. "New Traditionalism and Post-Feminism: TV Does the Home." In *Feminist Television Criticism: A Reader.* Ed. Charlotte Brunsdon, Julie D'Acci, and Lynn Spigel. Oxford: Clarendon Press, 1997. 126–37. Orig. *Screen* 31 (1988): 147–59.

Schweickart, Patrocinio. "Reading Ourselves: Toward a Feminist Theory of Reading." In *Feminisms: An Anthology of Literary Theory and Criticism.* Ed. Robyn Warhol and Diane Price Herndl. New Brunswick: Rutgers University Press, 1997. 609–34.

Shugart, Helene A. "Isn't It Ironic? The Intersection of Third-Wave Feminism and Generation X." *Women's Studies in Communication* 24, no. 2 (2001): 131–69. Infotrac.

Siegel, Deborah L. "The Legacy of the Personal: Generating Theory in Feminism's Third Wave." *Hypatia* 12, no. 3 (1997): Infotrac.

Stasia, Cristina Lucia. "'Wham! Bam! Thank You Ma'am!': The New Public/ Private Female Action Hero." In *Third Wave Feminism: A Critical Exploration.* Ed. Stacy Gillis, Gillian Howe, and Rebecca Munsford. New York: Palgrave, 2004. 175–84.

Vance, Carole S., ed. *Pleasure and Danger: Exploring Female Sexuality.* London: Pandora, 1989.

White, Mimi. "Ideological Analysis." *Channels of Discourse, Reassembled: Television and Contemporary Criticism.* Chapel Hill: University of North Carolina Press, 1992. 161–202.

Williams, Linda. *Hard Core: Power, Pleasure, and the 'Frenzy of the Visible'.* Berkeley: University of California Press, 1989.

———. "Why I Didn't Want to Write This Essay." *Signs: Journal of Women in Culture and Society* 30, no. 1 (2004): 1264–71.

Willis, Ellen. "Rock, etc." *The New Yorker.* 23 October 1971. 168–75.

I

GANGSTER FEMINISM:

THE FEMINIST CULTURAL WORK

OF HBO'S *THE SOPRANOS*

MERRI LISA JOHNSON

While *The Sopranos* "is not," following reviewer Rebecca Traister's phrasing, "a show that goes in for 'very special episodes' about abortion or bulimia … , it has tackled some women's issues that may be even more uncomfortable." Given the regularity of scenes on HBO's five-season gangster drama that correspond to recognizably feminist issues – for example, Janice claims the identity of feminist despite letting Richie hold a gun to her head during sex; Dr. Jennifer Melfi is brutally raped and subsequently experiences symptoms of post-traumatic stress; Meadow's room-mate, Caitlin, suffers from an anxiety disorder and self-medicates with Absolut Vodka; Carmela grapples with mixed feelings about her husband's adulterous relationships – *The Sopranos* clearly qualifies as a site of "primetime feminism," fulfilling quality television's role, formulated eloquently by Bonnie J. Dow as "an important ideological forum for public discourse about social issues and social change" (xi). In its representations of rape, battering, and spousal murder, the third season of *The Sopranos*, even more than the series as a whole, persistently takes up the feminist cultural work of examining "the economic and social roots of violence," mirroring a key tactic in cutting-edge cultural studies (Jenkins, McPherson, and Shattuc 11).

The graphic nature of these scenes, however, prompted critics and fans alike to ask whether *The Sopranos* went too far (Owen and

Vancheri). Others asked why the charge of going "too far" came up only in relation to violence against women, while the more prevalent violence against men on the show frequently went unchallenged. These inquiries into the sexual politics of *The Sopranos* recall similar critical conversations about the 1980s cult TV phenomenon *Twin Peaks*. "What's new about television exploiting our love affair with the interfaces of sex and death, or our hunger for seeing women dead or maimed or mutilated or suicidal or raped or helpless, especially if they're sexually active?," asks Diana Hume George, in an essay cleverly titled "Lynching Women" (a pun on film *auteur* David Lynch's name). "Prime time business as usual," she answers, "only a little worse because even feminists let it go by, behaving like charmed backsliders involved with a man so charismatic that we just couldn't think straight" (110). Hume George directs this charge in part at her own fanship as she sheepishly admits to being a "Peaks freak" and struggles to come to terms with the conflict between her viewing pleasure and her "objections to its sexual ethic, which [she] regard[s] as reptilian" (119). She writes also in response to Randi Davenport, who proposes that "*Twin Peaks* is informed by, rather than at odds with, recent feminist discussions about sexual violence" (255). Their stalemate evinces a "crisis of spectatorship" in feminist media studies, a point Judith Halberstam makes in relation to gay and lesbian critical responses to the 1991 film, *Basic Instinct*: "We simply do not know how to read imagined violence: all too often representations of the pernicious effects of homophobia, racism, and sexism are collapsed by the viewer into homophobia, racism, and sexism themselves" (253). The texts as well bear responsibility for this crisis, given the nature of media imagery "as a field of contestation with forces of domination and resistance, repression and struggle, co-optation and upheaval," as Douglas Kellner describes contemporary media culture (29). A tight weave of competing political energies – feminist, antifeminist, and pseudo-feminist – riddles recent films and cable series.

It is within the context of these debates over how to read gendered violence in media culture that I wish to situate my reading of episode 32 of *The Sopranos*, "University," in which Ralphie, a disgruntled Sopranos crew member, brutally murders his pregnant girlfriend, Tracee, a stripper at the Bada Bing! While I concede at the outset the difficulty of distinguishing between representations

of violence against women that reinforce sexism and representations of violence against women that critique sexism, the following
analysis trades the "too clearly identifiable patriarchal villain" (Williams 1271) of seventies film theory in for a postmodern map of
intersectionality, tracing the intersecting oppressions that structure
the settings and psyches of each character. Indeed, the feminist cultural work of *The Sopranos* resides specifically in the show's attention
to intersectionality, well represented by the richly textured portraits
of Tracee and Ralphie, and productively brought to the surface
through the critical lenses of sex worker feminism and feminist
masculinity studies.

THE STRIPPER AS RESISTING READER

Throughout the episode "University," two stories are carefully inter-
woven. One narrative strand follows Tracee, a dancer at the Bada
Bing! strip club, as she attempts to create a traditional family dynamic
in her life. In the opening scene she approaches Tony with a gift of
homemade date nut bread and is gently reprimanded for trying to
shift roles within the binary of good and bad womanhood. In Tony's
layman's terms, "You can't be doing stuff like this."

Silvio, Tony's consigliere, dismisses her more abruptly with an
ironic jab at the ludicrousness of a stripper who bakes. "Let's go,
Betty Crocker," Silvio instructs as he taps his watch, sending Tracee
back to her assigned position as working girl.

When Tracee discovers she is pregnant, she entertains hyperreal
fantasies of a future home life with her gangster lover, Ralphie
Cifaretto, despite his domineering personality and erratic behavior.
Tracee's domestic desires measure the extreme distortions produced
by the dominant ideology of family values, as she pictures a stereotypical 1950s' conclusion for her story: a loving marriage, a fulfilling
motherhood, and a well-run house – all tidily poised at the end curve
of a New Jersey cul-de-sac. Tracee's actual experiences of the nuclear
family as a violent space – her mother burned her hand on the stove
when she was a child, and she repeats the act by burning her infant
son with cigarettes – are erased by her media-driven nostalgia for
home. This narrative strategy of contrasting the cultural imagery of

home as safe, peaceful, comforting, and fulfilling with the frequent reality of home as violent, artificial, coercive, and lonely constitutes a major element of this episode. Tony's oft-cited nostalgia for 1954 can be grouped with Tracee's delusions as part of this series-wide pattern.[1] Like Tracee, Tony longs for a pastoral domestic space from a past that never existed. Indeed his own home in 1954 was far from peaceful, complete with a borderline personality mother threatening to stick a fork in his eye and mobster father cutting off a man's pinky finger in front of him, then spending the night with his mistress while his wife suffers a miscarriage.[2] In its contrapuntal line of nostalgic delusion and nightmarish memories, *The Sopranos* reenacts a widespread cultural wrestling match with the "miscarriage" of family, home, and the American dream. This popular subgenre characteristic of HBO original series – the "it's not TV" of family drama – produces a paradoxically utopian relief from empty master narratives of family values. "University" mobilizes this contrast between utopian and dystopian visions of home in the service of Tracee's complex characterization as a fallen woman with class-driven aspirations to redeem herself in the eyes of her gangster boss and boyfriend, thereby gaining access to the good life.

It is in fact a commonplace of the feminist movement against domestic violence that classism is responsible for the misleading idea of home as a safe retreat from the dangers of the public world. Middle- and upper-class homes are not necessarily free of spousal abuse and other sexist social ills. Through strategic editing, "University" echoes this insight, repeatedly collapsing the violence of strip club spaces against the performed comfort of home life to underscore the continuities between stigmatized and socially sanctioned arenas, asserting that they are not as separate or opposite as our symbolic register suggests. For example, in his capacity as manager of the Bada Bing!, Silvio slaps Tracee and slams her down on the hood of his car after she misses three days of work, as Ralphie laughs vindictively from the window of his house. The scene change uses his laughter as its transitional element, melding seamlessly into laughter at the family dinner table with his high-status mob-widow girlfriend, Rosalie Aprile, and their guests. Their dinner party conversation is structured by stereotypical dialogue from the "war between the sexes," as the women trade clichéd complaints about empty milk cartons in the fridge and "the football trance." Men have, as Rosalie says, "the attention span of children." This lame rehearsal of the popular men-are-from-Mars discourse red flags a lethargic antagonism beneath the surface of everyday domesticity, a tension amplified significantly by the previous scene. Ralphie's laughter, an obviously false performance of warmth and hospitality, replicates the disingenuous facade of "family values" often used to demonize strip clubs and justify violence towards the women who work there. Tracee's disposability, signaled by her exclusion from the dinner party and by Ralphie's approval of Silvio's corporal punishment, is dramatized as a sacrifice to the social-ladder-climbing middle-class family – her eventual death at Ralphie's hands a back-alley abortion of sorts. By positioning Tracee's murder at the intersection of sexism and classism in this way, the episode exposes the cold and calculating ideological construction work behind the bourgeois family, returning to the critical Marxist connection between "family as haven" and "heartless world" (Lasch 42). One necessitates the other – the "brutal world of commerce" creates our need for an emotionally supportive retreat within the family – and the Soprano dinner party shows the precise conceptual sites where *haven* borders on *heartless*.

The second narrative strand follows Meadow, Tony's daughter, as she negotiates romantic mythologies and imperfect relationships in her first year at Columbia University. Fully aware of the limitations of family, Meadow often embodies a perspective within the show that sees through the barriers Tony erects between blood family and business. Meadow's savvy subverts our expectations that daughters are sheltered and naive while strippers are worldly and cynical. In a brief essay on the father–daughter dynamic on *The Sopranos*, psychologist Josephine Gattuso Hendin argues that "Meadow and Tony are a matched pair, the flip sides of coercive vulnerability and coercive power," using the episode "College" to demonstrate their shared skills in subterfuge and strategic honesty (67). Meadow is thus more "gangster" than Tracee and is often posited as the more likely *heir apparent* to Tony's position as head of family than his son A.J. Her loss of virginity in this episode works as a counterplot to Tracee's quest for domesticity. The "good" daughter becomes sexualized, as the "bad" stripper seeks the legitimacy of love, marriage, and baby carriage. These blurred boundaries between stereotypes enact the poststructuralist dictum that each pole is haunted and inflected by its supposed opposite. Tracee and Meadow hold within their separate social roles *traces* of the other, calling directly into question the good girl/bad girl binary of traditional western thought and, once again, pointing beyond gender to class as a defining axis of feminine respectability.

This transvaluation is deliberately crafted through twinned scenes and rhetorically pointed segues in which Meadow's body fades into Tracee's. In one exemplary set of paired scenes, Meadow and her mother, Carmela, chat cozily in bed about Meadow's new boyfriend, Noah. When Carmela asks her daughter if she is in love with him, Meadow responds, "At this point I'd better be." Carmela follows up, "At what point?" but Meadow demurs, "We are *so* not having that conversation." In a previous scene we saw Meadow under Noah as he unwrapped a condom. Meadow is clearly referring to the birds-and-bees conversation that makes for such predictable humor in family television. In her most sardonic teenage knowingness, Meadow is not "going there" with Carmela, resisting the genre of *very special moments* that shapes much mother–daughter television dialogue. The dialogue is thus at odds with the setting, creating a jarring discord between the viewer's conditioned expectations for harmonious comfort and the scene's oppositional trajectory into unresolved tension. The next scene deftly reproduces the daughter/parent dyad in a conversation between Tracee and Tony. Tracee tells Tony she's pregnant and that the baby is Ralphie's. Instead of taking place in the protected bedroom of the family home, this conversation happens outside the strip club in the vulnerable public space of a gravel parking lot. Inverting the relationship between dialogue and setting, the dialogue here clings to domestic harmony, while the setting casts this hope literally out in the cold. Positioned in relation to Tony in this scene as a daughter figure, Tracee seeks advice and support, but, as unwed mother and sex worker, she takes on the hybrid role of deviant daughter, doubling Meadow's newly deflowered status. Tony reminds Tracee of her run-ins with the Department of Family and Children's Services (D-FACS) over her first child and mocks her innocent question, "If I have it, do you think he'll help me support it?" "Oh sure, it'll be *Father Knows Best* over there," inadvertently implicating television history in Tracee's deluded vision of Ralphie. In a perverse revision of "father knows best," Tony recommends an abortion.

On one textual level, then, Meadow and Tracee are tracked into separate socially classed material spaces: Meadow is inside while Tracee is outside; Meadow is home while Tracee is in a commercial setting; Meadow is with family while Tracee is with her boss; Meadow is enclosed and enfolded in the comfort of bed and maternal embrace while Tracee stands literally and figuratively at arm's length from Tony, hanging on to the inanimate metal of his car door window frame; Meadow is bathed in soft lighting while Tracee squints in the harsh morning sun. The two characters are set up through this series of contrasts, yet they articulate desires that "belong" in the other space. Meadow refers indirectly to her loss of virginity and confesses uncertainty about her feelings for Noah, whereas Tracee indicates reluctance to get an abortion and maintains stubborn optimism for making a home with Ralphie for a new baby. In the language of feminist narratologist Minrose Gwin, the material spaces of home and strip club do not correspond with the cultural spaces – the ideologies of gender, class, and sexuality – typically attributed to them (416). Meadow and Tracee are "in different places," mentally and emotionally, than their scripts and settings would have them. The episode title, "University," for instance, names a social institution that seems diametrically opposed to the Bada Bing! despite the fact that many college students work as exotic dancers. The title's off-center relationship to Tracee reproduces the cultural marginalization of strippers on the surface, while implicitly acknowledging the flow of women between the spaces of school and strip club, or respectability and sexuality. Both Tracee and Meadow are being "schooled" in the possibilities and limitations of their assigned cultural scripts, and the viewer is offered a lesson on universities and strip clubs as mutually reinforcing disciplinary structures, not "good" and "bad" places. It is on this textual level – where the cultural scripts and physical settings do not articulate properly – that a critique akin to sex worker feminism emerges.

In particular, the commonly noted point in sex radical feminism that the whore stigma affects all women structures this episode's exploration of character and morality. Jill Nagle, editor of *Whores and Other Feminists*, urges her readers "to problematize not only choices *to*

participate in the sex industry, but also choices *not* to," and through
this lens Meadow's experiences can be viewed as a comment on
whore stigma along with Tracee's. Not becoming a stripper – a
decision usually taken as evidence of a choice to be good, or to
respect oneself – can be reinterpreted as a concession to limits on
public displays of the respectable female body, a matter of social
class rather than morality. Meadow's body is as circumscribed by her
cultural script as Tracee's is. For, as Nagle writes, "Whores, too, are
something that women are not only supposed to not *be*, but also,
not be *mistaken* for. This division translates into a mandate to not
only *be* virtuous, but also to *appear* virtuous, to again demonstrate our
affiliation with the privileged half of the good girl/bad girl binary."
The parallel between Tracee and Meadow dismantles this tenacious
binary, constructing portraits of young women in the space between
categories and asking, to borrow Nagle's language, "what purposes
are served by using *any* sexual categories to describe women (4–5).

In an interview with Terry Gross on NPR's "Fresh Air," *Sopranos*
creator David Chase identifies "University" as the most heavily
misunderstood episode of the series, and his comments indicate a
conscious (if not terribly articulate) engagement on his part with
progressive visions of social responsibility. Chase asserts that the
episode tells "a story about this girl that nobody cared about." His
description of her as "expendable" lends itself to a reading of Tracee
at the intersection of gender, social class, and sexual stigma, as he
situates the episode in the context of the pervasive "violence against
women" that happens "every day" in American culture (Gross). The
series's use of extreme violence to explore the social and economic
roots of violence recurs in the fifth season in episode 58, "Senti-
mental Education," devoted in part to the theme of violence against
Asians. While some viewers might interpret episodes 32 and 58 as
simple reiterations of stereotypes in which strippers and minorities
are targeted for unproblematized attacks, the scripts clearly link this
violence with the perpetrators's financial and gendered insecurity. A
"diagnostic critique" of these episodes in the tradition of Douglas
Kellner's media studies reads for the social forces that encourage
violence as an acceptable response to economic pressures as long as it
is directed at expendable targets. Tracee's status as "whore" seems to
make her vulnerable to attack, as Ralphie mentions it several times to

excuse himself for killing her, but Tony eventually recognizes Tracee and Meadow as the same, not as opposites, indirectly challenging Ralphie's bigoted perspective. In the following episode, Tony looks at Meadow and *sees* Tracee.[3] This visual merger of the two women's bodies refutes easy designations of some women as less deserving of safety and sexual freedom than others.

It is particularly important to excavate the significance of Tracee's story in relation to representations of sex workers instead of reading her as a symbol of something else, since, as Wendy Chapkis insightfully points out, "the use of the sex worker as a symbol has served to obscure the real complexity of her life" (32). While Tracee's murder is about the problem of "compulsory virtue" for all women, it is also about the very particular situation of female sex workers, whose bodies and labor remain vulnerable to exploitations strictly legislated out of most socially legitimate work environments. As Jane Arthurs notes in *Television and Sexuality*, in her chapter on televised documentaries about strippers, the International Union for Sex Workers (IUSW) has "call[ed] for an end to stereotypical portrayals in the media through recognition of the diversity among sex workers and their clients" (99). In a gesture of solidarity with sex workers, then, or at least offering insight into the psychological impact of stigma, the episode encourages the audience to sympathize with Tracee as we see her humiliated and hurt in a thousand small ways before the scene of her death. She tries to show Tony her braces and is reprimanded by Silvio for fraternizing. She offers a kiss to Ralphie and he turns away, demanding in a patronizing tone, "*How* many cocks you suck tonight?" She says hi to Tony with a huge smile, but he waves her away and goes into a room with another stripper, closing the door behind them. Standing there in her too-tight tomato-red dress, hair swept up in an approximation of classiness and elegance, she has that look of gangly girls in six-inch heels for the first time. With this shot, the stripper is transformed from impervious fantasy girl into wallflower. As the camera lingers on Tracee's disappointed face and awkward retreat, she becomes someone we recognize, someone we can identify with, someone we have in fact been.

She becomes a fool.

The viewer can perhaps sympathize with Tracee's foolishness – feeling out of place or not good enough – but beyond this sympathetic portrait of girlish insecurity, I use the word "fool" here primarily in its Bakhtinian connotation, and I apply it with delicacy, since many feminists have historically had trouble seeing the stripper as anything other than a fool. Hardly an accusation of false consciousness, the narrative function of the fool, as Dale Bauer explains in "Gender in Bakhtin's Carnival," is that she doesn't understand social conventions, and in the absence of her understanding she prompts "a dialogue about those very interpretive norms." In this way, the fool acts "as a resisting reader within the text" and "provid[es] the means of unmasking dominant codes" (715). In her role as resisting reader within the text, Tracee reminds us that the stripper body has often been a site of struggle over what can be seen or not seen, and under what circumstances, a struggle over what is "obvious" – in other words, an ideological struggle.

In several scenes, Tracee forces other characters to explain the social conventions that structure their relationships. Tony turns down the date nut bread because he already has a family, and he struggles to spell out the difference between that gift-giving dynamic and the more limited employer–employee relationship he expects her to maintain with him: she can't give a gift because (*pace* Gayle Rubin and Luce Irigaray) she *is* a gift. Tony is pushed to articulate a cultural belief he does not necessarily understand. "Bread," he muses as she walks away. In this moment, the audience is meant to see more of the picture than Tony and Tracee perceive. "The role of the reader" when confronted with the fool, to return to Bauer's theory, "is to question and restructure the 'cultural and intertextual frames' in which the character operates and is made foolish" (715) The viewer's role, in the moments we witness Tracee's troubled relationship with her stigmatized position, is to recognize the frame as the problem. Tracee experiences these moments as inexplicable, but the text communicates with the audience on a level of meaning not available to her, consistently linking her mistreatment with broader social systems of misogyny.

The murder scene effectively demonstrates the ideological controls that shape individual desires and pit Ralphie against Tracee. Her desire to live with Ralphie, the motivating factor in this scene, returns us to the destructive effects of the dominant ideology of home as safe haven, for it is Tracee's unwavering psychological investment in this fiction that blinds her to the dangers of making a home with the wrong person, and her insistence on entitlement to this home triggers his violence against her. The following dialogue takes place, once again, behind the Bada Bing!

> *Tracee*   Fuck you. Three days you don't call, even to see how I am.
> *Ralphie*   Baby, I'm busy. I gotta work. How else am I gonna take care of you when you're nine months pregnant?
> *Tracee*   You serious?
> *Ralphie*   Of course I'm serious. We'll get a little house, in a cul-de-sac. I know that guy who's a mortgage broker.
> *Tracee*   Really? (Ralphie nods) Ralphie, I love you.
> *Ralphie*   I love you too, baby. I tell you what. If it's a boy, we'll name it after me. If it's a girl, we'll name it Tracee, after you. This way she can grow up to be a cocksucking slob just like her mother. *Are you out of your mind?*

When Tracee questions Ralphie's seriousness in the above-cited dialogue, he reacts defensively with verbal violence, at first seeming to insist on his good intentions, then turning the question back on Tracee by denouncing her worthiness as wife material. They continue this mutually abusive conversation as Tracee calls Ralphie a "Guinea mother-fucking piece of shit" and Ralphie greets her girl punches with more taunting and name-calling: "That's right, that's right, get it all out, you little whore." Finally she slaps him and draws blood. Ralphie becomes suddenly serious, punching her once in the face. Tracee further escalates the violence: "Does that make you feel good? You feel like a man?" In response, Ralphie beats her to death, punching her several more times in the face, then bashing her head into the guardrail. Ralphie ends the scene with the predictable blame-shifting words of abusive boyfriends everywhere: "Look at you now." Tracee wanted Ralphie to provide attention, affection, and a little house. He sees these requests as evidence that she is "out of [her] mind" – doesn't she realize that he too yearns for the idealized domestic life he sees in Tony's family, and that a stripper wife could never be part of that picture? In failing to recognize herself as an unwanted class marker, Tracee runs into the brick wall of Ralphie's fist. Like the nineteenth-century prostitutes targeted by Jack the Ripper – a complex instance of violence against women documented by feminist historian Judith Walkowitz in *City of Dreadful Delight* – Tracee's victimization results from sex worker stigma, a combination of traditional misogyny and class disgust (218).

In the final scene, a new dancer is being trained as Tracee's trademark song, "Living on a Thin Line" by the Kinks, haunts the background with a reminder of the thread-like boundary between good girls and bad girls, daughters and strippers, useful female bodies and disposable ones, putting to music what Jay Parini calls the "desperately thin line between realism and satire" in *The Sopranos* (76). In his essay, "The Cultural Work of *The Sopranos*," from which I derive my title, Parini describes the ambiguous presentation of violence on this series as "both a satire on violence and a presentation of that violence," and in this formulation he pinpoints the difficulty of performing a feminist analysis of the stripper-bashing scene in this episode (84). The show both problematizes violence against sex workers and reproduces the pernicious visual cliché of the dead stripper, in the same way that, as Sarah Projansky argues in her postfeminist analysis of the 1988 film *The Accused*, "the graphic rape scene functions, paradoxically, both to challenge rape myths from a feminist perspective and to contribute to the existence of violence against women in media culture" (96). The murder scene in "University" – adding another dead stripper to a long necrology of murdered sex workers in film and television – weighs heavily against the feminist cultural work of the episode towards dissecting the social and economic roots of violence against sex workers, separated by a desperately thin line between realism (stripper murder) and satire (a critical comment on stripper murder).[4]

As this episode of *The Sopranos* closes, three strippers walk across the screen, exchanging gossip about Tracee at the beginning of a shift. One says she heard Tracee went outside with Ralphie and never came back. Another cautions, "Keep what you hear to yourself." Feminist platitudes aside, they know their silence *will* protect them, or that it is their best option in the short term. Tracee lost her life because she did not adhere to this sort of advice. She criticized Ralphie, calling him on his failures as a man, refusing his characterization of her as inadequate mother and substandard girlfriend, and, as Kim Akass and Janet McCabe write about another character on the show, "This powerful narrative position – to say what should not be said – is, however, a precarious one" (154). Tracee finds out just how precarious as Ralphie reinstates his self-serving definitions with thirteen lethal blows to her face and head. Yet the gruesome text of Tracee's lifeless body remains before our eyes, confronting Tony and the audience with the foolishness of the frame, a haunting critique of whore stigma.

A GANGSTER IS BEING BEATEN

While the obvious focal point of a feminist analysis of "University" might seem to be the shocking and excessive reproduction of the punished female body in this murder scene, the episode cannot be adequately addressed without noting the ideological ligatures connecting the murder scene to the scene in which Ralphie is beaten by Tony for the murder. After killing Tracee, Ralphie goes inside the Bada Bing! and shoves his raw knuckles into an ice bucket. The other men quickly realize that something has happened to Tracee. When they go outside and find her dead body, Tony demands that someone bring Ralphie out. Ralphie returns to the scene of the crime and denies his involvement: "Can I help it if she's a clutz?" His cover story, that Tracee fell, recalls the theme of sexual transgression, concretizing the metaphor of the fallen woman. Her body has literally fallen – or been knocked – to the ground, revealing the masculinist agency behind the fall of the fallen woman. The scene then rapidly shuffles roles, repositioning Ralphie on the receiving end of the beating, where Tracee recently stood. The girl-beating is revised as gangster-beating, the gangster reduced to girlish vulnerability.

To the extent that feminist audience pleasure was thwarted in the violence towards Tracee by the sounds of the relentless beating, with its sobering horror and gore, it is let loose in triplicate at the sight of Ralphie getting what's coming to him. But before we indulge too freely in this pleasure, it is useful to note that the viewer is positioned as Ralphie's double in this scene. We are implicated in his behavior and lined up to share his punishment. The beating is shot through the chain-link fence against which Ralphie's body falls, and the viewers are on the other side of the fence, seeing Tony's fist and angry face coming at us with a very schoolyard-bully feel, his crew gathered around in a tight huddle. We experience the vulnerability of the male body being asked to account for itself. As Tony moves toward his target, Ralphie shouts in indignation that he's a made man. His status should make him safe from the sort of attack he unleashed on Tracee; his body should be off-limits to Tony. The terminology "made man" begs deconstructive gender analysis, highlighting the social construction of masculinity as an illusory surface of hardness and self-assurance. Furthermore, in asserting himself a "made man," Ralphie concedes the question's validity. The statement betrays an anxiety surrounding this status, operating paradoxically to mark the moment when Ralphie's claim to dominant masculinity is rendered most unstable.

In feminist masculinity studies, the point has been made that it is possible, even crucial, to examine the ways men are constrained and let down by the dominant fiction of masculinity without casting them as victims. Judith Kegan Gardiner asserts that a feminist masculinity studies will "help deconstruct static binaries in gender studies between victims and oppressors, difference and dominance, and hegemonic (or socially validated) and alternative masculinities." In the same volume Robyn Weigman's "Unmaking Men" calls for attention to interlocking systems of oppression in masculinity studies (35). In such an analysis, Ralphie's male privilege can be seen as alternately consolidated and undercut by its articulation with his white skin, Italian-American ethnicity, eleventh-grade education, blue-collar background, and masochistic fantasies.

Ralphie cannot be cast simplistically by feminist critics as a misogynistic killer because his character is not fully accounted for by the role of oppressor. In this point, I take as my model the work of bell hooks, who similarly rejects one-dimensional feminist analyses of the African-American rapists of the Central Park Jogger, insisting that the story cannot be fully grasped as an instance of "male violence against women" or "yet another horrific and brutal expression of patriarchal socialization," for these readings leave out the factors of race and racism. "[S]ince male power within patriarchy is relative," writes hooks, "men from poorer groups and men of color are not able to reap the material and social rewards for their participation in patriarchy. In fact they often suffer from blindly and passively acting out a myth of masculinity that is life-threatening" (*Yearning* 63). Indeed, Ralphie's violence must be situated at the intersection of gender privilege and class bias in order to grasp his motivations for "acting out a myth of masculinity that is life-threatening." He does in fact risk his life with his frantic macho behavior. In addition to being beaten in this episode for killing Tracee, he is killed and decapitated in a subsequent episode, arguably as payback for Tracee's death.[5] In this reading of Ralphie, as in hooks's analysis of the rapists, excusing the offender is not the point. Rather, an intersectional analysis links the sexism of violence against women with systemic violence against men in the forms of classism, racism, and/or heterosexism. Without taking the pressure off him for being psychotic and misogynistic ("I don't give a flying fuck, my brotha, what any little slit thinks of me"),[6] the episode explores his position within a differential network of power relationships and the unequal parceling out of privilege among men.

Much of this episode focuses on Ralphie's hysterical performances of masculinity as he overcompensates for his slow rise through the gangster ranks. Ralphie's underappreciated ability to "earn" for the guys above him in the mafia hierarchy, a fact he mentions frequently, makes him an intriguing figure of the contemporary American blue-collar worker. At this point in the season he has asked to be promoted to captain and been denied. He borrows Russell Crowe's lines from *Gladiator* to practice bravado: "I have come to reclaim Rome for my people." And to indirectly admit despair: "We are all dead men; all we can do is choose how to die." In one scene, Ralphie enters the club's backroom and harasses the bouncer, Georgie, calling him an idiot for not having seen *Gladiator* and then putting a cigar out on his inferior's black tee-shirted chest. In a show of status thinly disguised as boyish play, Ralphie slings a chain and padlock around until he (kind of, sort of) accidentally hits Georgie in the eye with it. Tony makes him take the injured man to hospital. Ralphie's cocaine-inspired delusions of grandeur grate uncomfortably against Tony's control and contempt. Like Tracee, Ralphie longs to be accepted by this patriarchal father figure and welcomed into the upwardly mobile Soprano "family," and, also like Tracee, Ralphie is ultimately excluded as déclassé.

Despite the clear inequality between Ralphie and Tracee, the two characters are similarly disenfranchised by lack of class access to institutions of higher education and the acquisition of cultural capital. In the same way that Tracee's class status made stripping not the least lucrative or liberating job choice, Ralphie too faced a limited range of career options with his eleventh-grade education. Becoming a member of the mafia in this sense is not unlike joining the military; rather than an exercise of power, it is often a reflection of economic necessity and an initiation into a violent, Darwinian, hypermasculine system in which many men are made to feel vulnerable and feminized. Ralphie brutalizes Tracee because she undermines his masculinity in front of his peers; his insecure class status makes it feel imperative to him to protect his masculinity, and his violence against her is a manifestation of this class anxiety, at least as much as it is an exercise of patriarchal power. Furthermore, if capitalism can be perceived as a system of prostitution in which all laborers sell their bodies, the struggle between Ralphie and Tracee is not merely between man and woman but between different kinds of sex workers, as Ralphie peddles his aggressive masculinity to improve his social position. Without eliding the difference between strippers and gangsters, or between "real" sex workers and figurative ones, it is important to recognize that Ralphie barters for status and wealth with his body, selling a fantasy version of himself – taller, harder, more fearless – for cash profits.

The series follows the thread of this suggestive association of the gangster-as-hustler in a more overt manner in episode 42, "Christopher": Ralphie entertains the fantasy of his own prostitute alter ego in a key scene that has indirect bearing on the paired scenes from "University" in which he gives and then receives a beating. His relationship to Janice Soprano, Tony's sister, reveals a perverse structure of desire in which Ralphie gets off on occupying the prostitute subject position while being anally penetrated. The shrill sounds of a vibrator fill Janice's bedroom. She works Ralphie from behind while they role-play pimp and prostitute in a cross-gender fantasy dialogue:

Janice   "How much money did you make today, slut?"
Ralphie   "Three hundred."
Janice   "That's all, bitch? I'll put you back on the street, ho. Make you work that ass."
Ralphie   "Put me back on the street baby, yeah."
Janice   "Work that ass you little cunt."
Ralphie   "Do you love me?"
Janice   "Mama's little tramp, mama's little whore. I'll pimp you out, bitch."[7]

A phone call from Rosalie Aprile interrupts the scene, and Ralphie modulates back into conventional domestic masculinity, assuring her he'll be home for dinner. Through Ralphie's relationship to Valentina La Paz (also in season four), we learn even more about his sexual peculiarities – she says he can't or won't "just fuck" her, that he wants her to hurt him, drip candle wax on his testicles, rub his dick raw with a cheese grater. He does not, in Tony's malapropism, "have penissary contact with her Volvo." Ralphie's desire for vulnerability, his preference for "bottoming from the top" in Janice's description to Tony, cracks open the dominant fiction of masculinity to reveal the latent anal eroticism of the all-male gangster arena. According to Tony's psychiatrist Dr. Melfi, Ralphie is a textbook masochist. His dominance over Tracee looks somewhat different when reviewed through the additional narrative layer of this later episode. The female sex worker's productivity and low status are translated into turn-ons in his fantasy landscape. Every time he rejects Tracee, or hits her, episode 32 expresses an inchoate recognition that he shares her position; thus Ralphie's masochism creates continuity between their characters in addition to the expected gender hierarchy. Like the film and literary characters included in David Savran's *Taking It Like a Man*, Ralphie is a "put-upon warrior" whose "penchant for pain by no means rules out the possibility of turning violence against others, especially women or feminized and racialized others who happen to get in the way" (208), but this lashing out, along with his disingenuous claims to victimhood ("What am I – the Invisible Man over here?"), do not entirely invalidate a Marcusean reading of Ralphie as the necessarily masochistic male subject of capitalism, self-disciplining to the point of absurdity (a cheese grater?!).[8]

While a full discussion of male masochism falls beyond the scope of this article, the series's connection between Ralphie's masochistic sex *play* with Janice and his sadistic *real-life* torture–murder of Tracee reproduces stereotypes of sadomasochism that are as limiting and misleading as those of sex workers currently under discussion. This spurious link between male masochists and psychotic killers acts as a reminder that media representations demonize men who don't adhere to conventional (male-dominant) sex roles, just as they demonize women who don't adhere to conventional (properly sanitized female) sex roles. Despite these misrepresentations of the "textbook masochist," *The Sopranos* contributes positively to conversations in feminist masculinity studies about male desire, departing from simple apprehensions of male sexuality as unremittingly dominant. For instance, in a much earlier episode, "Big Girls Don't Cry" (in season two), Tony tells his psychiatrist about his exhilaration in listening to the sounds of his crewmember Furio tearing up a tanning salon and beating the owner and his wife. "I almost wished it was me," he shares. Dr. Melfi is all too quick on the uptake: "Giving the beating, or taking it?"[9] This recurring imagery in which a gangster is being beaten breaks up the monolithic representation of masculinity as smoothly equating to power, pleasure, and discursive agency, allowing the viewer to perceive the more complex workings of power in which men participate.

Midway through episode 32, a brief sex scene encapsulates this complexity in microcosm. Tracee is participating in a threesome to fulfill her roles as girlfriend and sex worker. Ralphie fills the left margin of the television screen, berating Tracee for crying. A uniformed police officer stands at the other end of Tracee's body with his dick in her mouth. Tracee's discomfort as she endures this double penetration takes center stage in this scene. Her body stretches across the screen in a striking representation of intercourse as violation – heterosexual penetration as an expression of hatred for women – offering a memorable visual of how, in Andrea Dworkin's words, the system of sexual subjugation is "carried on the backs of women in the doggie position" (159). What is less obvious, but no less important or interesting to notice, is that *no one* in that room seems to be getting much pleasure. Ralphie scowls and pushes; the cop sucks in his breath as Tracee's braces scrape tender penis tissue. Tony's sexual encounter with another stripper later in the same episode likewise produces less pleasure than one might expect. Instead of a marker of privilege and hedonism, this blowjob is a study in exertion and dissatisfaction. He can't get there, no matter how hard he concentrates, how tightly he closes his eyes. The strip club provides a telling setting for these thwarted orgasms. The utopic pleasure represented by the strip club is exposed as another flimsy dominant fiction. Men go there to get away from it all – the strains and demands of post-sexual-revolution families and workplaces – and in this compensatory capacity it points paradoxically to what is missing or uncomfortable in these men's lives. Linda Williams's analysis of the utopian kernel in hardcore pornography illuminates moments like this one in the back of the Bada Bing! as she looks behind the escapist desires they enact to discover "compensatory fantasies designed to make up in the domain of sexuality the power that is denied men in their work and political lives" (*Hard Core* 163). Cultural anthropologist Katherine Frank likewise posits men's visits to strip clubs in terms of dissatisfaction with the everyday arenas of work and family, their desire to "relax" a measure of this dissatisfaction: "[A]lthough customers' motivations are indeed related to existing power structures and inequalities, their visits are not necessarily experienced as exercises in acquiring or wielding power" (86). To the extent that the strip club operates as a space of escape from feminist critiques of patriarchy, Frank notes "that these men [nevertheless] experienc[e] their visits to the clubs … within … a framework of confusion and frustration rather than simply one of privilege or domination" (96). Ralphie and the police officer dominate Tracee in the threesome scene, for example, but they experience their *ménage à trois* within a framework of confusion and frustration, occupying a blue-collar class status far from the space of prestige where masculinity pays off in material comfort without manual labor.

A conversation between three crew members amplifies this working-class anxiety, a perhaps unexpected subplot of the seemingly glamorous life of gangsters, as Tony's nephew Christopher cracks wise that if he wanted to work eighteen-hour days he'd get a job at Denny's, only to hear Silvio retort, "Like they'd hire you." With this background haze of blue-collar dissatisfaction in mind, Ralphie can be usefully read alongside Douglas Kellner's analysis of *Rocky* and *Rambo* as not merely "expressions of white male paranoia which present males as victims" but also "as symptoms of the victimization of the working class" with their "resentful, inarticulate, brutal" and "educationally deprived" protagonists. In the same way that "Rambo's neurotic resentment is less his own fault than that of those who run the social system in such a way that it denies his class access to the institutions of articulate thought and mental health" (64–5), Ralphie's gendered defensiveness and his lashing out at Tracee can be "read diagnostically" as symptoms of the limits his working class position enforces on the rewards he can reap from the patriarchy.

In this way, the scene of Ralphie's violence can be placed in the service of feminist critiques of patriarchy, pushing the audience (or, less broadly, the feminist fan) to ask what kind of system produces this sort of "monster."

The episode, not unlike Robin Wood's reading of *Raging Bull* in his book *Hollywood from Vietnam to Reagan*, "counterpoints two forms of violence: violence against women and violence against men." "While the motivations for these different manifestations of violence may seem quite distinct," writes Wood, "a true understanding of the film depends on our ability to grasp the relationship between the two" (252). Repressed homoeroticism is the joining factor between these two kinds of violence. Fear of being questioned as a "real" man, of being taken for a woman or a queer, motivates the aggression we have come to associate with masculinity. The cultural significance of violence against men in *The Sopranos* may not be far removed from "the cultural significance of boxing itself as licensed and ritualized violence in which one man attempts to smash the near-naked body of another for the satisfaction (surely fundamentally erotic) of a predominantly male mass audience" (254). Recall the scene where Christopher is forced to his knees in front of Tony, who aims his gun at Christopher's head. Or picture Councilman Zellman in his boxer shorts on the bedroom floor while Tony beats him across the back with his belt, ending with a final shot across the thin boxer-covered buttocks. The homoerotics of gangster violence create strong parallels between scenes that target women and scenes that target men, as they share a sexualized humiliation. In the fifth season, the anathema of overt gangster homosexuality appears as a brief subplot when Vito is caught in the act of giving a security guard a blowjob. Again, Woods's words on *Raging Bull* apply equally well to *The Sopranos*, as both media texts are "concerned with chronicling the disastrous consequences, for men and women alike, of the repression of constitutional bisexuality" (258). Tony, Ralphie, Christopher, and the Councilman are locked in a tense embrace with masculinity, desiring and fearing intimacy with other male bodies. The frustrations they take out on the female bodies that surround them point simultaneously at the sexist, classist, and heterosexist notions of masculinity that drive them to exhaustion as well as to murder.

While Ralphie's excessive violence against Tracee fills the screen and dominates the viewer's memory, the episode presents Ralphie as one point on a spectrum of patriarchal hurtfulness towards women. Jeffrey A. Brown criticizes the genre of "stripper revenge" movies for not going far enough in its structural analysis of violence against strippers: "The films manage to encapsulate systemic misogyny within a few symbolic male characters who are ridiculed as ineffective leerers or portrayed as violent psychopaths eventually killed off by the heroines" (74). In contrast, *The Sopranos* links Ralphie's violence to an established set of rules that everyone knows and is expected to abide by. After Tony hits Ralphie in anger at Tracee's death, Silvio gently reminds Tony that Tracee was not his wife or goomah, was not related to him by blood or marriage, and that he therefore had no "legitimate" grounds for avenging her loss. Ralphie's actions are clearly marked as reprehensible, but they are equally marked as part of *the way things are*, not a deviation from the norm.

The parallel subplot of Meadow's relationship with Noah brings out this sense of a patriarchal continuum. Meadow describes Noah to her mother in terms that apply to Ralphie: "[O]ne minute he's all affectionate and then the next he's a totally different person." Carmela soothes Meadow with a not terribly comforting thought: "That's just how some men are." This Jekyll and Hyde imagery characterizes Noah's behavior as monstrous, connecting him with Ralphie through the shared masculine trait of unpredictability. A scene in which Ralphie shouts armchair movie critic remarks at *Spartacus* is intercut with Noah flipping out over the C– he got on an essay, again linking their volatility. Immediately after the paired beating scenes (Tracee's beating, then Ralphie's), the show cuts to Meadow and Noah in the library. He tells her he thinks they've been seeing too much of each other. She asks why, but he resists answering her question, making evasive comments at first, and finally giving only partial explanations that don't match what we've seen of their relationship. Although he says she's too negative, the audience has reason to believe that she's not classy enough for him and his high-powered entertainment lawyer father. Noah's move from affection to indifference mirrors Ralphie's trajectory from "I love you" to "you cocksucking slob." Furthermore, Noah's biracial identity undercuts his claim to dominant masculinity, indicating a legitimate insecurity that parallels Ralphie's class anxiety. Tony's crudely racist treatment of Noah is not unlike his open disdain for Ralphie, marking the two characters as similarly subordinate masculinities. The break-up scene between Noah and Meadow replays stereotypical masculine behavior through Noah's lack of empathy and sudden inarticulateness. By juxtaposing these traits with the murder scene and its aftermath, the episode explores the possibility that despite their seemingly radical difference – the clean well-lit library in opposition to the dark wet ditch behind the Bada Bing!, the civil conversation in contrast to the screaming match and battering – Ralphie and Noah are different in degree rather than in kind. This is a radical feminist perspective, dramatically revoking what Lynn Phillips calls the "normal/danger dichotomy" of male heterosexuality: the belief "that healthy and abusive relationships are mutually exclusive" (52) and that dangerous men "are distinct from the men with whom women share their everyday lives" (55). *The Sopranos* thus expresses "the sense of disillusionment and betrayal" that arises "when the very men expected to protect women from danger become the ones who ultimately violate them" (55). The Noah/Ralphie co-plot mirrors the normal/danger dichotomy, and the parallels between their characters work in the feminist vein of problematizing the dichotomy, thereby revealing the "Noah" in "Ralphie" and the "Ralphie" in "Noah" (i.e. the behavioral spaces in which the "normal" guy and the "danger" guy turn out to be one and the same man). While Ralphie's violence is admittedly drawn in such excess that it might be difficult for the casual viewer to pick up on the connection between Ralphie and Noah, the parallel is nevertheless there.

Indeed, what I see when I watch this episode – as a former stripper – may differ significantly from what non-sex-workers see. My efforts to amplify the latent feminism in this episode of *The Sopranos* could be categorized as a subversive reading, as Mimi White defines the term:

> Sub-cultural readings are carried out in the interest of a willful subversion of dominant ideology by social and cultural groups whose interests are not centrally addressed, or are largely ignored, by television's system of representation with its plurality of voices. The claim is not … that television in general offers radical representations as an alternative to dominant social-cultural values. Rather, 'against the grain' readings are interested in the latent possibility of alternative viewpoints erupting within the multiple strategies of appeal that are normally at work in the medium. (191–2)

My situated and social constructionist viewpoint highlights all the ways that Tracee's work conditions and low status lead to the scene behind the Bada Bing! where she is murdered. Other viewers might be more likely to see Tracee's choices as the main causes of her death. She chooses to work as a stripper, chooses to blur the lines between stripping, dating, and hooking, chooses to get involved in a relationship with a dangerous man, and then chooses to taunt him recklessly. These arguments aren't wrong, exactly, but their atomistic vision obscures social responsibility for individual lives and deaths. In contrast, my intentionally activist interaction with representations of strippers, sex workers, and sexual women foregrounds meanings that may primarily be visible to the politicized sex workers in the audience. Despite this concession to the possibility that I am "reading too much into this text," a charge with which cultural studies professors are all too familiar, I nevertheless adhere to the position, forged by Wood in relation to Hitchcock's films, that while the *narrative* of "University" may seem to move toward the restoration of the patriarchal order, the monstrous oppressiveness of the order has been exposed, and the episode's *attitude* towards this restoration is, if not ironic, at the very least tragic (246–7).

THIS FEMINIST THING OF OURS:
TOWARDS A THIRD WAVE FEMINIST MEDIA THEORY

Finally, my reading of "University" operates on a metacritical level as a reflection on feminist media studies, diverging intentionally from a pattern of binaristic thinking about media texts as *either* radical *or* conservative in search of "a more dynamic model than that of certain forms of Marxism or feminism that primarily see the dominant culture as one of domination and oppression," as Kellner describes diagnostic media criticism in *Media Spectacle* (29). By unpacking the characterizations of Tracee and Ralphie as dynamic rather than static "victim" and "villain," I have tried to move the conversation in feminist media studies to a new plane, apart from the "love/hate struggle" described by Susan Bordo in *Twilight Zones: The Hidden Life of Cultural Images from Plato to O.J.* as a "rebellious but often dazzled, beguiled but skeptical, always intimate relationship with cultural images" (1). The same trope appears in Susan Douglas's

Where the Girls Are: Growing Up Female with the Mass Media: "If we are honest, we have to admit that we have loved the media as much as we have hated them – and often at exactly the same time." Even as I accept her assertion that "The war that has been raging in the media is not a simplistic war against women but a complex struggle between feminism and antifeminism," I long to move outside the conceptual trap of "guilty media pleasures" (12–13). In the same way that third wave feminists have asserted an interest in recuperating certain pleasures that were infused with conservative political significance during the 1970s – the pleasures of the sex wars, ranging from BDSM and pornography to make-up, marriage, and intercourse – a third wave feminist media theory might usefully revisit visual pleasure, once marked as irreparably patriarchal by Laura Mulvey, to insist on the feminist potential of media culture.

Whereas hooks powerfully models the intersectional analysis I have conducted here, her essays on popular culture focus almost exclusively on the absence of adequately progressive images of women and minorities. This pattern of reading for what is not enough in contemporary film models perceptive ideological analyses, but it can overwhelm at times with its negative focus. A brief sampling from *Reel to Real* demonstrates this relentless conclusion:

> Whereas *Crooklyn* attempts to counter racist assumptions about black identity, it completely valorizes and upholds sexist and misogynist thinking about gender roles... (44)

> *Kids* celebrates patriarchal phallic agency. It in no way critiques. Merely showing that females are violated so that teenage boys can feel phallic potency in no way serves as a critique.... There is nothing in *Kids* that indicates a concern with highlighting nonsexist perspectives. (66–7)

> Even though filmmaker Spike Lee may have intended to portray a radical new image of black female sexuality, *She's Gotta Have It* reinforces and perpetuates old norms overall. Positively, the film does show us the nature of black male–female power struggles, the contradictions, the craziness, and that is an important new direction. Yet it is the absence of compelling liberatory reconciliation that undermines the progressive radical potential of this film. ... While we can applaud Nola's feeble attempt to tell a new story at the end of the film, it is not compelling, not enough – it is not satisfying. (235)

It is, likewise, "the absence of a compelling liberatory reconciliation" between the feminist cultural work of "University" and the pernicious visual cliché of the battered and murdered stripper that troubles my interpretation of episode 32 of *The Sopranos*. Is this combination of progressive and conservative content just a way to appeal to a wide variety of audience members? Does the show offer us liberal-minded images of sexual women and then, in a strategic move of containment, take it all back?

bell hooks makes this argument even about the films she most admires, for instance asserting that *Leaving Las Vegas* offers a progressive vision of a prostitute who is self-assured and smart, and then takes it all back in a rape scene that "undermines the more progressive narrative in the film" (*Real to Real* 24). Regarding *Pulp Fiction*, hooks criticizes Quentin Tarantino's tendency to "titillate with subversive possibility … but then everything kinda comes right back to normal" (48). Tania Modleski makes a similar argument in *Feminism without Women* about *Gorillas in the Mist*, as I note in the introduction above.

In place of this rhetoric, Amanda Lotz advocates a new critical paradigm that aptly frames my reading of *The Sopranos* as an agent of (partially) feminist cultural work:

> Examining the intricacy of these images provides a much more productive route for feminist media criticism than simple categorization of new characters and series as anti-feminist because of character flaws or moments of conservative ideology. Especially when series and characters resonate with audiences to the degree that many recently have, we must explore what is in these texts with an eye to their complexity instead of quickly dismissing them as part of a hegemonic, patriarchal, capitalist system. (114)

This "eye towards complexity" is certainly warranted by *The Sopranos*. Tracee's story accentuates some of the most complex questions of postmodern feminist media theory (perhaps a clearer and less inflammatory term than "postfeminist" or "third wave" television criticism): how to read representations of violence as *both* reiterations of sexism *and* primetime feminist challenges to sexism, how to oppose "the nonconsensual treatment of women as *only* sexual bodies while simultaneously challenging the cultural hierarchies that devalue and stigmatize sexual bodies," as Jill Nagle writes (6), and how to read masculinity as it refracts through social class subordination and masochistic fantasies. We might begin developing this theoretical model, using "University" as a practice text, by working to read this stripper-bashing scene without lapsing into the seductive but simplistic reactions of bashing sex work or bashing men or bashing the media.[10]

NOTES

This article is reprinted from *Feminist Studies* 33, no. 2 (Summer 2007) by permission of the publisher, Feminist Studies, Inc.

1. Episode 11, "Nobody Knows Anything." Original air date: 21 March 1999.
2. Episode 7, "Down Neck" (original air date: 21 February 1999); episode 29, "Fortunate Son" (original air date: 11 March 2001); episode 59, "In Camelot" (original air date: 18 April 2004), respectively.
3. Episode 33, "Second Opinion." Original air date: 8 April 2001.
4. For the concept of a necrology of dead strippers, I am indebted to the necrology section in Vito Russo's *The Celluloid Closet: Homosexuality in the Movies*. I develop this necrology in more detail in my essay, "Stripper Bashing: An Autovideography of Violence against Strippers."
5. Episode 48, "Whoever Did This." Original air date: 10 November 2002.
6. Episode 47, "Mergers and Acquisitions." Original air date: 13 November 2002.
7. Episode 42, "Christopher." Original air date: 29 September 2002.
8. While I depart from Savran in my conclusion to this point, I have relied on his thorough and provocative overview of masochism in Freud and Marcuse to substantiate my reading of Ralphie as disenfranchised under capitalism.
9. Episode 18, "Big Girls Don't Cry." Original air date: 13 February 2000.
10. This chapter owes a significant debt to the anonymous reviewers at *Feminist Studies*, as well as to the Barnard Center for Research on Women, the University of West Georgia, and the Cultural Studies Association for providing opportunities to discuss portions of this work as it developed, and to Carol Siegel and Katherine Frank for their keen feedback.

REFERENCES

Akass, Kim and Janet McCabe. "Beyond the Bada Bing!: Negotiating Female Narrative Authority in *The Sopranos*." In *This Thing of Ours: Investigating the Sopranos*. Ed. David Lavery. New York: Columbia University Press, 2002. 146–61.

Arthurs, Jane. *Television and Sexuality: Regulation and the Politics of Taste*. London: Open University Press, 2004.

Bauer, Dale. "Gender in Bakhtin's Carnival." In *Feminisms: An Anthology of Liter-*

ary Theory and Criticism, Ed. Robyn R. Warhol and Diane Price Herndl. 2nd edn. London and New York: Routledge, 1997. 708–20. Originally published in Dale Bauer, *Feminine Dialogics: A Theory of Failed Community* Albany NY: SUNY Press 1988.

Bordo, Susan. *Twilight Zones: The Hidden Life of Cultural Images from Plato to O.J.* Berkeley: University of California Press, 1997.

Brown, Jeffrey A. "If Looks Could Kill: Power, Revenge, and Stripper Movies." In *Reel Knockouts: Violent Women in the Movies*. Ed. Neal King and Martha McCaughey. Austin: University of Texas Press, 2001. 52–77.

Chapkis, Wendy. *Live Sex Acts: Women Performing Erotic Labor*. New York: Routledge, 1997.

Davenport, Randi. "The Knowing Spectator of *Twin Peaks*: Culture, Feminism, and Family Violence." *Literature Film Quarterly* 21, no. 4 (1993): 255–9.

Douglas, Susan J. *Where the Girls Are: Growing Up Female with the Mass Media*. New York: Three Rivers, 1994.

Dow, Bonnie J. *Prime-time Feminism: Television, Media Culture, and the Women's Movement since 1970*. Philadelphia: University of Pennsylvania Press, 1996.

Dworkin, Andrea. *Intercourse*. New York: Free Press, 1987.

Frank, Katherine. *G-Strings and Sympathy: Strip Club Regulars and Male Desire*. Durham NC: Duke University Press, 2002.

Gardiner, Judith Kegan, ed. *Masculinity Studies and Feminist Theory: New Directions*. New York: Columbia University Press, 2002.

George, Diana Hume. "Lynching Women: A Feminist Reading of *Twin Peaks*." In *Full of Secrets: Critical Approaches to "Twin Peaks."* Ed. David Lavery. Detroit, MI: Wayne University Press, 1995. 109–19.

Gross, Terry. Interview with David Chase. "Fresh Air." *NPR*, 2 March 2004.

Gwin, Minrose. "Nonfelicitous Space and Survivor Discourse." In *Haunted Bodies: Gender and Southern Texts*. Ed. Anne Goodwyn Jones and Susan V. Donaldson. Charlottesville: University Press of Virginia, 1997. 416–40.

Halberstam, Judith. "Imagined Violence/Queer Violence: Representations of Rage and Resistance." In *Reel Knockouts: Violent Women in the Movies*. Ed. Neal King and Martha McCaughey. Austin: University of Texas Press, 2001. 244–66.

Hendin, Josephine Gattuso. "Tony and Meadow: *The Sopranos* as Father-Daughter Drama." *LIT: Literature Interpretation Theory* 14 (2003): 63–7.

hooks, bell. *Yearning: Race, Gender, and Cultural Politics*. Boston MA: South End Press, 1990.

———. *Reel to Real: Race, Sex, and Class at the Movies*. New York: Routledge, 1996.

Irigaray, Luce. "Women on the Market." In *This Sex Which Is Not One*. Trans. Catherine Porter. Ithaca: Cornell UP, 1985. 170–91.

Jenkins, Henry, Tara McPherson, and Jane Shattuc, eds. *Hop on Pop: The Politics and Pleasures of Popular Culture*. Durham NC: Duke University Press, 2002.

Johnson, Merri Lisa. "Stripper Bashing: An Autovideography of Violence against Strippers." In *Flesh for Fantasy: Producing and Consuming Exotic Dance*. Ed. R. Danielle Egan, Katherine Frank, and Merri Lisa Johnson. New York: Thunder's Mouth, 2006. 159–88.

Kellner, Douglas. *Media Culture: Cultural Studies, Identity, and Politics between the Modern and the Postmodern*. London: Routledge, 1995.

————. *Media Spectacle*. New York: Routledge, 2003.

Lasch, Christopher. "The Family as a Haven in a Heartless World." *Salmagundi* 35 (1976).

Lotz, Amanda. "Postfeminist Television Criticism: Rehabilitating Critical Terms and Identifying Postfeminist Attitudes." *Feminist Media Studies* 1, no. 1 (2001): 105–21.

Modleski, Tania. *The Women Who Knew Too Much: Hitchcock and Feminist Theory*. New York: Metheun, 1988.

————. *Feminism without Women: Culture and Criticism in a "Postfeminist" Age*. New York: Routledge, 1991.

Nagle, Jill, ed. *Whores and Other Feminists*. New York: Routledge, 1997.

Owen, Rob, and Barbara Vancheri, "Going off-key?: 'The Sopranos' Takes Some Hits for Graphically Portraying Violence against Women." *Post-Gazette.com* (10 May 2001), www.post-gazette.com/tv/20010510sopranos2.asp (accessed 23 April 2004).

Parini, Jay. "The Cultural Work of *The Sopranos*." In *A Sitdown with the Sopranos: Watching Italian American Culture on T.V.'s Most Talked-About Series*. Ed. Regina Barreca. New York: Palgrave, 2002. 75–87.

Phillips, Lynn. *Flirting with Danger: Young Women's Reflections on Sexuality and Danger*. New York: New York University Press, 2000.

Projansky, Sarah. *Watching Rape: Film and Television in Postfeminist Culture*. New York: New York University Press, 2001.

Rubin, Gayle. "The Traffic in Women: Notes on the 'Political Economy' of Sex." In *Toward an Anthropology of Women*. Ed. Rayna R. Reiter. New York: Monthly Review Press, 1975. 157–210.

Russo, Vito. *The Celluloid Closet: Homosexuality in the Movies*. New York: Harper & Row, 1981.

Savran, David. *Taking It Like a Man: White Masculinity, Masochism, and Contemporary American Culture*. Princeton: Princeton University Press, 1998.

Traister, Rebecca. "Is 'The Sopranos' a Chick Show?" *Salon.com*, 6 March 2004, www.salon.com.

Walkowitz, Judith. *City of Dreadful Delight: Narratives of Sexual Danger in Late Victorian London*. Chicago: University of Chicago Press, 1992.

Weigman, Robyn. "Unmaking: Men and Masculinity in Feminist Theory." In *Masculinity Studies and Feminist Theory: New Directions*. Ed. Judith Kegan Gardiner. New York: Columbia University Press, 2002. 31–59.

White, Mimi. "Ideological Analysis." *Channels of Discourse, Reassembled: Television and Contemporary Criticism*. Ed. Robert C. Allen. 2nd edn. Chapel Hill: University of North Carolina Press, 1992. 161–202.

Williams, Linda. *Hard Core: Power, Pleasure, and the "Frenzy of the Visible"*. Berkeley: University of California Press, 1999.

————. "Why I Did Not Want to Write This Essay." *Feminist Media Studies* 30, no. 1 (2004): 1264–71.

Wood, Robin. *Hollywood from Vietnam to Reagan*. New York: Columbia University Press, 1986.

2

FEMALE HETEROSEXUAL SADISM: THE FINAL FEMINIST TABOO IN *BUFFY THE VAMPIRE SLAYER* AND THE ANITA BLAKE VAMPIRE HUNTER SERIES

CAROL SIEGEL

With all apologies to Sui Sin Far's "Leaves from the Mental Portfolio of a Eurasian," I ask you to think of the following two anecdotes as film clips from the mental home movies of a feminist sex radical. I draw on Sui Sin Far's title because I feel, as I assume she did, the discomfort of critiquing, from the standpoint of my own apparently atypical experience, the accuracy of representations that sometimes it seems the whole world agrees on. Yet like so many feminists who came before me, I see no other way to call into question traditional views of women as a group than evoking the particularities of the lives of those whose experiences lie outside what is commonly represented as our true desires and essential nature. Such questioning is urgent for me due to my growing frustration with the failure of popular culture to recognize some crucial differences in women's sexuality and of feminism to address this failure. Opening with an apology also seems appropriate because while I wish my mental home movies could provide an emulation-inspiring record of the joys of sexual liberation, they too often chronicle a lifelong battle with both mainstream media and a majoritist feminism that deny my experience and observation of the workings of sexuality.[1]

CLIP ONE

Lying on the couch with the most beautiful person in the world in my arms, we enjoy Àlex de la Iglesia's *Perdida Durango*, a wild ride of a film about two Mexican criminals' last crime spree. The eponymous heroine (played by Rosie Perez) and her accomplice, Romeo (Javier Bardem), kidnap two innocent blond teenaged American suburbanites and entertain themselves by sexually tormenting their hostages until the conclusion, when Romeo dies and Perdida decides to free them both. Although she and the boy seemed to have bonded, he runs away and leaves her weeping with loneliness, all her tough defensiveness gone.

As the credits run, I turn to my lover and say, "Well that was certainly disappointing! Why can't we ever see the pretty blond and his sadistic dark lady stay together, happily ever after?" He replies, "That never happens in fiction, only in real life." I laugh, but remain disappointed.

CLIP TWO

A friend calls me and exhorts me to start watching the sixth season of the television series *Buffy the Vampire Slayer*. I am dubious, but she assures me that Buffy's affair with the vampire Spike is "just the sort of S/M stuff you like to see." I dutifully tune in and watch the next three episodes, but instead of what I like to see, I see what makes me feel near despair. Shortly afterward I shock her by shouting, after a few drinks, "What was the point of women's liberation anyway? Over thirty years of continuous struggle and we still have no sexual freedom at all!"

FLIRTING WITH VAMPIRES

Of course at calmer moments I recognize all the progress our movement has brought, but I remain deeply disappointed that we continue to pathologize certain sexualities, and specifically that female domination of men undertaken for mutual sexual pleasure, rather than to make money or get revenge, still remains outside the pale of feminism. Sometimes I think if it were not for Laurell K. Hamilton's "Anita Blake Vampire Hunter" novel series, I would

give up. In this chapter I compare this series to the Buffy series
in an attempt to understand why feminism, now in its third wave
as a movement, cannot seem to accept the expression of female
sexual sadism within consensual heterosexual relationships as potentially consonant with our political goals, and what might happen if
feminism could. We can in fact read Hamilton's novel series as a
response to Joss Whedon's *Buffy the Vampire Slayer* television series,
and we can recognize Hamilton's response as revisionary in a mode
similar to that of slash fiction – sexual fantasies about favorite
characters written by and circulated among cult TV show fans.
While Whedon's series engages with third wave concepts of female
identity – such as the combination of toughness and femininity,
self-assertion and voluptuous yielding – to address the problems of
sexual expression attending the greater social power young women
gained from feminism's second wave, Hamilton's series takes ideas
of female sexual empowerment much further, and, in imagining
female sadism as other than evil or pathological, breathtakingly
refreshes old concepts of gendered sexuality.

To begin, I will provide a brief synopsis of the three episodes
from *Buffy the Vampire Slayer* mentioned above, followed by some
questions they raise. First a little explanatory background. In episode
63 of season four, Spike is captured by the Initiative, a commando
group that fights supernatural monsters, and implanted with a chip
that makes him experience unbearable pain if he hurts a human. In
episode 82, season five, an erotic dream brings him to realize that
rather than hating Buffy, he is in love with her. Season five ends
with Buffy choosing to die in place of her younger sister Dawn in
order to save the world. In season six, she is resurrected through her
friend Willow's magic ritual but feels embittered about being pulled
out of Heaven. Buffy's newfound attraction to Spike is attributed to
this darkening of her personality. She no longer enjoys ordinary life
and secretly longs to return to the peace of death. Thus her affair
with Spike is negatively coded with a Freudian allusion to S/M as
linked to "the death drive." The affair is further coded, through
continually crosscut sequences, as a self-destructive addiction parallel
to the inability to stop using magic that has taken over Willow's life
and ended her loving, mutually supportive affair with Tara. (Willow
is very explicitly figured as a junkie trying to kick in "Wrecked,"

episode 110, when she lies curled up on her bed shaking and crying.) In episode 108, "Tabula Rasa," Buffy kisses Spike, and in episode 109, "Smashed," continues that theme.

"Smashed" was the first episode I watched in the Buffy series. The structure of the series, like that of many soap operas, is a series of crosscuts from one group of characters to another. This episode opened with a sequence that seems particularly significant. Spike confronts Buffy in an alley expressing anger because she aroused him with her kisses in the previous episode and now continues to leave him frustrated. They tussle and he learns, to his delight, that because she "came back wrong" from her resurrection in the previous season, the microchip implanted in his brain that causes him pain when he hurts other humans will not respond when he treats her violently. Buffy seems transformed into a monster, like Spike and his fellow vampires, with whom he is able to follow his impulses without restraint. This means she is now suited to him as a sex partner. Cut to Willow talking to her fellow witch Amy, who is in the form of a rat due to a magic spell; Willow says that attachment to others always ends in abandonment and pain. Since Willow is a lesbian, her assertion carries over from the classic feminist critique of heterosexual relations a general suspicion of romance and adds to it the normative concept that both pain and impermanent sexual bonding are always bad. This speech will be echoed in Buffy's explanation to Spike when they meet again later that she cannot continue to have erotic contact with him because "it always ends badly" when she has a sexual experience with anyone, a conclusion that, as I was later to learn, the entire series strongly supports.

Another echo is delivered thematically. Amy, now returned to her human form, goes with Willow to the Bronze, a local nightclub, and Amy dances with two young men. When she leaves them to talk to Willow, still mourning the loss of her relationship with Tara, the guys pursue Amy and accuse her of getting them "all worked up" and not following through, just as Spike has accused Buffy. One of the two grabs Amy's arm roughly. When Willow intervenes they gay-bait her, calling her "Ellen." Amy uses her magic powers to turn the boys into near nude tinsel-clad dancers in cages above the dance floor and makes them do an obscene pelvis-thrusting dance. The guys have suggested that dancing, a network-friendly symbol of sex, would relax Amy, and now she laughingly tells a jubilant Willow that she does feel more relaxed.

Among the messages conveyed in this sequence is that working men up through flirtation will result in the men forcing unwanted sexual attentions on you; sexual arousal, in other words, causes violence. Lynn Phillips's *Flirting with Danger*, a study of chronologically third wave young women's responses to the contradictory messages about sexuality with which they are currently plagued is particularly pertinent to these disturbing representations. As Phillips observes, "Young women are simultaneously taught to solicit and feel flattered by male sexual attention, to protect themselves against it, and to control men so they do not express it" (18). Resentful of a cultural discourse of male sexuality that blames "teases" for their own violation (58–63), some rebel by courting male attention and then frustrating it: "these women reason that their ability to arouse men (and their ability to withhold sexual gratification)" is their only avenue to powerful sexual expression (129). No wonder, then, that both heterosexual Amy and lesbian Willow discover that men are most fun and relaxing when their sexuality is exhibited as a caged and shaming spectacle.

This scene, in addition to the next, in which Buffy's loyal friend Xander stresses the importance of controlling "wild" desires, sets us up for the sex scene between Spike and Buffy, which will be crosscut with scenes from the Bronze to the tune of the song "Here" by Virgil, with the much reiterated line "What is wrong here?" Clearly what is wrong, according to the logic of the series, is S/M, reflexively equated with unrestrained sexual expression, letting go, and being wild. In the "sex" scene, Buffy and Spike fight each other in an abandoned house. He says, "I'm in love with you." She sneers, "You're in love with pain," and accuses him of following her because "you enjoy getting beat down." He answers smugly that he is a vampire – he is thus supposed to want sex on "the dark side" – and then snarls, "What's your excuse?" But we've already heard her excuse in their first confrontation in this episode when she explained that she kissed him because the loss of her Watcher, Giles (a protective father figure), coming so closely after her mother's death, left her emotionally vulnerable. This still does not explain why she would want to get close to Spike through S/M, which he constantly, coyly, alludes to as the center of their mutual attraction. In the midst of a physical battle, she kisses him aggressively and unzips his pants. She climbs up his body and opens her eyes very wide, symbolic in soft-core scenes of sexual penetration having been achieved, and they slam each other around in a tight clinch. Finally they fall through the floor into the basement, Buffy on top.

When Spike and Buffy reappear in the next episode, "Wrecked," naked on the floor, she acts amnesiac, asking when the building was damaged, and then seems aggrieved. His body is covered with bloody scratches, and a huge purple bruise marks his face. Red bruises likewise cover Buffy's face and body. Spike's suggestive hints make fairly clear that these marks are the result of S/M play, not just the initial fight, a point made repeatedly as he refers to their ongoing "degrading" lovemaking. Buffy expresses shame and regret, but, like Willow who fails to control her urge to cast spells, Buffy repeatedly responds sexually to Spike's taunting seductions, her self-hatred increasing each time.

In the subsequent episode, "Gone," Buffy begins what will turn out to be a slow movement toward making her relationship with Spike platonic as, again like Willow, she gets control of her "addiction." The parallel here stresses the series' reliance on the addiction metaphor to code unconventional sexual choices as sick, escapist, self-destructive, and damaging to society. S/M is figured as the ultimate sexual addiction, a classically Freudian manifestation of the death drive. Due to various epiphanies, Buffy no longer wants to die, thus an S/M relationship no longer appeals to her. Instead she recognizes it as a mistaken attempt to escape her "true" feelings.

Alas, this is far from being the sort of depiction of S/M I like. Among the questions it raises for me are:

- Why is the expression of male desire, even toward heterosexual women like Buffy and Amy, regarded as a sort of revolting assault?
- Why is no distinction made between the desire to dominate another and the desire to submit? Although there are many references to S/M, the series primly avoids showing us anything that Buffy or Spike actually do sexually or revealing what roles they play in relation to each other.

- Why does Buffy feel disgusted by her own sexual pleasure, even though she is not otherwise especially prudish?
- Why does the desire to dominate sexually, or to submit, have to be accounted for in ways other types of desires that differ from the norm, for example Willow's lesbianism, do not?
- Why is it depicted as comical and admirable for Willow and Amy, and other women throughout the series, to humiliate and hurt men for entertainment, but not for mutual sexual satisfaction?

One answer is provided by Thomas Hibbs, who argues that the Buffy series "replays themes about eros, sex, and love from classic *noir*, where sexual desire is typically seen as incompatible with conventional American life. Acting on that desire unleashes unanticipated consequences and rarely brings the happiness or even the pleasure sought" (59). The series has at its core "insistence on the inevitable and usually destructive consequences of sex" (Hibbs 60). No wonder then that Buffy's traditional feminist realization that "she does not need a lover to be complete" releases her into the happiness of "chaste bed-sharing love" (Kaveney 28–9). This outcome, perhaps more than any other in the series, exposes the limits of majoritist feminist critiques of sexual politics which cast men in the role of oppressors except where eroticism excludes genital sexuality and violence in favor of cuddly friendship. But the most fundamental answer to my questions seems to be that the series agrees with both mainstream culture and majoritist feminism that sadistic desires are pathological in women.

I am, therefore, especially grateful for Hamilton's Anita Blake series, which, in contrast to Buffy, provides us with a different sort of narrative of S/M sex. A short summary of a scene in one of her novels will serve to illustrate the tone of her depictions of consensual S/M. As with Buffy, the complexity of the series' plot demands some preface to discussion of the scene. In *Narcissus in Chains*, necromancer and vampire hunter Anita Blake must contend with two major problems that interfere with her heroic work to save the world from an insane shape-shifter. First, as the leader of a group of wereleopards, she must protect their most vulnerable member, Nathaniel, who is "one of those rare sub[missive]s who are almost incapable of saying no," whose "idea of pain and sex could be very extreme. Which meant that he might say yes to things that were very, very bad for him" (6). And, second, she must deal with her own combination of an overwhelming, supernatural need to feed on sexual excitement called "the *ardeur*," which often causes her to lose control and hurt others, and she must at the same time harness the energy that comes to her through the "*munin*" (ghostly presence) of a vanquished foe, Raina, a sexual sadist who "had no stopping point" (81).

Although Anita feels strongly that she should not take advantage of Nathaniel because his inability to set limits makes using him sexually "like child molesting ... the same as rape" (244), she finds she must give him regular S/M sex to protect him from life-threatening abuse by less caring others. Eventually she gives in to the *ardeur* and indulges in a lengthy S/M session with him, of which she, as narrator, gives pages of description, such as "I bit the flesh of his back, drew him into my mouth, and this time I did not stop until I tasted the sweet metallic taste of his blood" (198). Checking with him frequently to make sure he remains enraptured by the torture, she inflicts wounds all over his body, concentrating on his beautiful buttocks and often pausing to admire his lovely skin, hair, and body shape. Afterwards they exchange tender words and are congratulated by their friends, who see this as a good solution both to Anita's problems with the *ardeur* and *munin* and to Nathaniel's propensity to take life-threatening risks. The community of supernatural beings and the human community, to which they exist in uneasy relation, will be much safer as a result. This begins a relationship that Anita and Nathaniel find very satisfying, which also increases her superhuman powers to the point that she becomes invincible in her battles against evil.

Interestingly the Buffy and Anita series developed along parallel chronological tracks, a coincidence that makes comparison of them a particularly useful approach to analyzing the development of feminism at the turn of the twentieth century. On 31 June 1992 a feature film entitled *Buffy the Vampire Slayer* opened for a short, unsuccessful theatrical run. Disappointed with the transformation of his story into a comedy, scriptwriter Whedon returned to his original vision when he was asked to re-create the story for the television series with the same name that debuted in the 1996–97 season. His version of the heroine, Buffy, looked the part of the standard horror film "blonde bimbo who dies in reel two," but was a serious, honorable young woman whose situation as a hereditary vampire slayer would force her into early maturity (Tracy 13). Her story eventually stretched out through seven seasons to the delight of an enormous fan base. Meanwhile, in the world of print culture, Hamilton's Anita Blake Vampire Hunter series premiered in October of 1993 with the novel *Guilty Pleasures*. Rising slowly from moderate success with fans of genre horror, fantasy, and mystery fiction, the novels, which focus on an aggressive young detective with supernatural powers inherited from her grandmother, began to appear on the *New York Times* bestseller list after the January 2000 publication of the ninth in the series, *Obsidian Butterfly*. With twelve novels now in print, Anita Blake is still gaining in popularity.

The consensus among fans, as represented by their web-posted comments, as well as from academics, seems to be that the two series are quite similar, as in some ways they are.[2] However, I concentrate here on differences between the two series that make them legible as a sort of dialogue between the authors, with their competing concepts of women's sexuality. The sharpest distinction between the two series' representations of female sexuality arises from their differing treatments of sadomasochism, and specifically the sadistic inclinations of their respective heroines. And this major difference between the two series can be seen as a microcosm in which the most incommensurate views of female sexuality typifying the most recent waves of feminism are represented.

Both series can be, and often are, understood as feminist in that their protagonists are strong independent women who offer protection to the weak and fight on their behalf against evil beings. Women's issues, such as rape and sexual exploitation, are often addressed in the episodes, as are the problems Buffy and Anita face with authoritative men who resent their power and try to dominate them. Moreover, both Buffy and Anita must contend with their relatively small stature and girlish appearances, which frequently cause even friendly men to treat them as inferiors. Both are likewise the recipients of unwanted sexual advances. These series advocate women's empowerment through physical self-confidence derived from athleticism, mastery of weaponry and martial arts, as well as willingness to injure and even kill others in self-defense or to help the more vulnerable. Despite their belief that such feelings are wrong, both protagonists experience a degree of exhilaration, often amounting to sadistic pleasure, when they hurt or kill their adversaries. In that they are constantly menaced by villains who are overtly sexually sadistic, these responses in themselves result in moral crises very reminiscent of those that have interfered with feminist solidarity for the last three decades.

THIRD WAVE SADOMASOCHISM

One could hardly overestimate the trouble disagreements over female sexuality have caused feminism. Contention over women's interest and participation in sadomasochism resulted in the so-called "sex wars" that split the movement in the late 1980s, destroying much of its political power for over twenty years.[3] And arguments about what women do – and should – desire still rage on. While numerous sex radical texts from feminism's third wave seek to reclaim female masochism from patriarchal narratives of it as a natural response to male superiority and articulate it in terms of Foucauldian *askesis* – that is, as a self-fashioning physical discipline – majoritist feminists continue female masochism's pathologization as a manifestation of trauma-induced false consciousness.[4]

Julia Flower MacCannell's 1999 book *The Hysteric's Guide to the Future Female Subject* is representative of such work. MacCannell uses Sade's *Philosophy in the Bedroom* as a template upon which to map out contemporary gender roles. To her the current popularity/visibility of S/M and its commodification through soft- and hardcore pornography, club fetish nights, and couples' workshops at educative sex supply stores, such as Good Vibrations, creates dangerous situations in which a perverse person "acts out his or her own fantasy, but ... must confirm its logic by inducing the hysterical other to go along" (50). She regretfully warns us that for the contemporary girl, "the most important relation for her sexual life today is to the pervert and not to her Mother or her Father" because of the pervert's "skepticism regarding the law, including the law of sexual difference" (30). Adopting this blindness to sexual difference enables the girl to refuse "to join society, the world of other subjects in which her joys would be restricted" (18). MacCannell posits an opposition between women's untrammeled sexual freedom and "the *truth* of the girl's experience" (26). To refuse gender identification as male or female is perverse and immature in MacCannell's view. She judges Judith Butler's writing on the performativity of gender "less a theory about than a reflection of the education of young people to hysteria today" (30). She emphasizes the importance of acknowledging inherent gender difference to understanding desire and sees as the most crucial element of women's freedom the "right to resist a sexual encounter" (196–8, 261). In keeping with the majoritist position that stable gender identification is necessary to mental health, she reads male gender flexibility as unproductive confusion: "This is the hysterical setup, uncertainty about sex, in action" (31). Thus MacCannell's discussion of sex and gender is structured by her insistence on what she sees as the inevitable binary difference between male and female that she asserts always links sadomasochistic expressions of desire to women's disempowerment.

For a sex radical perspective we might turn instead to Linda S. Kaufman's 1998 book *Bad Girls and Sick Boys: Fantasies in Contemporary Culture*, where she defends the liberatory potential of S/M play for those seeking to avoid traditional, patriarchal gender identifications. In contrast to MacCannell, Kaufman rightly describes male masochism as an even more intense problem for majoritist second-wave feminism than female masochism in that it confounds the view of women as victims of patriarchy so central to this philosophy (21–6).

Still more problematic is female sadism. While male masochism has often been described by feminists as a ruse to disavow real social power, female sadism seems inexplicable in the terms of majoritist second-wave feminism. It constitutes a category crisis. As it does in popular culture generally, which avoids representation of sadistic desires in women as anything other than grotesquely unnatural and evil. This is strongly in contrast to post-sexual revolutionary naturalization within pop culture of male sadism and female masochism, so long as they are relatively mildly expressed within a mutually caring relationship, as for example in the recent film *Secretary*. As is often the case with third-wave art products, the film replays the tragedy of women's condition as a farcical romp by revising what was compelled and inescapable into a parodic, exaggerated, and knowing performance. But some aspects of the standard majoritist feminist account of S/M remain unchanged. And it is through brief consideration of them that we can begin to understand how to read Hamilton's Anita Blake series as a sort of slash response to Buffy that takes popular feminism further into the areas of unrestricted female sexual expression that the third wave has begun to explore.

The adaptation of Mary Gaitskill's short story "Secretary" into a film by sex radical feminist playwright Erin Cressida Wilson, co-author of *The Erotica Project*, provides an instructive case in the sex radical re-visioning of majoritist feminist thinking on S/M. Gaitskill's protagonist, Debby, is a classic victim of patriarchy of a sort familiar to any reader of majoritist feminist literature intended to effect consciousness-raising. She lives at home with a profoundly depressed mother and sister and a caricatured domineering father for whom "beer and kielbasa sausage" must be purchased daily and who can be heard "yelling at my mother" for hours every evening (137). Although her age is not mentioned, we can assume Debby is no older than her late teens based on her turns of phrase as first-person protagonist, together with her absolute lack of knowledge of male sexuality even to the point that she seems unable to understand what has occurred when her employer masturbates and ejaculates on her buttocks.

Like her mother and sister Debby seems not only depressed but nearly paralyzed by despair about her potential to find pleasure in life. When she secures a position as a secretary to a lawyer she experiences what seems to be the first contentment she has ever known because at last her life seems to have purpose. "I was useful" (137), she explains. But this period of relative pleasure lasts only two weeks. Then her boss begins to criticize her work as faulty and a waste of his time, to ask her disturbingly personal questions, and finally to spank and otherwise humiliate her. Confused and distressed by his behavior but also sexually aroused, she submits until the day when he masturbates on her. After that, she continues to be sexually obsessed with what has occurred but never returns to work. The conclusion of the story, when she rejects an investigative reporter's attempt to get her story about the lawyer, who is now running for mayor, shows us Debby subliminally identifying with the corpse-like discarded Barbie dolls in her parents' basement and recognizing that she has become disassociated from her own body. Despite the last line, "And it really wasn't such a bad feeling at all" (147), we are left with little option but to read Debby's foray into S/M as traumatic and her former boss's behavior as abusive.

The film presents a completely different vision, one more in keeping with Wilson's radical vision of female heterosexuality as a potential playground for women's powerful experimentation. First of all, the main character, now renamed Lee, who has just been released from a mental hospital, compulsively cuts and wounds herself to alleviate her feelings of frustration, anxiety, and depression. And her employer, no longer a glowering bully with "dense immobile shoulders" (Gaitskill 134) but instead a man of rather delicate physical beauty (played by the exquisite James Spader), seems sincerely caring as he draws her out about her emotional distress. When the spankings and other punishments begin, the predominant response we see in her is intense excitement. She not only clearly enjoys the S/M encounters, she does all she can to elicit them, while he shows considerable ambivalence, culminating in his refusal to continue due to an overwhelming self-disgust. Yet his self-disgust seems unwarranted, derived from a conventionally prudish revulsion at his own perversity rather than based on any idea that his behavior is damaging Lee. The film repeatedly establishes that in fact their S/M play has a profoundly therapeutic impact on Lee. And in contrast to the lawyer in Gaitskill's story, who reinforces pathetic Debby's conviction that she is worthless, making her repeat "I am stupid" (135), Edward, the film's lawyer, makes clear that he inflicts ritual punishments on Lee not because she is incapable of doing her job well but because she willfully defies his authority and makes deliberate mistakes – and because it turns them both on when he does so.

Lee's true love for him overcomes Edward's self-hatred and consequent fear that he is unlovable, just as his obviously affectionate discipline overcomes her nearly incapacitating anxiety about not being good enough. The film concludes by presenting them as a consensual S/M couple happily settled into a marriage that is otherwise conventional in that he works while she stays home and keeps house. Her embrace of domesticity made entertaining by sexual submission is presented as a choice, not something she gives in to because she sees no other options, a conclusion reinforced by her earlier rejection of a sweet and devoted boyfriend because he could not satisfy her need to submit to S/M discipline.

Both versions of the Secretary narrative attribute sadistic and masochistic desires along conventionally gendered lines, following

Freudian psychology: masculine sexuality is active/initiatory and dominating, female sexuality is passive/responsive and submissive. The sense that S/M reinforces traditional and unjust power divides is carried over from Gaitskill's story to the film in that both implicitly locate S/M in the workplace and distribute the dominant and submissive roles according to social status and power. Moreover, both versions pathologize masochism by presenting it as a response to bad parenting and resultant severe anxiety and depression. The main difference is that while Gaitskill's story has a sad tone, the film jocularly exhorts us to enjoy our symptoms. This is by no means a minor difference. The film serves as an effective argument for freedom of sexual expression, representing the consensual activities indulged in by adult women as deserving of tolerance and perhaps even respect. In its celebration of free sexual expression, the film aligns nicely with third wave feminist insistence on the primary importance of pleasure and refusal to emphasize victimization.[5] Like certain other third wave texts, the film draws on psychoanalytic theory not to diagnose putative illness, but to insist on the liberatory aspects of its descriptive potential. Third wavers like Laura Kipnis and Mandy Merck emphasize the ways classic psychoanalytic theory calls into question gender binarity rather than agreeing with the normative Freud, but despite the film's refusal to represent S/M as deathly it still fails to imagine the possibility that free expression of sexuality could depart very far from what have been traditionally regarded as specifically female desires. Submission is still represented as woman's deepest sexual desire.

We must turn from narratives with some pretensions to realism, like the Secretary stories, to ones more clearly marked as fantasies in order to bring to light the defense of female sexual sadism that is now beginning to appear within pop cultural products. Arising from the ongoing vampire craze that began with Ann Rice's 1976 *Interview with the Vampire* and fed by the Goth subculture now entering its third decade, the Buffy series provides a context for understanding the evolution of Hamilton's Anita Blake series from its short and relatively restrained first novel about a rather prim religious girl disturbed by her necromantic powers to its current cult status as unabashed sadistic eroticism for women in which the now overtly dominant heroine learns the utility of her deviant sexuality.

Hamilton took the series from apparent complicity with the most sex-phobic elements of feminist second wave ideology – that women crave domestic security more than orgasm and that seduction is a form of rape – the sort that mainstreamed in the 1980s when feminism became popularly associated with the right's war on recreational sex and pornography, to a defiantly third wave sex radical position on S/M: that women have a right to use sex as a form of intensely exciting entertainment. The story of this attitudinal progression within the series also provides an implicit dialogue, imaginatively extended in the writings of many fans, between Hamilton's work and the cult that grew for seven seasons around *Buffy the Vampire Slayer*.

Second wave feminist literary criticism and theory developed out of consideration of intertextuality, as academics traced influences and established female traditions in order to create a women's canon. But the concept of sisterly affiliation in solidarity against patriarchal heterosexuality that structured this newly revised canon was exploded by the sex wars from which feminism's third wave emerged as a movement defining itself largely in contrast to the feminisms that had previously gained cultural legitimacy, as I discuss in *New Millennial Sexstyles*. While African-American theorists, notably bell hooks, pointed out that the first two waves of feminism had mainly aimed to liberate white middle-class women, third wave feminism defined itself as both multiracial and global, particularly when it came to refusing the simple division of the human race into men who were all understood to benefit from patriarchy and women who were all understood to be victimized by it. Working from her recognition that imperialism – "not patriarchy" – is the biggest obstacle to women's liberation in the world today, hooks calls for an end to the "common" second wave feminist idea that "the woman who is emotionally and sexually committed to an individual man is necessarily incapable of loyal woman-identified political commitment," and goes on to assert, "Just as the struggle to end sexual oppression aims to eliminate heterosexism, it should not endorse any one sexual choice, celibacy, bi-sexuality, homosexuality, or heterosexuality" (*Feminist Theory* 128, 152). Yet this truly radical position remained on the margins of the feminist movement prior to the millennium, as her book's subtitle, *From Margin to Center*, indicated. It was not until the third wave that feminism generally acknowledged the shared political interests of oppressed peoples, even when these interests cut across gender binarity. Thus while second wave feminists came to be understood by the media as determined to regulate sexuality, not without reason, third wave feminists rebelliously insisted on the right of consenting adults to absolute sexual freedom. No longer marginalized, the agenda hooks attributes to truly radical feminism, "claiming the dark in resistance to the bourgeois world of repression, order, boredom, and fixed social roles" (*Outlaw Culture* 74), became central to feminism's third wave.

In the aftermath of this struggle, popular culture studies generally became the province of third-wavers due to the association of popular culture with pleasures second wave feminists deemed complicit with women's exploitation. Erotic texts created by and for women were often particularly despised by the second wave of feminism. As Ann Barr Snitow famously observed, genre romance has functioned as women's version of pornography (254–60). And pornography was seen as intrinsically harmful to women. Pat Califia sums up his opponents' position well in saying, "The antipornography movement espouses a traditional view of women's sexuality, including the belief that women do not enjoy pornography, casual sex, genital sex, or sex outside the context of a romantic relationship; women are so different from men that there can be no such thing as pornography created by or for women" (*Public Sex* 111). Such sweeping claims about what is proper or natural to women and consequently how our desires should be represented split the second wave of the women's movement. The anti-pornography movement united political conservatives with feminists in a common affirmation of traditional views of gender difference, and women who sought sexual experiences deemed inappropriate found our pleasures roundly condemned by majoritist feminism.

One reaction to the denigration or dismissal of their pleasures by women caught up in the production and consumption of pop pornography/eroticism is deliberate opposition to feminist politics, as Constance Penley notes when she discusses the writers of slash fiction who understand themselves as rebels against identifications that would be assigned to them by "a middle-class feminism that disdains popular culture and believes that pornography degrades women" ("Feminism, Psychoanalysis and the Study of Popular Culture" 492).

While, as Paula Graham argues, fan fictions created by the Buffy enthusiasts can be understood as an attempt to "reproduce and extend online" the "idealised female-centered community" represented by Buffy's friends, the Scooby Gang (28), quite a bit of the Buffy slash (erotic fan fiction) could be placed in the category of rebellious female-centered pornography. Kristina Busse comments that it often exceeds the typical slash "hurt–comfort" model "with its variety of fics resembling traditional sadomasochistic porn. These intensely erotic stories constitute an understandable response to a show that prominently features vampires; after all, the vampire symbolically connects pleasure and pain" (212). Busse provides numerous examples of fan fics that conflate nurture and S/M in "the image of the vampire suckling on the breast," such as Saber Shadowkitten's "Master of Puppets," in which Spike, in bed with both Buffy and Angel, is "suckling her tit like a babe, quickly slicing the tender skin around her nipple so her blood flowed like a mother's milk" (214).

Less maternal imagery occurs in many fics. For example, in "Feel the Fever," by Lady Raven, when a magical fever causes Buffy and Spike agonizing sexual arousal, this is the result:

> Angel gave Giles a crooked half-smile that definitely was one, and slid off his jacket and turned around. Giles let out a slow breath as he fingered the long rents in the back of Angel's T-shirt, the edges crusted with blood.
> "Buffy did that with her nails alone in less than a minute."

Or in Herself's "Leather," a piece that revisits Buffy's affair with Spike, dwelling on her domination of him, Spike initially resents her slapping him around and her fetishization of his black leather duster, but comes to submit to her entirely, even as "the idea came to her that she'd rejected him – rejected his skin, his real body, the man who wanted to make love to her, in favor of the leather coat, his demon and his disembodied cock. And having done that, she'd not even let him finish." The theme of Spike's involuntary abject devotion to Buffy and her cool indifference to his suffering structures many fics. This first-person narrative "Slave," by Spikelovin, is typical:

> She smiles a dirty little smile and lets me know that she knows. That she knows that I'd do anything. Anything. She'll take me up on that. Don't you bloody doubt it. She'll ask me to do some

unspeakable thing, some unforgivable thing, and I'll do it. I'll do it and smile.... I worship her. Because she's everything. Because she's the whole bloody world and she's giving me so many little slices of nothing. I've never been so grateful.

Stories of Spike as a sex slave who will eagerly fulfill every fantasy, giving his body to whatever abuse his beloved chooses to inflict upon him, and of Buffy as his exploitive, sadistic partner clearly fascinate a substantial number of fans, as is suggested by one fan fic website's title, "Love's Bitch," taken from Spike's self-description, in episode 42, "Lover's Walk." We can easily read the aggressively pornographic style of this Buffy slash as an assault on the bourgeois values of majoritist feminism which demand that the sexuality of girls, even girl vampire slayers, be constrained within the bounds of propriety.

Yet we need not assume such responses fall outside all feminism. Feminism, like all radical political philosophies, is meant to provide an alternative viewpoint to that which, at any given moment, the dominant system of power–knowledge offers as normative. When fans imaginatively rewrite both Buffy and Anita as figures with the potential to defy externally imposed definitions of female sexuality, as necessarily constrained by romantic love and the desire for domesticity, their writings often virtually – in every sense of the word – engage third wave sex radicalism. Katinka Hooijer's rejection of majoritist second wave "feminism's impractical theories and universal sexual norms" is characteristic of sex radical third wave critiques arising from the realization that pornography can generate "new realities of pleasure" for women (267, 278). The television series *Buffy the Vampire Slayer* follows a pattern similar to that of the sex-regulating feminism that became majoritist in the second wave, while the Anita Blake series, like many of the pornographic Buffy fan fics, could hardly be less in compliance with previously accepted ways of understanding female heterosexuality.[6]

SLAYAGE AND FEMININITY

From the onset Buffy and Anita were conceived as almost diametrically opposed characters, despite their resemblance in what Hilary M. Leon calls "many superficial characteristics" (1). Blonde, slender, and athletic, with a conventionally pretty face, Buffy embodies the high-school cheerleader ideal. And her personality initially matches her outward appearance. Cheerleaders are by definition conventionally feminine. Their role in the spectacle of high-school sports reflects their acceptance of secondary status, celebration of the dominant male, and narcissistic desire to be objects of desire. Buffy embraces this identity, exhibiting the narcissism of a conventional American teenaged girl expressed through obsession with shopping and fashion model slimness, as is dramatized in "Bad Eggs" (12 January 1998) when she argues with her mother at the mall about a dress she wants and brags about how thin she is. It does not seem accidental that her mother's objection to the dress is that it, in her view, makes Buffy look like a prostitute, and that the focus of the episode is on a school lesson about accidental conception that goes horribly awry because the eggs the students are given to care for are filled with monsters that possess human hosts. The combination of this hideously exaggerated vision of the horror of teen pregnancy with parental caution about looking sexually available drives home the series' typical message that while it is normal for girls to want to excite desire, sexual activity is always life-threateningly hazardous for them. As early as the first episode of the series, while Buffy courts attention for her high-status appearance, she expresses concern that she might be seen as a "slut," a term she and her friends use to describe girls who present themselves provocatively not just to excite admiration but to get sex.

Buffy also expresses an increasingly hopeless longing to be normal, which she repeatedly defines as conforming to white bourgeois sub-urban concepts of feminine identity, including a central role in life landmarks of narcissism such as appearing as Homecoming Queen and later as the gorgeously attired bride at an elaborate wedding. In her expressions of sexuality she conforms to current bourgeois norms for youth. Buffy seems to be aroused by participating in acts of violence, although "this troubles her deeply" (Marinucci 72). However, given that noisily interactive horror film viewing (including cheering on the killers) and mock battles, such as paintball fights, as well as video combat-gaming competitions, are standard courtship activities among young people, this in itself does not depart from norms. Buffy's disgusted rejection of the sadomasochistic displays and practices of the vampires reinforces the sense that she is a "good girl" after all, as does her commitment to serial monogamy.

More troubling, as the first episode establishes, Buffy would easily fit into Sunnyvale High School's in-crowd if it were not for her special powers as a preordained vampire slayer. As her creator Joss Whedon frequently explains, her struggles are meant to symbolize typical adolescent problems. Thus we are pushed to read the slayer powers symbolically. Buffy's attempts to construct a sexuality which can satisfy her need to feel feminine and virtuous while also helping her protect her loved ones and herself strongly reflect the dilemma of would-be good girls within the mainstream culture, but the series' Gothic premiss, which provides abundant supernatural interference in Buffy's life plans, suggests other dynamics beneath the surface. Buffy is more able than most of those around her to perceive evil. That the evil she sees is supernatural symbolically suggests that the hidden truths available to her enhanced perception concern what her world considers unnatural deviations from the socially established norm. She is compelled by her own nature to fight to destroy such manifestations. Most troubling of all, the figures who embody the evil she must fight often appear to be outcasts, punks, Goths, and anyone noncompliant with the sexual and gender mores that connote respectability in suburbia, such as bisexual boys, young women who engage in sex for its own sake, older women who pursue recreational sex especially with younger males, and, most frequently, practitioners of ritual S/M.

"[P]erversity such as s/m sexuality is the kind of 'fun' Buffy neither needs or enjoys" (34), as Elyce Rae Helford observes of the initial *Buffy the Vampire Slayer* episodes. Later, as Buffy does begin to enjoy S/M with Spike, the sad results reinforce the sense that her earlier attitude was morally correct, for, "in the Buffyverse there are two kinds of sex: human (vanilla) and vampire (BD/SM). Normative, heterosexual sex is vanilla" (Larbalestier 207). Buffy, then, becomes a misfit because she feels compelled to combat immorality as it is understood by high-school prudes. The values that drive the policing actions that define Buffy's "misfit" violent behavior seem placed in the overlap between the religious right (despite the show's parodies of it) and the most puritanical strands of second wave feminism, the latter in that she extends her protection and friendship to lesbians so long as their relationships are monogamous and egalitarian, as we see after the Tara and Willow affair begins with episode 66, "Hush."

In contrast, while Anita is initially primly accepting of the sexual restrictions imposed on women by religiously informed concepts of respectability, she is never in conformity with white middle-class American norms. In fact, from the first novel in the series, an important part of Hamilton's development of Anita's character is that Anita does not consider herself white, although she is light-skinned enough to pass. Instead, she suffers from unresolved grief at the loss of her Mexican mother, who died when she was a small child, and from the bitterness of her subsequent rejection by both her father's racist second wife and her first love, who broke off their engagement because his parents could not accept a Latina daughter-in-law. Far from cultivating a femme appearance like Buffy's, Anita often wryly remarks her inability to look or behave like a "girl," which she seems to define as a vain consumerist. In the first novel she tells us, "I hate to shop. I consider it one of life's necessary evils, like brussel sprouts and high-heeled shoes" (*Guilty Pleasures* 125). Her clothing choices are generally determined by what best conceals the weapons she carries while still giving her quick-draw access, although many of her outfits put her on the wrong side of "the fashion police" (*Guilty Pleasures* 91). About one outfit with a bulky sweater bunching over her shoulder holsters, she says, "I'd rather look less than fashion perfect and live" (*The Lunatic Café* 76). Glamour has little appeal to her even when she prepares for romantic encounters. Since lingerie is rarely comfortable, she sleeps "in oversize t-shirts, and slipping on jeans [is her] idea of a robe" (*Circus of the Damned* 278). She also lets us know, "I don't wear make-up often" (*Guilty Pleasures* 130). Anita seems completely comfortable with the fact that her lovers are better looking than she is. A moment in *Cerulean Sins*, when she and Jean-Claude exchange lines from Christopher Marlowe's *Dr. Faustus*, with her addressing him as Helen ("Was this the face that launched a thousand ships?" [213]), is typical. As is her caressing "the faint tracery of whip scars on his back, which were just another part of his perfection" (*Cerulean Sins* 211). Asked by a dominant female vampire "It doesn't bother you that you are not more beautiful than the men?" Anita answers, "I had to make my peace with being the homely one of the group a long time ago" (*Cerulean Sins* 54).

Anita's relative lack of interest in her appearance is not only consonant with many third wave feminists' matter-of-fact views of the female body in a way that Buffy's obsession with her own glamour is not. It is also significant in that an important part of advertising in general, and the beauty industry in particular, is conveying to women the message that only those who conform to current concepts of female attractiveness deserve a sex life. Mainstream media consistently represent as ridiculous and repulsive women who want an active sex life but fail to be thin, regular-featured, smooth-haired, and toned enough to merit one. The difference between Anita's and Buffy's self-images is quite significant in that, as Carolyn Sorisio argues, endorsement of consumerist materialism is typical of "postfeminism" as represented by rebels against the second wave like Katie Roiphe and Naomi Wolf. For these women, rejecting the "victim feminism" they believe the second wave fostered entails claiming their right to the sort of power capitalism confers on economically privileged males who derive a large part of their social status from purchasing and displaying expensive, fashionable commodities (Sorisio 139–43). But for the woman, one of the objects she displays is her own body, enhanced by fashionable attire and cosmetics, if not plastic surgery. Its adherence to beauty standards and consequent publicly acknowledged desirability gives its possessor power. For the postfeminist, owning her own body then becomes a source of power in a different way than envisioned in feminism of any wave. Sorisio argues convincingly that such empowerment betrays the principles of feminism and constitutes a license to exploit Third World peoples and the poor. The hierarchy of glamor, in which beauty depends to a large degree upon the ability to purchase specific products, reinforces socio-economic inequities. Like most third wave feminists, Sorisio sees feminism as synonymous with a commitment to human rights and rage against their violation, and consequently as opposed to the mainstream that excuses imperialistic exploitation because it seems necessary to the privileged attainment of status through consumerism. Buffy's pursuit of media-defined glamor not only has these unpleasant overtones, it also reinforces the isolating message of postfeminism: women are competitors who must internalize capitalist individualism as they receive value from having more purchased signifiers of beauty than other women.

Anita, despite her self-image in the early books as a loner, depends far more than Buffy on community for a sense of worth. But her community is less recognizable as such because of its placement far outside the mainstream. Carol Queen's comments on the S/M community, and other queer sex spaces, help explain what Anita's world offers women whose fantasies are of acting on desire rather than merely arousing it in others. While in the ordinary world, "[w]omen who refuse to adjust their looks to fit the straight-gal norm are often rewarded with scorn and abuse," within S/M community circles "[i]t's not *how* you present yourself, it's *that* you present yourself," being there and ready for erotic pleasure is enough (Queen 64–5). We learn from Anita that the stunningly beautiful vampire "Jean-Claude preferred ... curves on his women. As he'd pointed out to me, the beauties of his day in the French court were today's size twenty" (*Incubus Dreams* 299). Nor is this a standard to which she feels she must adhere. Instead, her attitude seems always to be that lovers should accept her as she is; she rarely concerns herself with whether she meets physical requirements of theirs or anyone's. She looks like a "dominatrix maybe, but nobody's toy" (*The Killing Dance* 311). Action oriented, Anita always insists upon being the subject of erotic play rather than its object; she is concerned with her own feelings rather than the expectations of others. She is proud of her battle scars, which in her view "aren't like freak show bad," just "interesting," and is so amused by their power to disgust or upset others that she has to be instructed by her employer to keep them covered in the office (*Burnt Offerings* 1).

Not meeting beauty standards is not a source of rage for Anita, but being outcast because of her deviations from other cultural norms is. She despises the many people who reject her for differences she cannot control, from her race to her necromantic abilities, and very much including the unorthodox sexual arrangements she enters into in order to be true to her feelings. Anita acts out her rage against mainstream society through the adoption of an anti-authoritarian outlaw persona. In the early novels she "dreams of white picket fences and domestic bliss, away from the monstrous world in which she lives, but does not accept that her future holds such potential" (Leon 19). Later Anita comes to understand that the outlaw persona is not merely a mask but something she values and sees as her true self.

From the onset she is uncomfortable with and often contemptuous of ordinary middle-class Americans, which causes her to bond with other rebels, including contract killers like her friend Edward, and in the later books with the monsters, vampires and shape-shifters who inhabit the underworld of the parallel universe in which the novels are set.

As one novel succeeds another in the series, the heart of this universe comes more and more to resemble the S/M subculture. Anita's powerful adversary in the early novels and lover in the later ones, Jean-Claude, the vampire master of Saint Louis, the city where they both live, owns and manages an S/M-themed male strip club called Guilty Pleasures. He and his vampire associates dress almost entirely in fetish gear whether or not they are on stage. Her second fiancé, Richard the werewolf king, presides over a monthly gathering of his lycanthropes where erotic blood rituals are enacted. Hamilton's lavish descriptions of these scenes are often reminiscent of Califia's recollections of the early S/M scene in San Francisco where the participants appear in his memory not like humans at all but as wonderful wild animals: "The leather they wore and the metal and ink they put in their bodies were not fashion statements, they were brave declarations of difference and affirmations of a passion for pain, power, and extreme degrees of penetration" (*PoMoSexuals*, 94). Hamilton's explanation of Anita's introduction into S/M culture evokes for me the excitement I felt upon discovering the intellectual community maintained in the writings of feminists who are not chronologically third wave but share the sexual radicalism that so influenced its ideology, such as Califia, Queen, and Shannon Bell, as well as pioneers of pro-sex feminist theory like Eve Sedgwick and Jane Gallop.

Anita's awakening to alternative sexual communities is as physical as it is intellectual, calling to mind actual communities that foster S/M play. In *The Killing Dance*, for instance, we have a scene at the werewolf lupanar (ritual gathering), where Raina, as dominant werewolf, presides over the group, "absolutely naked except for a sprinkling of gold body glitter, done thick enough on her nipples to make them seem metallic" (317), and Anita experiences her first taste of unleashed S/M power: "it wouldn't be just sex. It would be magic, and it didn't seem shameful or pagan or wrong" (319). As opposed to a heteronormative culture that "has devoted a great deal of energy to guaranteeing that a penis plus a vagina will always equate zero – no social change, no insight, no shared understanding," Califia celebrates queer culture for "its honesty: the willingness we have, as queers, to face the truth of our own fantasies and desires and choose to own them and follow them, even if we face horrendous penalties" (99). It is in a similar atmosphere of queered desire that Anita comes to know and accept herself as she is, sadomasochistic desires included.

SLAYER SEXUALITIES

In their relationship to their own sexualities and to male objects of desire, Buffy and Anita superficially resemble each other, especially in that both series present a progression in which the heroine gains self-knowledge. But as the series develop the differences also become increasingly marked. Buffy has three main love interests in the course of the series: Angel, a vampire who initially appears to her as a protective and mentoring figure; Riley, a mortal demon fighter; and Spike, the vicious vampire who begins as her enemy, falls in love and seduces her, only to be ultimately sexually rejected by her. Anita also has three main love interests: Jean-Claude, Richard, and Micah, leader of the wereleopards. Buffy has a foil in the cold and cruel Faith, a conscience-less Slayer who unambivalently enjoys killing and is identified as a "bad girl precisely because she falls down on the male side of [the] equation, wanting sex not intimacy" (Larbalestier 218), while Anita has as her contrast character, Raina, the alpha werewolf and snuff-film pornographer whose sexual sadism defines her. In addition Buffy and Anita also come to belong to groups of people with shared goals. Buffy's group, the Scooby Gang, is composed of her high-school friends who join her in fighting evil. Anita's group, the wereleopard pard, is a unit of lycanthropes organized to offer each other support and protection.

   Their interactions with these figures develop Anita's and Buffy's ethics and sense of their own sexualities in sharply differentiated ways. Buffy is initially attracted to Angel, her first lover, because of his combination of physical beauty and his protectiveness of her, and Anita is attracted to Jean-Claude for similar reasons, although she distrusts him because he is a vampire. Buffy's trust in Angel is revealed to be foolish when she loses her virginity to him in the episode "Surprise" in season two, and as a consequence he loses his soul and reverts to his murderous, monstrous Angelus persona, fully realized in the next episode, "Innocence." Thomas Hibbs points out that "Angel is thus a stand-in for the predatory male, whose true and truly vile self is revealed only after he gets what he wants" (58). Justine Larbalestier goes even further in claiming that "he has become the brutish demon that we are taught lies at the heart of all men" (204). Both of these observations reveal just how strongly the series endorses the traditional message that where sex is concerned young women and men can only be deadly enemies because of the incommensurability of their desires. For the man to realize his desire means the destruction of the girl's purity, value, and dreams. And in addition he will inevitably hurt her even further because he can only despise what he has conquered. Buffy is the loser because the failure of this affair is predictive of her future, in which "finding someone who can both accept who she is and offer her the emotional release she needs, has so far been a fruitless quest" (Tracy 27).

Conversely Anita's distrust of Jean-Claude is gradually revealed as foolish, and their increasing love and trust provide a pattern for her other affairs. After having sex with him for the first time in *The Killing Dance* she begins a relationship about which she is ambivalent. She realizes in *Burnt Offerings* not only that "I'd been virtuous for so long, but when I lost it, I lost it big time" (246), but that she can no longer understand virtue as defined primarily by chastity. In the next novel, *Blue Moon*, she and Richard also become lovers, but she subsequently decides to withdraw into celibacy from their jealous competition and from her own confusion. *Obsidian Butterfly*, published in 2000, takes Anita in a new direction. Anita finally accepts that traditional sexual chastity simply does not work for her and begins to experiment with unconventional sexual arrangements. Whenever she hesitates to act on her desires because the seeming immorality of some sexual activity makes her uncomfortable, she has to give in to save others. These thoughts in response to an advance from Jean-Claude are typical: "He had me there. A moment of personal weakness against the lives of two people. What a choice" (*Circus of the Damned* 57). She finally accepts both Richard and Jean-Claude as her lovers.

While Anita does encounter some very bad people, both male and female, whose cruelty appears to be intrinsic to their personalities, in most cases when she finds men cold or harshly judgmental, she later learns that they suffer from emotional problems caused by earlier experiences of sexual pain and humiliation. Unlike the males in Buffy's world, who usually either conceal an evil and mortally dangerous dark side, like Angel, or a sort of nasty weakness, like Spike, Anita's male acquaintances have almost all been raped – by women as well as men – and subjected to demeaning sexual abuse that results in their construction of a hard, defensive posture that belies their inner sensitivity to others. In the presence of her strength and unfailing decency, and her compassion for their victimization, they melt and show their true natures, which are almost invariably good. While in Buffy's world masculinity signifies the power to victimize others, in Anita's it is constantly revealed to be a mask over vulnerability, just like that of women.

Consequently Anita changes from someone who thought of vampires as walking corpses, shape-shifters as monstrous animals, and men as hardly less grotesquely inhuman, to someone who recognizes the common humanity all these creatures share with her. This recognition allows her to advocate for men, even defending Richard from rape charges in *Blue Moon*, where, of course, her insistence on his innocence turns out to be right. Here the pervasive influence of gender and masculinity studies on third wave feminism is evident in the recognition that men's sexuality is neither monolithic nor automatically productive of enmity to women.[7]

As I hope even this brief comparison suggests, the two series proceed from very different concepts of the truth of gender difference and follow opposite trajectories of feminist critique. Having sex is always wrong for Buffy. This is the case because in Buffy's world the truth is that masculinity and femininity are biologically determined attributes in those who, like Buffy, are not mentally disturbed. Moreover, masculine and feminine sexual needs are incompatible; since men inevitably dominate women sexually, all sexual activities between them will occur at the woman's expense. Besides the disastrous affair with Angel, which can only be resolved by Buffy's complete renunciation of him, she experiences a humiliating one-night stand in "The Harsh Light of Day" with Parker, who just uses her sexually. Then she becomes lovers with Riley in "The I in Team," season four, only to cause a string of problems from an unleashing of deadly poltergeists through their passion in "Where the Wild Things Are" to Riley's obsession with vampire prostitutes which ends their affair in "Into the Woods." Her affair with Spike is even more ill fated. Their brief S/M affair ends in "As You Were" because, as Hibbs explains, "[t]he sexual liaison with Spike brings shame" (58). The return of Riley, now happily married, makes Buffy realize how revolting she finds her relation to Spike. Her response is to suppress, with great effort, the lust she feels. Ultimately she is able to love him because, in accordance with conservative ideology that reads sexual activity outside procreative monogamy as anti-romantic, she has rid herself of all predatory erotic feelings and killed his desire to act on his. Because in the Buffyverse gender is always either masculine or feminine, and masculinity is always locked by sex into a destructive opposition to femininity, they can only feel affection for each other in the ungendered space of asexuality: "When there is love, they don't have sex at all" (Larbalestier 216).

Having sex is, conversely, always right for Anita because in her world the truth of gender is that it is performative and not linked to biological sex. Dominance and submission are the real genders, as in the S/M community. Because Anita is dominant by nature, her needs will be met by the partners to whom she is spontaneously drawn, those able to submit to her to some extent. As her honesty about her own desires grows, her affairs yield more and more satisfaction. Her reunion in *Obsidian Butterfly* with Edward the contract killer of monsters, a character somewhat parallel to Riley, includes her recognition that he is able to compartmentalize his life enough to enjoy a loving relationship in which he plays the part of an ordinary guy and his partner is a conventionally feminine woman. But she finds this a sort of dishonesty to which she is unwilling to stoop. Anita does not reject her own sexuality because she cannot express it in ways that the mainstream approves without misrepresenting herself, as Buffy – like so many women – does.

Given that within the Buffyverse all sexual arousal, let alone consummation of it, results in dire, life-threatening problems, Buffy's rejection of sexuality is understandable. The lack of sexual activity among the members of the Scooby Gang provides a protective retreat for Buffy and makes them a more effective force against evil. The Scoobies give

Buffy a place to retreat from troublingly sexualized interactions with vampires. Vampire power is explicitly linked to sexual allure, and in scenes between Buffy and her vampire lovers, Angel and Spike, "the distinction between sex and death is blurred" (DeKelb-Rittenhouse 148). Numerous episodes suggest that in the Buffyverse there is little difference between casual sex and rape, or between consensual S/M play and the eroticization of murder. This attitude is very much in line with mainstream therapy culture. As Califia notes, the 1994 revision of the *Diagnostic and Statistical Manual of Mental Disorders* partially depathologizes S/M by designating it a sexual disorder only when it resulted in intense distress or disruption of ordinary function still did not "distinguish between consensual S/M and violence" (*Public Sex* 141). Because it questions the possibility of perfectly egalitarian sexual relations, without any trace of violence or competition, the Buffy series implicitly identifies chastity as the precondition for the development of women's, and non-macho men's, empowerment. The moral message of the Buffy series falls too close to that of the religious right, as Michael P. Levine and Steven Jay Schneider sum it up: "Far from being subversive in any positive sense, *BtVs* in fact embodies questionable values and stereotypes on a number of levels.... [T]he show does not challenge sexual and gender stereotypes (except superficially), or those about romance and true love, but instead reinforces them" (300). Several Buffy episodes, including the two that show the loss of her virginity and its horrific aftermath, could actually double as didactic after-school specials.

Anita's third wave sex radical universe forcefully opposes this vision. First of all, Anita, unlike Buffy, cannot control her own sexual desire, not because she is immoral or self-indulgent but because the *ardeur* must be regularly fed with sexual activity lest it drain the energy of the two triumvirates of vampires and lycanthropes to which she belongs, endangering the lives of her friends and all their dependants.[8] She is schooled in her own alpha nature through interactions with the formal groups of vampires and lycanthropes, which, unlike the egalitarian Scoobies, are always hierarchical and structured through rituals of dominance and submission. Early in the series, circumstances force Anita to accept "vampire marks" from Jean-Claude, transforming her so that she partakes of his powers and can communicate with him telepathically. According to vampire hierarchy and tradition, this makes her Jean-Claude's human servant, but her strong resistance to the role or even the name of "servant" finds affirmation in the later novels where she and Jean-Claude resignify the term as he bows to her necromantic as well as her amorous will. What she has to learn, her progression through the books suggests, is that by overcoming her fear of her own desires she can emerge a true heroine, powerful enough to right wrongs done to the weak and shield the vulnerable from exploitation. In *Blue Moon*, she faces the fact that "sexual energy was one of the ways I performed magic" (217) and subsequently learns that subjecting another person to her "lust" can heal his physical injuries (412). Her rejection of Richard in *Narcissus in Chains* because he cannot accept his own beastliness, which includes sadistic impulses, and her replacement of him with Micah, who worships her strength and is "one of the most easygoing people I'd ever met" (*Cerulean Sins* 302), illustrates how far she has come in self-acceptance and departure from her early dreams of normalcy.

In *Cerulean Sins* Anita briefly reunites with Richard, continues her affair with Micah, has her first episode of casual sex with the werewolf Jason, and also begins a *ménage à trois* with Jean-Claude and his former lover Asher, and each of these sexual events increases her own strength and adds to that of her lovers, as well as being instrumental in averting tragedies, including the destruction of the human race. *Incubus Dreams* (2004) takes Anita even deeper into acceptance of her sexual desires as she adds the vampire Damian to her growing group of occasional lovers, learns to accept her sexual kinks, becomes much more comfortable with casual sex, successfully instructs Richard in sexual self-acceptance, relaxes enough to play at S/M role switching with Jean-Claude, and gives in fully to her longing to treat Nathaniel as a "wife." Furthermore, she finally comes to understand that sex can be loving and healing without needing to be enclosed in monogamy or to result in a permanent relationship. Instead of the agonized soul-searching she used to do over each sexual encounter, Anita begins to congratulate herself on being able to do what is necessary to help others and save lives, and is no longer troubled that this usually entails sorts of sexual activities she once would have condemned. If Buffy learns that she cannot act on her desires without causing trouble, Anita learns that she cannot refrain from acting on hers without tragic repercussions.

It is in these lessons that the two series carry on the dialogues about sadomasochism so central to the feminisms of our times. The Buffyverse implies, as does MacCannell, that what girls must learn in order to become women is a truth about sexual difference that precludes the lifting of restraint. Even Willow and Tara's mutually nurturing, egalitarian lesbian affair eventually leads Willow to a dangerous and soul-threatening addiction to magic. Affairs with men much more rapidly unravel into destructive violence. Successful female maturity in the Buffyverse means accepting that sex is dangerous for women because it always involves power imbalances and emotional, if not physical, violence, and thus we must renounce our desires for the good of society and our better selves. Surely the series means to suggest that we must *sometimes* do so, but, because sex never leads to anything but problems in Buffy's world, the implication is that women are better off without engaging in any sexual activity. Anita's universe more closely resembles that of sex radical third-wavers and third wave visions of sexual freedom like the film *Secretary*, in that it insists that women's sexual gratification is important, perhaps even necessary, to the preservation of the human race. But Hamilton goes beyond even this feminist sex radicalism by positing absolute female pleasure as predicated on absolute sexual power. The popularity of the novel series calls the deviance of this position into question.

Certainly the Buffy series does important feminist work in reminding the young women who have gained from feminism's previous wave considerable freedom to define their own sexualities that sexual activity still carries serious dangers for women. Many girls and women, like Buffy, want to experience their gender identity narcissistically; they want to shop and adorn themselves and be the objects of male desire. They want to tease men and refuse sex to affirm their own power. And when they do have sexual relations, they want to submit to a strong, powerful man. Sex radical third wave feminism correctly insists that women have a right to express such feelings without being punished for them. And the Buffy series is right to warn its audience that in our unjust, sexist world this sort of expression is often followed by horrific punishments.

The Anita series speaks to another audience, or perhaps the same audience in another mood. It rightly asserts the existence of other desires in women and girls. Its wish-fulfillment fantasy of a world in which women's pursuit of untrammeled sexual power is always rewarded represents another sort of feminism, the kind that allows us to relax our vigilance and fall into pleasure. For second wave sex radicals it was often extreme enough to assert, as Lynne Segal does, that "The way to fight the continuing victimization of women cannot be to abandon notions of sexual liberation. Or to make women's pursuit of heterosexual pleasure incompatible with women's happiness" (309). For feminists in the more inclusive and sexually sophisticated third wave, however, sex radicalism can go further, and Hamilton takes it all the way. In a move that encompasses – and may even be seen as going beyond – Hooijer's assertion that "porn *is* feminism" (273), Hamilton's series suggests that in its most utopian expression, female sadism *is* feminist sexuality.

CLIP THREE

Walking into B. Dalton's bookstore in the mall, I am musing on my embarrassment at buying another Anita Blake novel. Guilty pleasures, indeed. I always fear that the clerk will give me the sort of disapproving stare to which I was regularly subjected in porn stores in the 1970s, when I was the only woman in the place. I anticipate the respectable-looking woman behind the counter fixing that humiliating gaze on me, and perhaps remarking, as a fellow feminist once did at an academic conference where I was presenting a paper on S/M, "You don't deserve to call yourself a woman!" Then I look up and see a great cardboard tower of books, all by Laurell K. Hamilton, standing next to the store's doorway. They have built something akin to an altar to her popularity with readers.

Finally, after all these years, I am among other women, and, to my pleasant surprise, discover I am not alone.

NOTES

1. See Gilles Deleuze and Félix Guattari. *Kafka: Toward a Minor Literature*, especially pp. 16–27, for an extensive discussion of the concept of majoritarian and minoritarian languages and representational systems. In brief, Deleuze and Guattari call discourses that have "official" status, that attempt mastery of signification in the name of cultural norms, majoritist, and give the language of "psychoanalysis today" as an example (27). The feminisms that support the current consensus of official power/knowledge on sexuality

are, thus, majoritarian, and would include, for instance, feminist claims that S/M reinforces patriarchal oppression and damages women.

2. See especially Hilary Leon's discussion of this.

3. Lisa Duggan and Nan D. Hunter's *Sex Wars: Sexual Dissent and Political Culture* provides an excellent third wave overview of the debates, as does Nan Bauer Maglin and Donna Perry's *"Bad Girls"/"Good Girls": Women, Sex, and Power in the Nineties*. The volume *Debating Sexual Correctness: Pornography, Sexual Harassment, and Date Rape*, ed. Adele M. Stan, offers a basic selection of writings representing those on both sides of the issue.

4. This is not to suggest that no feminists of the second wave argued in favor of women's freedom to pursue S/M relationships; however, third wave feminism, with its strong emphasis on making space for previously marginalized voices, seems especially invested in crossing the boundary between domesticated, safe sexualities and dangerous, wild ones.

5. Almost all feminist writings coming out of the third wave distinguish between the repressive attitudes popularly associated with majoritist second wavers and the more open, pleasure-oriented attitudes that typify their own feminist generation. In "Taking Feminism to Bed: The Third Wave Does the Sex Wars" (88–114), a chapter of her study *Not My Mother's Sister*, Astrid Henry gives an overview of this trend.

6. Addressing the cultural work of fan fiction, major theorists such as Henry Jenkins and Matt Hills stress fans' resistance to all that is normative, whether it comes out of cultures marked as masculine, feminine, or even feminist.

7. Feminism's third wave is far more inclusive of male voices than the previous waves were, with most essay collections featuring contributions by feminist men. And, as Judith Kegan Gardiner's 2002 collection, *Masculinity Studies and Feminist Theory* reflects, many third wavers have come to understand the two fields as interrelated.

8. This plot device interestingly resembles one of the most popular in early *Star Trek* slash fiction, *pon farr* stories in which Spock goes into heat and must have sex or die. See Constance Penley's discussion in "Brownian Motion: Women, Tactics and Technology" (158).

REFERENCES

Buffy the Vampire Slayer. DVD. The Complete Seven Season Series.

Busse, Kristina. "Crossing the Final Taboo: Family, Sexuality, and Incest in Buffyverse Fan Fiction." In *Fighting the Forces: What's at Stake in "Buffy the Vampire Slayer"?* Ed. Rhonda V. Wilcox and David Lavery. Lanham, MD: Rowan & Littlefield, 2002. 207–17.

Califia, Pat. "Identity Sedition and Pornography." In *PoMoSexuals: Challenging Assumptions About Gender and Sexuality*. Ed. Carol Queen and Kate Bornstein. San Francisco: Cleis, 1997. 87–106.

———. *Public Sex: The Culture of Radical Sex*. San Francisco: Cleis, 1994.

DeKelb-Rittenhouse, Diane. "Sex and the Single Vampire: The Evolution of the Vampire Lothario and Its Representation in *Buffy*." In *Fighting the Forces: What's at Stake in "Buffy the Vampire Slayer"?* Ed. Rhonda V. Wilcox and David Lavery. Lanham, MD: Rowan & Littlefield, 2002. 143–52.

Deleuze, Gilles and Félix Guattari. *Kafka: Toward a Minor Literature*. Trans. Dana

Polan. Minneapolis: University of Minnesota Press, 1986.

Duggan, Lisa and Nan Hunter. *Sex Wars: Sexual Dissent and Political Culture*. New York: Routledge, 1995.

Gaitskill, Mary. "Secretary." In *Bad Behavior*. New York: Vintage, 1988. 131–47.

Gardiner, Judith Kegan, ed. *Masculinity Studies and Feminist Theory*. New York: Columbia University Press, 2002.

Graham, Paula. "Buffy Wars: The Next Generation." *Rhizomes 4: Cyberfeminisms*. www.rhizomes.net.

Hamilton, Laurell K. *Blue Moon*. New York: Ace, 1998.

———. *Burnt Offerings*. New York: Ace, 1998.

———. *Cerulean Sins*. New York: Berkley, 2003.

———. *Circus of the Damned*. New York: Ace, 1995.

———. *Guilty Pleasures*. New York: Ace, 1993.

———. *Incubus Dreams*. New York: Berkley, 2004.

———. *Narcissus in Chains*. New York: Jove, 2002.

———. *Obsidian Butterfly*. New York: Ace, 2000.

———. *The Killing Dance*. New York: Ace, 1997.

———. *The Lunatic Café*. New York: Ace, 1996.

Helford, Elyce Rae. "'My Emotions Give Me Power': The Containment of Girl's Anger in *Buffy*." In *Fighting the Forces: What's at Stake in "Buffy the Vampire Slayer"?* Ed. Rhonda V. Wilcox and David Lavery. Lanham, MD: Rowan & Littlefield, 2002. 18–34.

Henry, Astrid. *Not My Mother's Sister: Generational Conflict and Third Wave Feminism*. Bloomington: Indiana University Press, 2004.

Herself. "Leather." February 2003, www.echonyc.com/~stax/Buffy/herself/Leather.htm.

Hibbs, Thomas. "Buffy the Vampire Slayer as Feminist Noir." In *Buffy the Vampire Slayer and Philosophy: Fear and Trembling in Sunnydale*. Ed. James B. South. Chicago: Open Court Publishing, 2003. 49–60.

Hills, Matt. *Fan Cultures*. London and New York: Routledge, 2002.

Hooijer, Katinka. "Vulvodynia: On the Medicinal Purposes of Porn." *Jane Sexes it Up: True Confessions of Feminist Desire*. Ed. Merri Lisa Johnson. New York: Four Walls Eight Windows, 2002. 259–80.

hooks, bell. *Feminist Theory: From Margin to Center*. Boston MA: South End Press, 1984.

———. *Outlaw Culture: Resisting Representations*. London: Routledge, 1994.

Jenkins, Henry. *Textual Poachers: Television Fans and Participatory Cultures*. London: Routledge, 1992.

Kaufman, Linda S. *Bad Girls and Sick Boys: Fantasies in Contemporary Culture*. Berkeley: University of California Press, 1998.

Kaveney, Roz, ed. *Reading the Vampire Slayer: The Complete, Unofficial Guide to "Buffy" and "Angel."* New York: I.B. Tauris, 2004.

Kaveney, Roz. "'She Saved the World, a Lot': An Introduction to the Themes and Structures of *Buffy* and *Angel*." In *Reading the Vampire Slayer: The Complete, Unofficial Guide to "Buffy" and "Angel."* Ed. Roz Kaveney. New York: I.B. Tauris, 2004. 1–82.

Larbalestier, Justine. "The Only Thing Better than Killing a Slayer: Heterosexuality and Sex in *Buffy the Vampire Slayer*." In *Reading the Vampire Slayer: The Complete, Unofficial Guide to "Buffy" and "Angel."* Ed. Roz Kaveney. New York: I.B. Tauris,

2004. 195–219.

Leon, Hilary M. "Why We Love the Monsters: How Anita Blake, Vampire Hunter, and Buffy the Vampire Slayer Wound Up Dating the Enemy." *Slayage* 1. www.slayage.tv/essays/slayage1/hleon.hym

Levine, Michael P. and Steven Jay Schriener. "Feeling for Buffy: The Girl Next Door." In *"Buffy the Vampire Slayer" and Philosophy: Fear and Trembling in Sunnydale.* Ed. James B. South, Chicago: Open Court, 2003. 294–308.

MacCannell, Juliet Flower. *The Hysteric's Guide to the Future Female Subject.* Minneapolis: University of Minnesota Press, 1999.

Maglin, Nan Bauer and Donna Marie Perry, eds. *"Bad Girls"/"Good Girls": Women, Sex, and Power in the Nineties.* New Brunswick, NJ: Rutgers University Press, 1996.

Marinucci, Mimi. "Feminism and the Ethics of Violence." In *"Buffy the Vampire Slayer" and Philosophy: Fear and Trembling in Sunnydale.* Ed. James B. South, Chicago: Open Court, 2003. 61–75.

Penley, Constance. "Brownian Motion: Women, Tactics and Technology." In *Technoculture.* Ed. Constance Penley and Andrew Ross. Minneapolis: University of Minnesota Press, 1991. 135–63.

———. "Feminism, Psychoanalysis and the Study of Popular Culture." In *Cultural Studies.* Ed. Lawrence Grossberg et. al. London: Routledge, 1992. 479–93.

Queen, Carol. "Introduction." In *PoMoSexuals: Challenging Assumptions About Gender and Sexuality.* Ed. C. Queen and K. Bornstein. San Francisco: Cleis, 1997.

Raven, Lady. "Feel the Fever." 7 July 2004, http://tns.bitchenvy.com/fiction/n_z/feel_the_fever.html.

Segal, Lynne. *Straight Sex: The Politics of Pleasure.* London: Virago, 1994.

"Slayers: Anita Blake and Buffy Summers." www.geocities.com/Area51/Shire/8109/main.html.

Siegel, Carol. *New Millennial Sexstyles.* Bloomington: Indiana University Press, 2000.

Sin Far, Sui. "Leaves from the Mental Portfolio of an Eurasian." In *Mrs. Spring Fragrance and Other Writings.* Ed. Amy Ling and Annette White-Parks. Urbana: U of Illinois P, 1995. 218–30.

Snitow, Ann Barr. "Mass Market Romance: Pornography for Women Is Different." In *Powers of Desire: The Politics of Sexuality.* Ed. Ann Snitow, Christine Stansell, and Sharon Thompson. New York: Monthly Review Press, 1983. 245–63.

Sorisio, Carolyn. "A Tale of Two Feminisms: Power and Victimization in Contemporary Feminist Debate." In *Third Wave Agenda: Being Feminist, Doing Feminism.* Ed. Leslie Heywood and Jennifer Drake. Minneapolis: University of Minnesota Press, 1997. 134–54.

South, James B., ed. *"Buffy the Vampire Slayer" and Philosophy: Fear and Trembling in Sunnydale.* Chicago: Open Court, 2003.

Spikelovin. "Slave." 30 November 2004. http://slayerfanfic.com/viewstory.php?sid=7133.

Stan, Adele, ed. *Debating Sexual Correctness: Pornography, Sexual Harassment, and Date Rape and the Politics of Sexual Inequality.* New York: Delta, 1995.

Tracy, Kathleen. *The Girl's Got Bite: The Original Unauthorized Guide to Buffy's World Completely Revised and Updated.* New York: St. Martin's Press, 2003.

Wilcox, Rhonda V. and David Lavery, eds. *Fighting the Forces: What's at Stake in "Buffy the Vampire Slayer"?* Lanham, MD: Rowan & Littlefield, 2002.

3

PRIMETIME HAREM FANTASIES:

MARRIAGE, MONOGAMY, AND

A BIT OF FEMINIST FANFICTION

ON ABC'S *THE BACHELOR*

KATHERINE FRANK

An attractive young man stands at one end of a room, facing a tray of fifteen long-stemmed red roses. Across the room, twenty-five aspiring wives in revealing cocktail dresses stand in a formation reminiscent of the Miss America pageant, running nervous fingers through their hair. The camera pans the lineup, then zooms in on each face to highlight the tension in the room. A pretty blonde bites her lip; a buxom brunette wrings her hands. Each woman focuses intently on the bachelor with her eyes, as if willing him to glance in her direction. Shiny noses, caked-on eye-makeup, and department store dresses infuse this highly staged moment with a dose of reality. These are not actresses; they are mostly "girls-next-door," nurses and teachers and bartenders, with the occasional makeup artist or swimsuit model thrown in for ratings. On this particular evening, the host has instructed the young man to "send ten women home" by offering a rose to each of the other fifteen ladies. As always, the viewers have been promised a "dramatic 'rose ceremony.'"

"This is so difficult," the bachelor says, his smile strained by his own case of nerves. "You are all so special." One by one, he calls out the names of the chosen ones. Carrie. Kara. Sarah W. Sara B. Relief floods their faces as they approach him for a hug and a rose.

"Thank you."

"Thank you."

Sometimes the women perform an overdone sigh of relief, sometimes they dance a little jig, and sometimes they admonish him for not picking them first. The other girls are then asked to leave, empty-handed and, for the most part, distraught. They hug each other without enthusiasm, offer congratulations to the new rose-bearers, and then make their way out of the mansion. Before they leave the premises, they are interviewed on camera. Teary and humiliated, Kristine proclaims her love for the bachelor and wonders how he couldn't feel the same way. Danushka, the model, decries his lack of taste in women. Although the interviews with the first few rejected women often draw on familiar defense maneuvers ("It wasn't meant to be"; "I didn't feel a connection with him, either"), these parting interviews become more emotional and less measured as the season progresses.

The camera then returns to the scene inside the house, as the bachelor and his selected women toast with champagne glasses. They have made it to another episode.[1]

READING *THE BACHELOR*

In the highly popular "reality" series *The Bachelor*, a carefully selected single man is introduced to twenty-five attractive and available women. Over the course of several weeks, with cameras following closely, he is offered the opportunity to date them individually or in groups, to kiss them (or more), to "connect with" them romantically, and to possibly fall in love with one or more of them. At the end of each week's show, in a highly ritualistic moment termed the "rose ceremony," the bachelor selects the women who will return for another week of growing emotional and sexual involvement with him, and, often, increasing rivalry among themselves. The rest of the women are sent home. The season finale occurs when the field has been narrowed to two women, and the audience is then kept guessing throughout a two-hour special as to which woman he will choose. His emotional equivocations and videotaped confessions are judiciously used to create suspense ("Tanya is beautiful inside and out, a wonderful girl; Mary is so caring; there is such a connection"). Finally, there is an emotional, on-camera break-up with one woman and the other is offered a proposal – for marriage, for a future engagement, or for a move to the bachelor's home town. The prize is love itself, it seems, along with fifteen minutes or more of tabloid interest in the new couple and the more interesting rejected or attractive competitors.

I have to admit it: I am a *Bachelor* junkie.

Since the program first aired on ABC in 2002, I've watched every episode of every season of *The Bachelor* and its counterpart in the name of equal opportunity, *The Bachelorette*.[2] During my pregnancy, I fervently hoped I wouldn't go into labor early and miss the final rose ceremony of *Bachelor 4* (and if you've been pregnant and felt your body swell incomprehensibly by that eighth month, you realize how bizarre such a wish is). In the end, my labor was conveniently induced a week after millionaire bachelor Andrew Firestone picked the blonde-haired, all-American Jen Scheft to be his fiancée.

The Bachelor, like many popular series, is best when watched in groups. At this stage in my life (married, with child, and living far from most of my girlfriends), I have resorted to phone calls during the commercials, conference calls to place bets on the last-lovelorn-lasses-standing after each week's rose ceremony, and follow-up emails to speculate on behind-the-scenes developments. I am definitely not unique in this desire to consume and reconsume this particular reality dating series – a brief Google search turns up message boards, discussion groups, and betting pools for those who do not have their own ready-made posse of viewing pals (or, perhaps, those who want to discuss it even more than their friends will bear). Weekly celebrity magazines, such as *People*, *In Touch*, and *Us*, feature stories about the bachelor and his "contestants," and *The Bachelor* has now earned its own hour-long *E! True Hollywood Story* on the Entertainment Channel. The contestants make appearances on talk shows and at special events, and several have capitalized on their newfound fame by writing books on dating and relationships. Spin-off shows have appeared on competing channels, each with a slightly different twist but few as compelling as the original. In addition to *The Bachelor* and *The Bachelorette*, for example, *Who Wants to Marry My Dad?*, *Mr. Personality*, and *Average Joe* have followed suit. Another string of reality dating programs plays on Americans' cultural ambivalence about the relationship between love and money: *Joe Millionaire*, *Who Wants to Marry a Multi-Millionaire*, *For Love or Money*, and the like. Indeed, reality dating and reality marriage constitute widespread cultural phenomena and warrant close critical scrutiny from feminist media critics.

There are a number of possible ways to "read" *The Bachelor*. One predictable feminist response might analyze the show as a startling example of normative gender expectations in the media, as well as a patriarchal primer for contemporary love and marriage: the women compete bitterly for the bachelor's hand and are lined up each week – like pageant girls or show dogs – for him to select the ones who will continue on to the next round (pretty with large breasts usually does fairly well; intellect seems less often important). Airtime for the women clearly correlates with sunbathing frequency, bikini size, and salacious tendencies towards late-night skinny-dipping or sexy lap dances for the bachelor. In this reading, the series appears one-dimensional and unremittingly sexist.

For a slightly less predictable interpretation, one could focus on the complex, contradictory, and contested performances of gendered interaction within the show. After all, one might observe, aren't the women drawing on heterosexist scripts and stereotypes to achieve their own goals of fame, love, or success? This critical lens might foreground the agency exercised by the female contestants in their relationships with the bachelor, each other, and the producers, even as their sexuality is harnessed by the show's producers for profit and even as the women are portrayed as desperate, marriage-hungry, back-stabbing bimbos fighting for the attention of a man. From this angle, the show demonstrates what Lynn Spigel calls "a postfeminist logic that embraces femininity and 'girliness' in the name of enlightenment and female empowerment" (1212). This postfeminist logic perhaps explains the pleasure that these women take in self-presentation, female–female competition, and the attraction of a highly desirable (at least in this contrived situation) male suitor. Following popular conceptual trends in feminist theory, one might usefully explore the racial politics of the show (there are always a few contestants of color who make it past the first cut but never to the final round) or the class dynamics that emerge quite pointedly at times (as when the young Southern contestant, Amber, asks millionaire bachelor Andrew Firestone if he likes the Olive Garden and is clearly dumbfounded when he responds that he does not eat there).

In light of this collection's focus on "sex radical spectatorship," I intend in this chapter to depart from these familiar approaches and use the dynamics of the show to pose a conceptual and practical challenge to feminists to rethink, once again, our understandings of how heterosexual women might practice our own relationships in the new millennium. After all, *The Bachelor* and its copycat programs are exploring contemporary relationship formation, and even though the shows are frequently dismissed as ridiculous (How could anyone really fall in love in two months, with cameras following them around? Why would you go on a game show, hoping to fall in love?), or offensive (Doesn't this kind of programming trivialize marriage? Doesn't it make women look desperate, catty, and insecure?), this exploration is strikingly relevant to female – and feminist – television fans. The fact of the matter is that for many of us, especially those of us in the middle classes, intimate relationships *are* forming and unfolding differently than in the past, and we tune in hungrily for the pragmatic and ethical dilemmas posed explicitly and implicitly by "reality dating" and "reality marriage" television. Su Holmes argues that scholars need to explore how reality TV is actually consumed by audiences, as well as to develop new theoretical tools to study it (Holmes and Jermyn 17). It might be useful, she suggests, to "foreground Reality TV as opening up space for experimentation and exploration" (18). I would argue that *The Bachelor*, and the pleasure derived from it by the viewers, opens up precisely that sort of space. The interaction between the bachelor and his bevy of beauties, so easily dismissed as simply patriarchal, can be interpreted as a potentially feminist opening for exploring the nature of relationship formation and experimenting in new ways with the negotiation and meaning of monogamous commitments. Through its practice of making private moments of romantic and sexual interaction, and sometimes extradyadic transgression, public – for the viewing audience and for the participants in the game – *The Bachelor* problematizes normative expectations of erotic relationship behavior, even as the "plot" draws us inexorably towards true love, marriage and the happily monogamous ever-after.

As a third wave feminist critic, I am not interested in simply pointing out the ambiguities presented by *The Bachelor* and its reality cousins with regard to sexual and emotional nonexclusivity or any other form of gendered interaction; rather, I am interested in *using* those ambiguities to challenge everyday thinking about the practice of monogamy in heterosexual relationships[3] – not to settle on a final answer (equal opportunity; "don't ask, don't tell"; serial monogamy; recreational swinging; polyamory; or any other singular option that might currently be available) but to insist that certain questions be repeatedly posed and held open to discussion, and to encourage as much creativity in feminist thought about monogamy as we have devoted to those perennial questions about the division of household labor or whether to keep or change one's last name. What do we want out of romantic relationships or out of marriages? What does sex mean in our relationships? What intimate ideals do we want to hold ourselves to, and why? What do monogamous dreams and promises mean in an era of increased premarital sexual experimentation, delayed childrearing, and a dramatically lengthened life span? Before reading further into the dynamics of *The Bachelor* – especially what I call the "harem fantasy" and its implications for the audience's own happy endings – a review of feminist arguments for and against monogamy in heterosexual relationships is in order.

MARRIAGE, MONOGAMY AND FEMINISM

Marriage has long been a site of critical analysis and debate for feminist theorists, and for each writer who has urged its abandonment as a patriarchal institution there have been others who argued for reworking heterosexual relationships into post-patriarchal forms that leave behind the institution's troubled history as a contract to secure men's property or an inequitable bargain for women.[4] In the past decade, self-identified third wave feminist writers – Naomi Wolf, Patricia Payette, Allison Abner – have openly expressed their desires to take up positions as wives and to employ the traditional rituals and symbols found in weddings in self-conscious and sometimes pioneering new ways. In addition to working for structural changes such as reform in divorce and property laws, part of making hetero-sexual relationships more equitable and desirable has involved revising the roles of husband and wife, redistributing household tasks and responsibilities, sharing responsibility for initiating sexual activity, participating in shared childrearing, instituting dual breadwinning (where the woman does not automatically give up her career after childbirth or to follow her husband), and challenging constraints on female sexuality before marriage (few American men may expect or even desire to marry virgins nowadays).

Among many of my heterosexual feminist peers, however, monogamy is the one aspect of contemporary marriage that is not up for "reinvention," that remains a steadfast and taken-for-granted expectation in their intimate relationships. Bring up the fact at a cocktail party that your husband has moved his new lover into your home or that you attend swing parties together several times a month and you may be met with stunned, angry, or horrified responses. Now granted, nonmonogamy has historically worked against some women's interests, especially when practiced surreptitiously by married men. Women have faced harsher punishments for their transgressions by the legal system, and male violence against women has also made it more difficult for women to pursue multiple partners – openly or secretively. Even when monogamy is practiced more openly, men have had certain ideological, economic, and opportunistic advantages over women when it comes to developing and maintaining sexual or intimate relationships outside of marriage. As Diane Richardson notes, a "connection was often made between sexual liberation and women's liberation" by feminists in the 1970s, as "the demand for the right to sexual pleasure was not only about gaining greater personal authenticity and equal sexual rights with men, it was also about seeking empowerment in a much broader sense." However, "with hindsight," she argues, "many feminists have since questioned this view," as sexual liberation also seemed to grant men greater access to women's bodies and at times made it more difficult for women to say "no" to sex (104). Other feminists questioned whether practicing nonmonogamy was simply an attempt to make women's sexuality more like men's and whether we should be refusing an equality based on nonrelational values (this idea, of course, includes a faulty assumption that nonmonogamy always belies intimacy and commitment, an assumption that is patently untrue in many cases). Open nonmonogamy has sometimes seemed like a difficult and ultimately unrewarding path for feminists to recommend for a variety of other reasons: the continuing salience of the double standard in discourses about male and female sexuality, persistent ideological attachments to the idea of "true love" and the supposed singularity of sexual desire for the beloved, lingering religious prohibitions, the psychological difficulties involved in maintaining alternative relationships (battles with jealousy, insecurity, selfishness, and possessiveness), and the practical issues that may make different forms of nonmonogamy more difficult to initiate and sustain for women than men (because of a lack of time or financial resources, worries about physical safety, the risk of unwanted or unplanned pregnancy, responsibility for young children, etc.). Secret nonmonogamy, once primarily a male prerogative in marriage, is arguably increasing among married women, though this kind of "equality" in opportunity and practice may be debatable as a worthwhile political statement, feminist or not, despite Laura Kipnis's creative attempts to theorize it as such. Yet sexual nonexclusivity is a crucial piece of sex radical feminist history and could play a stimulating role in the third wave project of reinventing and re-envisioning marriage for heterosexual feminist women and men.

Unfortunately, I notice, along with feminists Stevi Jackson and Sue Scott, that in recent years "the critique of monogamy has become so muted as to be almost inaudible" in feminist writing (151). Political investment in monogamy, they argue, "declined in the 1980s with the shifting terrain of sexual politics," as it became associated with "a libertarian, individualistic, hedonistic pursuit of sexual variety" (153). There is no longer "a widely accepted feminist language" with which to question the taken-for-granted character of monogamy, but instead "an (often unarticulated) assumption that in heterosexual relations it is women who are damaged by nonmonogamy" (154). Yet, and here I reiterate Jackson and Scott's call to action, a critique of monogamy is essential if we are to think critically as feminists about sexuality and the institution of heterosexuality.

Early feminist writers like Emma Goldman and Victoria Woodhull raised heavy challenges against the practice of monogamy in marriage.[5] During the second wave of feminism in the 1970s, nonmonogamy was seen as a challenge to the oppression wrought by heterosexual relationships and was "central to the politics of the personal" (Jackson and Scott 151). In addition to serving the interests of men and capitalism, some writers argued, monogamy often serves to separate women from each other by leading them to invest their time and energy into a single man instead of a network of relationships

(Robinson 144). Often practiced unequally (that is, ex
enforced for married women but not necessarily for marri
monogamy might simply be another name for sexual dominati
some polyamorous communities, and among some gay and les
groups, sexual nonexclusivity is still considered a political statemen
and a revisionary practice because of this historical misuse of the
monogamous pledge.

Relationship expert and African-American activist Audrey
Chapman, although not writing explicitly as a feminist, put forth
the idea of "man sharing" in books, articles, and seminars, and offers
practical advice for women who find themselves in nonmonogamous
relationships, even suggesting that forgoing romantic ideals may
result in self-actualization and female empowerment. According to
Victoria Robinson, writing more recently, questioning heterosexual
monogamy in a contemporary context allows feminists to "argue for
the rights of single mothers" and to develop new ways of relating
as lovers, partners, and parents, as well as to respond "imaginatively"
to new social trends such as divorces and remarriages and the kinds
of families created by them (145) Nonmonogamy, she argues, can
also "serve to disrupt some of the assumptions monogamy makes
about human behavior," such as the belief that we "are inherently
jealous and possessive" (144). Similarly, Jackson and Scott argue for
practicing nonmonogamy and for challenging heterosexual privilege
by (1) ceasing to recognize the couple as a primary form, (2) recognizing the contradictory view that sex is what makes a relationship
"special" and intimate, and (3) putting an end to the equation of
monogamy with security. Despite acknowledging the practical and
emotional difficulties many individuals have with practicing sexual
nonexclusivity, Jackson and Scott stand their theoretical ground on
the value of the effort:

> We continue to feel that it is worth retaining our commitment to
> non-monogamy and working to make it possible rather than allow-
> ing our lives and the lives of others to be circumscribed by our
> most negative emotions (jealousy, possessiveness, insecurity, etc.).
> It may not always be easy, but overall we think it worth the effort.
> Moreover, it is not all a case of 'po-faced' political correctness
> – there is a considerable amount of pleasure and enrichment to be
> gained from non-monogamy. (153)

There are important indications, in fact, that we live more and more of our lives in states of nonmonogamy, whether we consciously accept this condition or not. New patterns of mobility, the increased presence of women in the workforce for longer periods of time, a delay in childbearing and -rearing, an increased human lifespan, and a host of other social and economic changes mean that young adults may spend more years dating and engage in more premarital sex than previous generations (and sometimes even more sex outside of a relationship in the search for additional marital partners). Women as well as men may have overlapping relationships, secretive or open, both before and after marriage. Like men, however, women are expected to shift to a more "mature" sexuality with marriage, to monogamous desire and practices. Yet although many people recognize the difficulty of following these prior sexual experiences with lifelong monogamous relationships, serial monogamy has been the primary (though not the only) means of reconciling these challenges. When one relationship fails, another takes its place – and when passion flees, so too do many bored spouses. People tend to mistake these trends as personal anomalies, however, rather than seeing them as significant cultural patterns in the evolving form of sexual and emotional intimacy.

WHAT REALLY TURNS US ON
ABOUT *THE BACHELOR*

The bachelor soaks in a hot tub full of women in string bikinis – his first group date – appearing as if he has just won the hetero-lottery. The scantily clad women wave their ever-present champagne glasses and tell stories about their exploits in the dating world, hoping to catch and keep the bachelor's attention through perkiness, sexiness, or silliness. This is not a time to be demure or traditionally modest – the competition is too stiff, the stakes too high. One woman hangs her head and begins to slur her words; several of the other women wonder aloud whether or not to remove her from the hot tub and eventually choose to do so (hey, one less competitor, after all). She is the youngest, quickly criticized for not being able to handle her liquor. One of the women clearly holds the bachelor's attention (is it her abundant cleavage or her witty rendition of high-school cheers? – the audience is left to make their own best guess); another woman breaks down in tears from "the pressure" and removes herself from the soapy scene to take refuge from cameras and competitors in the bathroom. As soon as possible, the bachelor slips away from the group with one of the women for some private time, which results in a quickly forged "connection" and some stolen kisses. In the documentary-style interviews that follow, the kissee then describes her attraction to the bachelor; the other women in turn express doubt about her motives and complain about her "aggressive" behavior. "She's not here for the right reasons," one young woman complains (insinuating that the kissee is seeking fame or victory rather than "true love").

The bachelor's next group date takes place at a winery, and again a woman drinks too much and breaks down from "the pressure," running from the room in tears. After consoling her with hugs and kisses outside, the bachelor returns her to the group. Shortly thereafter, he takes a pretty brunette to the wine cellar for a tour, and kisses her as well. In her post-date interview, she excitedly expounds upon the depth of their connection. (Too bad he doesn't offer her a rose later on!)

Of course, these are the kind of women who kiss AND tell; what a perfect way to create tension for the evening's rose ceremony! They dish among themselves — was it right for him to kiss Christy? Was she pretending to be upset just to steal him away? Isn't she just a little bit "psycho"? And what about the brunette? Wasn't she a bit too forward for going to the cellar with him anyway? And aren't both of them proving to be aggressive drama queens who just aren't here for the right reasons but seem intent on warping the bachelor's heart and mind with their calculated moves?

Much of the intellectual commentary on *The Bachelor* focuses on the antiquated gendered roles and stereotypical self-presentations made by the eager and hopeful contestants (Pick me! Pick me!), as well as the unquestioned ideals of marriage and heterosexual relationships that shape the series and its spin-offs. Reviewer Caryn James, for example, writes of the appeal of *The Bachelor* as "nostalgia." "And like all nostalgia," she explains, "it speaks to the longing for an idealized past. We're in an age where sexual roles are fluid, and 'The Bachelor' offers an escape from ambiguity, a temporary and knowingly false return to an era in which male and female roles were clear – stereotypical, but clear" (19). Expressing similar concerns about nostalgia and gender relations, Barbara Dafoe Whitehead addresses the reverse series, *The Bachelorette*, asserting that "despite its contemporary trappings, the show is actually about courtly love," "a leisurely world where gallant young men devote their energies and imaginations to winning the hand of their chosen fair lady" (2). In a world where the language and practice of romance have "faded" and young would-be-daters settle for "hook-ups" and casual sex instead of formal planned dates, Whitehead sees *The Bachelorette* as a revelation of "the longing of accomplished young women for the romance of earlier generations" (2). I have no doubts that these gendered romantic fantasies appeal to some of the viewers of the show, and there is also no doubt that the producers have selected romantic dates for the participants in order to produce an air of liminality, an escape from the everyday world into a zone where love and "connection" are produced seemingly effortlessly (the beach in Hawaii, the candlelit dinner, the spa massage for two).[6] Any man wondering about how to create such consumptive "romance" for the woman in his life could easily use the show and its featured commodities as a primer.

There are other fantasies that may also be indulged in by the viewers and other anxieties that are given shape as the season unfolds: for example, the fantasy that true love exists and can be recognized instantly through the magic of "connection"; the worry that in a contemporary, U.S., middle-class world of choice and opportunity in sexual and dating partners, one will ultimately make the wrong decision in love and select a partner that is "wrong," the fear of being a perpetual wallflower, sent packing on a walk of shame despite one's best efforts to win love and happiness. The more jaded commentators argue that *The Bachelor* is nothing more significant than an opportunity to ogle young women as they catfight in string bikinis, and I admit, as well, to the possibility of a more pornographic motive for some viewers.

In place of these accusations of nostalgia and pornographic pleasure – or, perhaps, alongside them – I maintain that the harem fantasy contains a kernel of feminist potential in light of the above-cited debates over monogamy and sexual nonexclusivity.[7] However historically inaccurate it may be, the image of the harem that continues to captivate American audiences and emerge in popular cultural forms is that of a group of attractive, sexually available young women under the control of a powerful man (though possibly the reverse), protected, secluded, used, and ranked according to his polygamous desires. This particular harem fantasy is a frequent source of erotic fascination and a recurring image in pornography. *The Bachelor* draws on this fantasy through its organization (twenty-five women competing for one man and interacting in intimate situations) and through clusterings of comments and representations that emerge in each episode. In the opening episode of each season, the bachelor is introduced to the ladies who will be living together and competing for his heart. As they step out of limousines, one by one, wearing cocktail dresses or evening gowns, they are simultaneously revealed to the bachelor and to the voyeuristic audience at home. The bachelor is continually reminded that the women are available to him (we usually assume sexually and emotionally) and that he will be selecting among them; the women are continually reminded that if they fail to compel the bachelor's interests, they will be asked to leave the "compound." Before the rose ceremonies, the women are often shown preparing for their meeting with the bachelor – choosing outfits, styling their hair, and applying make-up – in the hope of advancing to the next round. The fall 2004 season exemplified this particular harem fantasy even more clearly, as bachelor Byron Velvick lived full-time with the contestants, rather than being sequestered in his own "bachelor pad" as the men had in previous seasons. The women were shown caring for him in a variety of traditional ways (cooking for him, delivering flowers and notes to his door) and less traditional ways (visiting him in their lingerie in the hopes of spending some time alone with him). Each bachelor has seemed aware that he is living a fantasy, proclaiming disbelief that "all of these beautiful women" have been assembled for his benefit and appear to feel so strongly about him. Though he sometimes resents their demands on his attention or struggles because he does not want to "hurt" anyone by preferring the company of another woman, he is also continually aware of his privileged position, and is sometimes apologetic for it.

The emotional trials and tribulations of living as a *member* of such a fantasy harem are also dramatized in this particular form of television competition. After all, because the women live together for most of the season, they are placed in direct competition for male attention and in daily interaction with each other. Further, although some of the women earn individual dates with the bachelor (usually for such ambiguous reasons as "first impressions," a "connection" forged through a brief conversation, or the occasional impromptu skill competition), the others must partake in "group dates" involving all of the twisted emotional sparring one might expect in such a situation. In *The Bachelor*, then, the fantasy of choice and access for the bachelor often constitutes a growing nightmare for the contestants, as they cry alone or in groups about their inability to compel the bachelor's attentions or over his transgressions of their supposed romantic bond. The contrived situation is designed to fuel jealousies as the women compete for the bachelor's attention, and the editing process reinforces this theme of competition among the women by letting specific and colorful rivalries emerge early in each season. The bachelor often kisses more than one woman on his group dates, an act that is perhaps expected in order for him to test his sexual "chemistry" with different women, yet is still emotionally jarring for the participants. Sometimes the women openly discuss their intimacies with the bachelor with each other; other times they are more secretive. Contestants are shown wondering what happened during his private encounters with the others: "Did she kiss him in the hot tub?"; "Why did Brooke return home without underwear?" When only three contestants remain, the bachelor takes them each on consecutive overnight dates, usually to well-known "romantic" travel destinations like Aspen, Hawaii, or an outdoor desert spa, where the option of choosing a late-night, camera-free "fantasy suite" is open to each couple. The women are each left wondering whether or not he indulges with the others, though they quickly learn that it is usually *not* a good idea to broach this subject directly with the bachelor. The contestants express their emotions to the cameras instead: "It's so hard to know that my boyfriend is dating two other women"; "I'm holding back because I know there are other women involved."

The overall situation constructed by the series seems less an idealized example of heterosexual romance than a potentially traumatic scenario, as fears of losing the game mingle with all of the disturbing emotions triggered by same-sex competition and by a mate's possible infidelity – jealousy, possessiveness, insecurity, anxiety, and depression. The camera loves nothing more than expressions of emotional distress, shame, or sorrow from the competitors. If there is a sure way for a contestant to get airtime, it is to shed some tears onscreen while bemoaning her fears of rejection, or, better yet, to throw up or have a panic attack on the way to a rose ceremony. When a contestant is rejected, the camera follows her into the limo for her ride away from the mansion, and this is a perfect opportunity for her to articulate her self-doubts to the television audience ("Why didn't he fall in love with me? What is wrong with me?") or to give herself a teary pep talk ("I know that my man is still out there, I just need to find him."). If a contestant has a particularly dramatic breakdown, it may be shown several times throughout the episode and in advertisements for the show. It is precisely this voyeuristic enjoyment of women's emotional pain that has led some commentators to wonder if *The Bachelor*'s female viewers are so competitive themselves as to have become sadistic, or whether the enjoyment stems instead from masochistic identifications with the rejected women.

In an article about the queer coupling of reality television and marriage, Judith Halberstam suggests that the emotion on the part of the bachelor and the members of his harem is not authentic, anyway:

> Of course, if they were honest, the studs and babes would admit that the chance to nuzzle, cuddle and smooch twenty-five hotties with impunity in a two-month span is reason enough to sign on for the rocky ride of reality dating. But honesty is not the best policy for bachelor/ettes. So as each potential soul mate confesses to "falling for" (the most overused phrase in reality marriage land) the man or woman of the hour, the bachelor/ette returns the love and longing in equal measure and commits to love, honor, and obey, forsaking all others, in sickness and in health, until death do they part, or at least until the next episode. (46)

Yet I would argue that the love story (the *after*-story, happy or not) is just as important as the hook-ups and break-ups and tensions of the harem phase, especially for those of us who reconsume the show in all of its different forums: many viewers found *Bachelor 4* Bob Guiney's season disappointing, as it became clear that he hadn't "really fallen for" any of the women and was seemingly just working his way through the women in the manner that Halberstam suggests, and the successful relationship of *Bachelorette 1* Trista Rehn and her final pick Ryan Sutter has remained a tabloid staple, even resulting in expensive made-for-TV nuptials. Also significant is the fact that on talk shows, in gossip weeklies, or on specials such as *After the Final Rose*, the "runner-up" is often shown both confronting the man who rejected her and "doing fine," recovering fully from the break-up even if she admits to a painful healing period. Significantly, the contemporary dramatic love story being told here is not one of the virtuous, taciturn woman pining away for the man of her dreams and waiting for him to recognize the fact that he is in love with her (the story we might expect given the critical focus on the show's "nostalgia" for "courtly love"); rather, it is of a woman who pursues romantic connection (perhaps a bit too recklessly), risks losing her dignity and facing emotional pain in the process, and emerges determined to keep trying even if she loses this particular battle in the end ("Someone will realize how much I have to offer"). The contemporary love story is played out here by experienced partners – that is, they may each have a noteworthy romantic and sexual past. Several bachelorettes have revealed previous marriages on *The Bachelor*, and a single mom made an appearance in *Bachelor 7*. Such revelations are dramatized on the show as moments of honesty and connection, but also often of turmoil for the bachelor. Real-life couples may negotiate this territory in different ways, choosing to remain discreet about their previous liaisons or to tell all, but part of the appeal of this particular harem fantasy is that deciding how to handle the historical non-exclusivity of our partners (even if it is not supposed to be part of a shared future) is actually a widespread conundrum for contemporary daters.

For some viewers (especially those ideologically and psychologically committed to monogamy), the show offers a vicarious opportunity to experience all of the emotions that go along with competing for romantic attention and witnessing a lover's transgressions, as well as to reaffirm the existence of the one true love and the importance of romantic and sexual exclusivity in a contemporary context. After all, though the bachelor's choice of and access to attractive women is celebrated throughout the early episodes of the season (which bachelor *didn't* look overjoyed with the attentions he received and the kisses he bestowed?), in the end he is asked to choose, with his final rose, the one woman who can offer him *everything*. The expectation, of course, is that once the final rose is distributed, the two will become monogamous, just like any other couple in love. Nonexclusivity is the story of the intimate past, not the story of the intimate future. Though the bachelor may have been shown equivocating in the final episodes to build dramatic tension, the last few moments of the season are designed so that he can renarrate his experience using the cultural tools so loved by romantics: "This was meant to be; "I have listened to my heart; despite the past, you are the only one; our connection is real; I knew it all along." On the other hand, for cynical viewers (perhaps not a distinctly different group), the bachelor's transgressions over the course of the season allow for a pleasurable challenge to normative ideas about love, sex, and commitment. After all, up until that final moment we could have pictured either one of the women leaving on his arm. The eventual break-up of the couple (only two of the bachelors have yet remained with their last-loves-standing) allows for a critical stance toward romantic ideals.

The reality for young couples seems more and more to be that lifelong monogamous commitment is difficult, if not impossible for some, and this sentiment is being dramatized in popular cultural productions like *The Bachelor*, along with the element of choice that goes into partnering. Do we choose our lovers rationally or does love choose us? Can we make a list of desirable qualities, check it twice, and "order up a compatible relationship," as a television advertisement for the Internet dating website e-Harmony claims? What is the nature of this "connection" that we feel for someone, anyway? Certainly, the language used by the participants still tends toward "soulmates," "true love," and "the ultimate connection," but the stories that we are left with in the end, especially on the dating shows, are far more ambiguous than that. Though ultimately the choice comes down to one paramour in *The Bachelor*, the fissures created in our understandings of contemporary relationships are not simply recuperated by the bachelor's proposal in the final episode.

LOVE, SEX, AND MARRIAGE IN YOUR LIVING ROOM

Judith Halberstam homes in on a central question posed by *The Bachelor*: "Why has marriage become prime-time fodder for a public that craves escapist 'reality' TV? Should we interpret these new marriage shows as evidence that the institution has completely crumbled or as a reinforcement of its ubiquity?" (44). She argues that "win a husband/wife" shows seem to trivialize the sanctity of marriage "and, in the process, turn straight coupling, for better or for worse, into pure entertainment." Such representations of reality romance within queer media theory oddly dovetail with conservative cultural fears about the contemporary decline of marriage. Reality TV has since its inception been accused of cashing in on or even creating simulated moral panics, of deliberately exploiting "controversial social or moral issues in its bid to attract an audience in the competitive television environment" (Holmes 21). Certainly, *The Bachelor* cannot be entirely excused for this sort of casting, scripting, and editing. In *Bachelor 5*, for example, Trish, one of the contestants, claimed to have slept with thirty-five men, at least one of whom was married, and this disclosure led to fiery debates on the show and in the multiple forums where the show is reconsumed about the state of female virtue. "How could she?", mused the other contestants.[8] Further, when the rejected Trish returned to beg the bachelor to give her another chance, *Bachelor 5* Jesse Palmer called her a "stalker." She was not the first female contestant to have been spoken about in these negative terms by the bachelor himself. *Bachelor 2* Aaron Buerge, for example, described one of the contestants, Christie, as having "a sort of *Fatal Attraction* thing going on."[9] Every season, it seems, features one or two women who are guaranteed to bring up controversial issues, act emotionally unstable, or escalate everyday roommate dynamics into television-ready histrionics. But part of the success and appeal of *The Bachelor* – it has, in fact, outlasted many of the more over-the-top or controversial reality programs and is preparing for its tenth season – is that it does not go too far in the direction of cultivating or cashing in on cultural panics and predictable melodrama.

Media theorist Misha Kavka argues that reality TV is based on contradictory impulses, both to "peddle the mores of the status quo back to as broad (and hence commercially viable) an audience as possible" and to "'queer the pitch' of the ordinary to keep that audience watching." Indeed, this is something that *The Bachelor* does quite well, even without the attempts by the producers to stir up controversy. Queering the pitch, Kavka argues, refers to the "in-built,

often barely controlled effects of excess in reality TV programmes
– too much emotion, too much information, too much visibility":

> Indeed, to perform intimacy in the public space of television
> viewing, as reality TV participants must do, is by definition to
> parade an incoherence of norms that in other contexts is closed
> down, or at least regimented, by the status quo. Because such
> performances queer the public–private divide, the spillage of
> reality TV has a tendency to work against the patriarchal and
> hetero-normative structures that may define the premise of the
> programme. (221)

"There is something queer," she writes, "about asking that people
play out their intimate moments in public view," despite the fact that
much "real-love television does not diverge from the heterosexual
premise of romantic union" (221). Almost "despite itself," real-love
reality TV opens up "productive fissures in the hetero plot" (222).

Unlike some of the dating shows, *The Bachelor* rarely relies on
carefully concealed video cameras in bedrooms or on stalker-style
night-vision recorders to capture intimate moments with multiple
contestants. Instead, "private" areas are set up on group dates (the
shower, the wine cellar, the hot tub) or overnight opportunities are
presented (the "fantasy suite") and the cameras follow along where
the other contestants are not allowed to go, making even these private
moments into public television fodder at a later date. But although
some encounters are "private" to the contestants yet visible for the
television audience, other moments track between visibility and invisibility for both parties. Though *Bachelor 1* actually took the viewers
inside the fantasy suites using hidden devices (stopping just short of
the pornographic – we heard about the chocolate syrup deployed by
the winner, Amanda Marsh, in the tabloids but did not actually get
to see its application and consumption by the couple in the fantasy
suite), the final limit for the following shows has been the bedroom
door in the suites, which almost all bachelors and their final three
ladies have stepped through (perhaps this is because our fantasies of
what is occurring inside prove much more interesting and titillating
than what is actually going on). The audience may see some passionate
kisses, a clothing change, a massage, or a steamy encounter in the hot
tub, but are left wondering if actual sex occurred with any or with

all three of the final women. Further, the audience is left with some of the same pressing questions as the other contestants – what really goes on in there? Does whatever "happens" behind closed doors with the other contestants impact the relationship between the bachelor and the woman he eventually chooses? Should it?

One of the questions that viewers puzzle over in conversations and on message boards is how the winning bachelorette will be able to handle observing the affections that her "boyfriend" bestows on the other women during the show or the sexual situations that come to light when the show is aired. After all, due to the fact that the show is pre-taped, each contestant is also a possible viewer and will eventually have the visible evidence of his encounters with the others that she was denied during the filming. Do not make the mistake of thinking that a competitor can escape witnessing this past by refusing to become a viewer herself – in fact, the women may also be taped as they watch scenes from the show for its companion episode, *The Bachelor: The Women Tell All*. Recently, the last two contestants were also asked to watch the final episode live with friends and family for another ABC special, *The Bachelor: After the Final Rose*. The winner of *Bachelor 6*, Mary Delgado, for example, was asked to watch the scenes of Byron Velvick with the other finalist, Tanya, and she was asked directly by the host, "Is it hard to watch Byron say those things and do those things with another woman?" Added to this post-date visibility, of course, is the ever-present invisibility of what happened in the fantasy suites, and it is hard for viewers to imagine which is more maddening for the contestants, whether they win or lose. After being chosen on *Bachelor 2* by Aaron Buerge, Helene Eksterowicz reportedly asked him to propose to her again after viewing the show. When their relationship ended in a much-publicized break-up, Helene was said to have been upset because Aaron could not seem to adjust to the fact that he was "no longer dating twenty-four other women" (Devinney). Now certainly, contemporary daters are not asked to be literal spectators of their partners' previous intimacies in such a direct manner. It is here, however, that such a fantasy becomes compelling for a viewer, where the "productive fissures in the hetero plot" are opened. What is that plot nowadays, anyway?

Yet it may not even be the passionate kisses that are the most diffi-cult to observe or, for the viewer, to imagine observing. The bachelor also shows himself, in subtle ways, to be a slightly different person with each woman. He may be more fun-loving and playful with the thin brunette; more cautious and reserved with the curvy blonde. He may picture one of them coming home with him and decorating his apartment; he may be planning on moving to a Southern state with another. And herein lies the trauma on the other side of the equation: *how* does he choose? Despite our understandings and everyday operations of our "selves" as coherent and even singular, many of us notice how a new lover brings forward a different side of us, how certain preferences, fantasies, and personality traits may shift to the fore in each relationship, and may shift again after a break-up as we "find ourselves" again. Sometimes this instability may play out through questions about our identities: Am I a country girl or a city girl? Do I want to have a family and a career or do I want to quit working to focus on my children? Do I want to breed at all? Is it a rugged man that makes my heart beat faster or a man in a suit? Do I want a man at all? Dating, in many respects, can be a game of make-believe: what will my life be like if this is the person I choose, or if this person chooses me?

Yet while we may each live out our own dramas of identity as we analyze or overanalyze our relationships, and, in effect, choose our intimate futures, we do not always have the chance to witness our partners doing the same, and those rare occasions when we do may prove unsettling. Some knowledge and conversation about our partners' past loves is inevitable in the dating world today, though for some couples it may involve the intimate details of each pairing and for others it may be limited to occasional glimpses of dusty photographs in a shoebox. An interest in other people's love-lives, on television or in the tabloids, is also a reflection of our interest in our own partners' past erotic encounters: How many were there? What were they like? Can we ever know the truth? Who was most skilled in bed? Who had the best body? Am I the last one on his (or her) list? Did I "win"? And it isn't just the ghosts of our partners' other sex partners that haunt us (though certainly some are more haunted and haunting than others, and the possibility of sexually transmitted disease brings a serious element to these specters), but also the ideas of who our partner might have become with a different person on his or her arm and who we might have been in a different context or relationship. These kinds of questions have a real salience in the world of dating in a place like the United States, where decisions about whom to marry are the responsibility of the individual, for the most part, and life partners are chosen, at least on an experiential level, through consideration of relatively intangible factors (connection, chemistry, creativity, perceived similarities and differences, preferences).[10] For the final contestant on *The Bachelor* or *The Bachelorette*, as well as for the person doing the choosing, love is bought with some very compelling visual evidence of this struggle to choose or to let oneself be chosen, once and for all.

There is also the question of whether or not the emotion we feel in our intimate relationships is truly authentic – a question that comes to life in color on *The Bachelor*, as contestants wonder about whether or not their connections are real, whether their emotions are generated by the man in front of them or the machinations of TV drama. In a series of interviews with husbands and wives in the United States, for example, anthropologist Naomi Quinn notes that when individuals narrated their relationship histories they often expressed a concern as to whether they really loved the person they were thinking of marrying. She found that they used a "metaphor of love as an *entity* that may or may not be the real thing, so that a person might be fooled into thinking that this love, even their own for someone else, is real when it is actually false" (10). Her interviewees performed mental tests to interrogate their emotions and to decide upon the authenticity of their relationships. After all, how does one ultimately decide on a spouse or a life-partner in this world that says we can have only one, *the* one? And how do we decide among all of the possibilities for our *selves*? We question and re-question love, rewrite past relationships (I never loved him even though I thought I did; I always loved her even though I just now realize it). What happens on *The Bachelor*, then, though accelerated and encapsulated, may not be so far removed from what actually happens in relationship formation, at least for some of us.

The Bachelor, like other reality shows, has been critiqued for not really being real – for being the product of judicious editing and scripted encounters. For example, James writes that it

> is the least realistic of all reality shows. You're more likely to be
> thrown into a pit of writhing snakes like the contestants on "Fear

Factor" than to have a romantic experience like this. The show's winking, playful distance from real life is the key to its success, a distance evident in its comical pretense that love at first sight and happily ever after do exist – if only you can find the right television producer to hand them to you. (19)

Yet, as Hearn argues, reality shows may also work to define a "post real world" (8): there is no longer any need to discuss authenticity in terms of the storylines themselves because both viewers and participants (not necessarily mutually exclusive categories) are aware of the conventions of such programs and have accepted them. The importance of authenticity here, I would argue instead, lies on a different level than that of determining whether or not a chain of events is represented correctly to television viewers or whether the same sort of things could happen in "real life." Instead, authenticity is important, and compelling, at an emotional level: is the love the contestants feel for each other authentic? This is a favorite discussion among fans and on talk shows devoted to analyzing the relationships developed on *The Bachelor*; sometimes the participants themselves don't even know what is real and what has been "produced" in the name of entertainment.

The Bachelor, after all is said and done, may actually be helping to queer one of the biggest public and private romantic myths there is: that of "The One." The language is used repeatedly throughout the season ("He's the One, I just know it"; or, for the losers, "I know that the One is still out there, and I will find him"), yet somehow this mantra-like repetition only serves to throw the contradictions of this ideology into starker relief. Contestants muse about how fate brought them to the set, not their own agency; how they had hoped, but doubted, that the One might manifest himself in such a contrived situation. The bachelor thoughtfully assesses the tangible qualities of his potential wives (their beauty, skills, demeanor, self-esteem), and ruminates on his realization that so many of them seem "perfect" and that it is "very difficult to choose." Only two of the bachelors thus far have remained with their final girl for any period of time (although one of the women from *The Bachelorette* has married her pick). The rejected woman, who also eventually becomes both a viewer of the show and a post-show viewee, is often seen later "realizing" that her emotions were either not authentic ("I was caught up in the moment," they say, watching their teary departure from the rose ceremony at a later date) or that she will heal ("I was hurt, but I'm getting on with my life"). We saw Meredith Phillips crushed by the rejection of *Bachelor 4* Bob Guiney, but then madly in love once again by the end of *Bachelorette 2*, where she was allowed to turn the tables and select her mate from twenty-five hot, successful men. And there, believe it or not, she found the One, Ian McKee (oops, now they've parted ways despite "great expectations for a happy ending").

The relationships of many twenty- and thirty-something viewers may not unfold with such lightning speed as those on *The Bachelor*, but there will undoubtedly be some common elements in precisely how those stories proceed. For many contemporary daters-to-marryers, romantic and sexual pasts, on both sides, are a fact of life. The chosen one must be reconfigured, not as an arbitrary person who was in the right place at the right time, or who had the desired conglomeration of traits and attractions, but as the One who was there, all along, waiting. The nonmonogamous past is thus swept away as a necessary evil, the form of the quest, not the shape of the future. And when life's contingencies and statistical trends later send many of these same individuals back into the dating and marriage market as serial monogamists, the story will be retold, though perhaps this time with a hint of cynicism or campiness. And it is in these retellings that take place with either more or less zest and need than the first (ten?) times around, that our heterosexual stories are being rewritten, whether we like it or not.

HAREMS FOR ALL?

It's down to the final two and the bachelorette, Meredith, is agonizing over her decision between two men. Crying backstage, she exclaims, "I don't want to choose." When she descends the stairway, still a bit teary-eyed, the bachelors inform her that they have something to say to her – a compromise. "We've decided to all stay together," they say, smiling. "It's obvious that you get different things from each of us, and we like each other as well. How about we live as a threesome and see how that works out?"

Or: It's down to just Tara and Jessica, two young blondes who look almost as if they could be sisters. As the show is concluding, they realize that neither of them is really in love with Jesse, the young football player they have been competing for all season. The final scene is set, and Jesse waits at the end of a red carpet, in a circle of flowers. Instead of approaching him singly, though, wondering if they are the selected or the rejected, they decide to confront him together. "It's been fun," they say, "but we've actually decided to forgo our opportunity to become football wives and head off together into the sunset."

With these admitted fictions in mind, I'd like to propose that we reconceive of monogamy as a fetish. (Here I use "monogamy" in its colloquial sense to mean sexual exclusivity in relationships, and "fetish" in its colloquial sense to mean a point of erotic fixation.) I call monogamy a fetish because I believe that there are some people who really, truly find the thought of having sex with just one person (and the practice of it), for the rest of their life, to be their preferred erotic experience. Just like there are people who find that thinking about, looking at, or masturbating into shoes is an unparalleled erotic experience. I don't know the actual statistics, but I'd guess that the numbers of people who are "into" shoes in this way are probably about the same as (but perhaps greater than) the numbers of people who are "into" monogamy in a purely erotic sense. Now, of course, there are many people who desire to be monogamous and find monogamy to be a valid ideal, whether or not they find it erotically compelling (that is, their fantasies may take them elsewhere, but they nonetheless desire to maintain a monogamous coupling). There are also people who are monogamous because of their religious beliefs, their cultural milieu, or their desire not to cause pain to a partner to whom they are pair-bonded. There are people who are monogamous because of economic circumstances. There are people who are monogamous because they in turn wish their partners to be monogamous, who cannot stand the thought of their beloved touching (or sometimes even thinking about) another person's body. There are people who are monogamous in cycles, and others through different stages of the life course. Some people are sexually monogamous;

some people are only emotionally monogamous. Despite the official story, there are many variations on the theme.

Though I do not believe that there is only one way for relationships to proceed that would be ideal for feminists, I do think that it would benefit us to think critically about the stories that we tell ourselves about monogamy, love, and sex. Asking questions about what the intimate future of the relationship might hold with regard to sexual exclusivity can help us rethink the way that the emotional and sexual balances in relationships change over time. What does it mean if passion fades in a long-term relationship? Is that relationship over? Should you trade it in? Was this person never "the One" to begin with? What if we decided to operate as if our intimate futures were not already decided when we made our choice of life partner? What if both parties were open to negotiation about sexual exclusivity (among other important things, of course)? And what about the meaning of sex? Why can we engage in recreational sex before marriage or when not committed (or, at least, some of us can) but once we are in a relationship the meaning of sex becomes fixed, immutable, non-negotiable?

Certainly, one should not even consider taking *The Bachelor* as a model for any kind of enlightened nonmonogamy. Most of the relationships on the show, between the bachelor and the hopefuls and between the contestants themselves, are plagued by a lack of honesty, by intense emotional drama, and even by psychological trauma, making it more of an advertisement for the contradictions and difficulties that exist because of our schizophrenic attitudes toward love and sex than a primer for more positive romantic imaginings. In an interesting twist, it appears that the friendships between the female competitors that are forged on *The Bachelor* are more stable than the romantic heterosexual bonds. Helene Eksterowicz and Gwen Gioia from *Bachelor 2* have remained close and collaborated on a book about dating (*Nobody's Perfect: What to Do When You've Fallen for a Jerk but You Want to Make It Work*), Tara and Jessica from *Bachelor 5* reportedly vacationed together after the show aired. However, the show's popularity and controversial nature should make it interesting to feminists who wish to rethink contemporary heterosexuality. Luckily, there are indeed some people who are systematically exploring new ways of multiple partnering and writing about it, developing ethics and guidelines that are designed to enable humane and fulfilling intimacies that fall outside of the acceptable molds. We may not exactly have the blueprints yet, but there are many architects out there working through the night, trying to figure out how to fit the loves of their lives into the frameworks they've been given and then remodeling until it all works a bit smoother.

I do have to admit that my own queer fantasy scenarios may never happen on ABC. Maybe on cable?

NOTES

1. These sequences are not meant to be accurate representations of scenes from *The Bachelor* but to serve as illustrations of its common narratives. Some names are indeed those of women on the show, but quotations and sequences have been reconstructed from memory.

2. As the dynamics of the shows are similar, and because there have been three times as many seasons of *The Bachelor* as *The Bachelorette* as of this writing, I will primarily discuss *The Bachelor* here, referring to "the bachelor" and "the women."

3. My focus here will be on heterosexual relationships because the show's dynamics are such; also, the critique of monogamy has remained more vital in queer theory than in feminism over the last few decades.

4. For further analysis, see Pateman.

5. For further analysis, see Donovan.

6. For further analysis, see Illouz.

7. Western understandings of harems do not match the reality of this social organization as it was actually practiced in different places and historical periods. In *Dreams of Trespass: Tales of a Harem Girlhood*, for example, Fatima Mernissi distinguishes between imperial harems and domestic harems in Turkey. She notes that it was the historical Ottoman imperial harem "that has fascinated the West almost to the point of obsession," inspiring hundreds of famous paintings of "luxuriously dressed and lasciviously reclined indolent women, with slaves standing by and eunuchs watching the gates." Domestic harems, on the other hand, were extended families, often made up of monogamous couples. What defines this kind of harem, she writes, "is not polygamy, but the men's desire to seclude their wives, and their wish to maintain an extended household rather than break into nuclear units" (34–5). These harems continued to exist even after the last Turkish sultan lost power and his famous imperial harem was dissolved in 1909.

8. Most of the other contestants, as Trish reminded us, were in their early twenties versus her more advanced age of post-thirty. I quickly did the math in my head, and wondered if I would announce my personal estimate on national television. What is the definition of sex anyway? What counts? Do you count blowjobs or overlook them? Sure, the national average for women is between four to six lovers, but many of my friends are boasting of triple digits (at least in their own small circles). My own response to the uproar was not panic but a certain smugness as I reflected that even though

I am married and living in the suburbs, I may still be on the cutting edge in some way.

9. This is a reference to the film *Fatal Attraction*, where a single woman pursues a married man so aggressively that she becomes a menace to his family.

10. See Illouz for a fascinating discussion of the political economic underpinnings of such factors when selecting intimate partners.

REFERENCES

Abner, Allison. "Motherhood." In *To Be Real: Telling the Truth and Changing the Face of Feminism*. Ed. Rebecca Walker. New York: Anchor, 1995. 185–93.

Califia, Pat. *Public Sex: The Culture of Radical Sex*. San Francisco: Cleis, 1994.

Chapman, Audrey B. *Man Sharing: Dilemma or Choice? A Radical New Way of Relating to the Man in Your Life*. New York: William Morrow, 1986.

Devinney, C. Brian. "The Bachelor: Aaron and Helen Tell All – Why I Hate Aaron." *Reality News Online* www.realitynewsonline.com.

Donovan, Josephine. *Feminist Theory: New Expanded Edition*. New York: Continuum, 1985.

Halberstam, Judith. "Pimp My Bride: Reality TV Gives Marriage an Extreme Makeover." *The Nation* 279, no. 1 (2004): 44–6.

Hearn, Alison. "Image Slaves." *Bad Subjects* 69 (2004): 2–9.

Holmes, Su, and Deborah Jermyn, eds. *Understanding Reality Television*. London: Routledge, 2004.

Illouz, Eva. *Consuming the Romantic Utopia: Love and the Contradictions of Capitalism*. Berkeley: University of California Press, 1997.

Jackson, Stevi, and Sue Scott. "The Personal Is Still Political: Heterosexuality, Feminism and Monogamy." *Feminism & Psychology* 14, no. 1 (2004): 151–7.

James, Caryn. "The Bachelor and His Barbies: Love at 25th Sight." *New York Times*, 17 November 2002, sec. 2: 19.

Kipnis, Laura. *Against Love: A Polemic*. New York: Pantheon, 2003.

Mernissi, Fatima. *Dreams of Trespass: Tales of a Harem Girlhood*. Boston MA: Addison-Wesley, 1995.

Pateman, Carole. *The Sexual Contract*. Stanford: Stanford University Press, 1988.

Payette, Patricia. "The Feminist Wife? Notes from a Political Engagement." In *Jane Sexes It Up: True Confessions of Feminist Desire*. Ed. Merri Lisa Johnson. New York: Four Walls Eight Windows, 2002. 139–70.

Quinn, Naomi. "Love and the Experiential Basis of American Marriage." Unpublished MS, n.d.

Richardson, Diane. *Rethinking Sexuality*. London: Sage, 2000.

Robinson, Victoria. "My Baby Just Cares for Me: Feminism, Heterosexuality, and Non-Monogamy." *Journal of Gender Studies* 6, no. 2 (1997): 143–57.

Spigel, Lynn. "Theorizing the Bachelorette: 'Waves' of Feminist Media Studies." *Signs* 30, no. 1 (2004): 1209–21.

Whitehead, Barbara Dafoe. "Forget Sex in the City, Women Want Romance in Their Lives." *Washington Post*, 9 February 2003, B02.

Wolf, Naomi. "Brideland." In *To Be Real: Telling the Truth and Changing the Face of Feminism*. Ed. Rebecca Walker. New York: Anchor, 1995. 35–40.

4

GETTING WET:

THE HETEROFLEXIBILITY OF

SHOWTIME'S *THE L WORD*

CANDACE MOORE

POOL SCENE #1

In the pilot episode of *The L Word*, the audience is introduced to Midwestern aspiring writer Jenny (Mia Kirshner), who moves to West Hollywood to live with boyfriend Tim (Eric Mabius). Busy setting up her writer's studio in the converted garage behind Tim's house, Jenny hears a woman's voice in the backyard next door assuring someone, "Tina said I could swim here whenever." Curious, she approaches the bamboo fence bordering the neighbor's pool to glimpse moppy-haired Shane (Katherine Moennig) unbuttoning her white shirt and throwing it carelessly to the side. Another woman pulls her blue floral-print dress over her head in one fell swoop. Embarrassed, Jenny ducks, and the camera cuts to a reverse angle shot of the space between the bamboo slats that stands in for Jenny's voyeuristic gaze. The subsequent reverse shot joins the spectator's gaze with Jenny's point of view and positions the fence as a frame around the cavorting lesbians to reinforce the explicit voyeurism of the scene. An overhead angle next offers the audience a bird's eye view of Shane's dive into the water – an omniscient perspective to which Jenny could not possibly be privy. The cinematography moves the audience purposefully from subjective to objective points of view – we're "with" Jenny one moment and apart from her the next. Shane tosses water from her hair and, from above, we watch the two women kiss. Then, foreclosing our omniscient perspective and limiting visual access to the lesbian sex scene which follows, the camera returns to a close-up of Jenny observing through the fence; she cocks her head sideways to get a better look. From Jenny's partially occluded point of view, we watch as Shane leads her lover over to the side of the pool, turns her around, and, kissing the base of her neck, wraps her arms around her waist and fucks her. The woman moans, already close to orgasm. Back to a close-up of Jenny, who looks down, then closes her eyes.

POOL SCENE #1, REENACTED FOR THE HET SET

Later that night, Jenny and her boyfriend face each other on their couch in the dim light, touching. Between kisses, Jenny asks, "The neighbors next door … Are they a gay couple?"

"Yeah, they are," Tim answers distractedly, looking down at Jenny's body. They begin to rub each other and breathe harder as they converse.

"I saw them having sex in their pool this afternoon," Jenny reveals.

"You sure you saw them getting down?"

"I saw them getting way down, Tim," she teases.

"Why don't you tell me about it?" They kiss passionately, her way of "telling him about it," before she continues with her narration. She is intentionally turning up the sexual heat.

"There was this girl with short black hair," Jenny starts, pulling Tim's undershirt off, "and she walks out, and she takes off her clothes in, like, two seconds flat."

"Like this?" Tim asks, as he pulls off Jenny's shirt.

"I think it was a little bit faster," Jenny answers coyly. "Then there was, um, this blonde girl," Jenny continues, "who had these really beautiful breasts … I wasn't really watching that closely," she says.

"Oh, I think you were watching," Tim whispers, rubbing Jenny's breasts, "Very closely. What did they do next?"

"The tough skinny one takes the blonde vampy one … backs her against the side of the pool, and then she begins to fuck her."

Tim throws Jenny down on the couch, yanks off her pants, pulls his own down, and climbs on top of her. "Like this?" asks Tim.

GAY STRAIGHT OR WHATEVER

In January 2004, Showtime, a pay cable network, launched the first ever lesbian-themed serial drama, *The L Word*, with a large-scale marketing campaign aimed at an urban demographic. Since the airing of its pilot episode, *The L Word* has become a breakout hit for Showtime, earning the fastest show renewal in the network's history.[1] Cultivating the appeal of HBO's explicit serial *Sex and the City*, but with a twist, *The L Word*'s early advertisements read "Same Sex. Different City." This slick double entendre implied the new program's homosexual subject matter while promising to deliver the overt sexual content of *Sex and the City*, then wrapping up its final season. As evidenced in this marketing pun, one of the show's most effective strategies has been to produce sex scenes that ensure appeal for a premium-paying straight audience, while offering specific pleasures for queer viewers "in the know." The show cultivated this polymorphous audience during its fledgling season and has gradually and strategically incorporated more frequent, more diverse, and more complicated visions of queer sex in season two. Showtime's top executive Bob Greenblatt in fact makes it clear in interviews that Showtime has had its eye on a "broad" (code for mostly straight, mostly affluent) market audience for the show: "It must be liberating for Ilene [Chaiken, *The L Word*'s lesbian creator/executive producer] to do a series about her own experiences… But ultimately, we want people everywhere to buy it. So yes, the women are all attractive and we make no apologies about that. It's television. Who wants to watch unattractive people, gay, straight, or whatever?" (Glock 26). By marketing *The L Word*'s plethora of girl-on-girl sex scenes as well as its "anthropologically specific" portrayal of the West Hollywood lesbian lifestyle to "people every-where" – or at least to those who can afford pay cable – Showtime encourages visual consumption of *The L Word* via the tourist's gaze, and the show's creators have capitalized on this gaze as an ambivalent lure for straight and queer viewers alike.[2]

Like many pop culture critics, I subscribed to digital cable and to Showtime specifically to witness the world's first lesbian TV show play out. Having seen a few pool scenes shot in person, months earlier when I interviewed cast members on location in Vancouver, I was especially keen to see how the pool (a huge set piece built inside the studio, causing oppressive humidity under the hot lights) was worked into the completed series, almost as if it were a character. As a regular writer and entertainment editor for the lesbian magazine *Girlfriends*, I tuned in with a specific set of hopes, expectations, and concerns about lesbian representation, and, again like many other critics, I was initially disturbed by how casual, exhibitionistic, and heterocentric the first scene's depiction of lesbian sex seemed (Shane and her anonymous poolside conquest), compared to the intimate close-ups and narrative complexity of the second scene's rendering of heterosexual sex (Tim and Jenny's play-by-play appropriation). After all, the voyeur getting off on two women "getting way down" is a standard trope of heterosexual male porn, and is thus easily dismissed by the lesbian or lesbian-positive spectator as "soft porn," hardly registering as progress on the trajectory of lesbian visibility. But after watching the series over the course of two seasons and returning to read closely these early scenes in the pilot episode, I now see them as part of the show's tutor text for straight viewers, and appreciate their subtle work in positing queer sex as the new standard. Consciously transforming the conventions of heteronormative visual pleasure, the first pool scene significantly puts a woman in the traditionally male position of the voyeuristic spectator, and this female spectator then directs the second scene's narrative "re-enactment." Her role as director further complicates and queers the trope of straight male pleasure in lesbian sex. The soft-core pornographic elements of the series thus offer a feminist, queer-positive political edge.

The arc of the show from season one to season two has seemingly operated to transform straight tourists into queer-friendly travelers. The tourist gaze is a particularly useful theoretical model for *The L Word*, both because of the dialectic of immersion and distance mobilized by the show through the camera work and visual rhetoric of the pool scenes, and because of its focus on sexuality and "anthropologically specific" representation, through which *The L Word* offers a tour, albeit fictionalized, of the Los Angeles lesbian world. Media technologies share with tourism the fetishization of the experience of "being there," while they simultaneously distance the viewer from the viewed, as Ellen Strain argues in *Public Places, Private Journeys: Ethnography, Entertainment, and the Tourist Gaze*. This theory is easily imported into television studies since the television set, traditionally nested in the domestic sphere, is conceived of as a "window" to a bigger world, as Lynn Spigel has pointed out (7). Spigel argues that "television — at its most ideal — promised to bring to audiences not merely an illusion of reality as in the cinema, but a sense of 'being there,' a kind of hyper-realism" (14). Problematizing the distinction between the tourist, who "gladly or unknowingly accepts Disneyland's versions of the world's wonders," and the traveler, who "seeks and knows how to recognize authenticity," Strain argues that perhaps these archetypes are, if not one and the same, both similarly victim to the notion that there is an "authenticity" available to be grasped, or misrecognized, in the first place. Without completely disregarding the likelihood that there is no authentic lesbian culture to be grasped in this mediated "Lesbian-Land," I would argue that *The L Word* cultivates the tourist gaze in politically positive ways, as the show explains references, for instance, that most queer audience members would not need to have explained, to encourage *heteroflexibility* in its straight viewers. Through this term, I am siding with those cultural critics who place a high value on the viewer's agency, as I mark the possibility, frequently encoded in this televisual text, that the viewer can access multiple desires and sensibilities, entering a text, or a desire within the text, in a queer fashion as a straight spectator.[3]

Sites of exotic leisure and mundane backyard approximations, pools are foregrounded throughout the series, relating sexuality and community, fluidity and pleasure. Whether stressing the confident plunge or the slow submersion, *The L Word*'s repeated trope of "wetness" couldn't be more explicitly sexual, even as it figuratively represents being "in the lesbian know" or becoming knowledgeable about "real" lesbian sex and relationships. In fact, it is largely through parallel-structured scenes set in and near this backyard swimming pool that The *L Word* thematizes the conceits of "complete immersion" and "voyeuristic distance" over the arc of its first two seasons. In each scene, *getting wet* signifies being (or, in season two, becoming) a local. Each scene also depicts a straight tourist (a possible stand-in for the audience member) who looks on, poolside, at the queer women in the water. The pool not only produced heat on (and presumably off) the set, it proved instrumental in *The L Word*'s symbolic rhetoric as a meeting place for lesbian locals and pay cable tourists — gay, straight, or whatever.[4]

STRAIGHT WOMEN GO GAY FOR SHANE

Underscoring *The L Word*'s success is the fact that it was crafted with crossover appeal in mind. In the pilot episode, explicit sex scenes between the token heterosexual couple, Jenny and Tim, compete with lesbian sex scenes for screen time. The lesbian sex that is depicted in the pilot, given that there are no butch main characters, takes place between women who, as femmes in lesbian roles, could seamlessly pass as straight, allowing for a straight male viewer with fairly traditional tastes to see them as sexual objects, drawing on tried-and-true porno movie plots involving straight men taking voyeuristic pleasure in sex between gender-conforming lesbians.[5] Straight female viewers might also relate better to these women, in theory, because, as beautiful, fashionably dressed career women, they are "just like them" (or like they wish to be) with the exception that the women on the show sleep with women. *The L Word* has even inspired the manufacture of a T-shirt for straight female fans proclaiming heteroflexible lust: "I'd go gay for Shane."[6] With this slogan, the political thrill of crossover appeal is revealed, in that "going gay" might well mean reconsidering one's sexual orientation apart from heteronormative pressures and assumptions.

Hetero defection drives the show's plot, after all. Doesn't Jenny, in fact, "go gay" as an indirect result of Shane's erotic appeal? Watching Shane in the pool with the unidentified "blonde vampy one" clearly turns Jenny on, and while she channels the erotic charge of what she witnessed earlier that afternoon into her sexual relationship with Tim, a queer element remains attached to her re-enactment. She attempts to make her excitement safe – and "straight" – by implicating her boyfriend in the scene and encouraging him to derive conventional pleasure from it too. During Jenny and Tim's erotic dialogue, the producers of *The L Word* cash in on the fact that within heteronormativity, objectifying lesbian sex as sexy is de rigueur. At first glance, Jenny even appears to be emphasizing the details for Tim's erotic benefit, but she soon reveals in her description and body language not only an appreciation for other women's bodies (a safely heterosexual feminine gaze), but just how much the thought of two women fucking excites her, making sex with Tim a potentially queer act.

For instance, instead of seeing this scene as an appropriation of lesbian sex, what if it is instead an approximation? The heterosexual couple re-enacts the lesbian couple's sex act, and Tim, who would typically hold a position of voyeuristic power as a consumer of porn lesbians, is cast in the rather emasculating role of lesbian top. If "queer" is, as David Halperin suggests, "by definition whatever is at odds with the normal, the legitimate, the dominant," if it "demarcates not a positivity but a positionality vis-à-vis the normative – a positionality that is not restricted to lesbians and gay men but is in fact available to anyone who is or who feels marginalized because of her or his sexual practices" (62) – then the straight couple that privileges a lesbian sex scene as the norm arguably achieves a queer positionality. While Tim's excitement might be considered traditional, Jenny's pleasure in lesbian sex stretches boundaries; her role in the exchange is the truly queer one, for it is not Tim who chooses the dominant role, but Jenny who requisitions him to it based on her fantasy. Desiring to be fucked by a woman, she wordlessly but distinctly insists Tim play Shane's role. She begins the pantomime by taking off his shirt as she describes Shane's clothes coming off. Jenny structures and ultimately controls this sex play with Tim. A writer delighting in creating a scene, she writes him into Shane's role, herself into the woman-who-has-the-orgasm's role. She sets things up, in other words, so that *she* can come. Focusing on Tim's pleasure within this schema of the hetero couple imagining and role-playing two women fucking, one might read the scene simply as a reiteration of the historical place of men in relation to lesbian images – men being the ones who generally consume and get off on them – but one might, with Jenny's subversive direction in mind, see the scene as a *commentary* by the producers of the series on straight porn featuring lesbians.

While common stereotypes suggest men's strongest erotic sense is visual, whereas women are more aroused by narrative – being told a tale – this scene flips the script. Jenny stresses the way things look, the blonde girl's "beautiful" breasts, while Tim gets excited by the story itself, by what happened, in what order, and how the act is described. Wide-eyed and pleasantly surprised at Jenny's ability to reproduce evocatively her erotic visual experience, "Like this?" is Tim's repeated refrain. Jenny first responds to this question in the negative. The clothes came off faster with the lesbians, she indicates. When Tim again asks, "Like this?" during intercourse, the camera cuts away before we hear Jenny's answer. As *The L Word*'s plot progresses, we are ultimately given her response to this increasingly central question in their relationship. No.

By the season's end, we see that Tim's "like this" – in other words, his lesbian topping skills – could not measure up to the "authentic" lesbian model. Presenting the erotic ploy of a man deriving pleasure from lesbian sex, *The L Word* eventually shows the standards of lesbian sex to be exactly those by which he fails.

The pilot episode's first pool scene and its retelling/re-enactment together act as subtle foreshadowing devices, while also offering a way into the series for straight viewers. The pay-off these scenes offer queer viewers comes later, after reflection on the queering of what at first appear to be straight sex scenes. The pool scene outwardly invites new potential heterosexual fans to take touristic pleasure in lesbian sex visually from the "straight" perspective (Jenny's) to which they are accustomed. The pool scene's re-enactment entitles straight viewers, male and female, to think of lesbian sex as hot, while it simultaneously entices them with the visual titillation of straight sex, making doubly sure they are able to find pleasure. Yet by accepting Jenny's eye line as their own, male viewers become feminized as they look on, and – given that Jenny's subjectivity is later revealed to be queer – female viewers inadvertently "go gay." The scene ultimately decenters hetero visual and sexual privilege. In fact, reversing the typical biased view of the lesbian top as an imitation male, this scene imports male viewers into the role of imitation lesbian top, a role in which they are (like Tim) shown to be inadequate.

At the same time, these two scenes subtly introduce straight viewers to an experience with which queer viewers are intimately familiar. Heterosexuality, as the assumed paragon of healthy sexuality – the "norm" – is the basis of nearly every sexual representation on the silver, and the smaller, screen. Homosexuals have been raised translating heterosexual love stories, reading texts, films, songs, and soaps, against the grain. By opening with queer sex and then patterning heterosexual sex on it, the show gives straight viewers a gentle version of the representational alienation well known to queers – that of eroticizing a scenario without recognizing oneself as a viable subject within it. *The L Word* cleverly offers straight viewers subjective entry points – whether through Jenny or Tim – into the fiction.

These opening scenes ostensibly welcome visitors to lesbian sub-culture and begin a process of instructive transformation, simultane-ously working to expand straight spectators' comfort zones, even as they serve as coded critiques of heteronormative tropes. It comes, of course, as no shock for queer viewers to see yet another straight sex scene played out, even on a lesbian television show. Within this revisionist scenario, however, a hetero couple not only enjoys playing out a lesbian sex scene, but for a woman's pleasure and under her direction, as Jenny acts as the voyeur, the conduit, and the director of the erotic, structuring visual and physical pleasure around her sexual enjoyment.

Jenny is the main vehicle for straight viewers to develop an insider's understanding of *The L Word*'s lesbian world. Jenny's poolside fascina-tion, a fascination the character tries at first to *straighten out* with her boyfriend, becomes the trigger that causes her to explore further a world – the West Hollywood lesbian community – in which she is initially a mere tourist in both a geographical and sexual sense. Soon after their lesbian-inspired erotic play, Jenny and Tim visit a party thrown by neighbors Bette and Tina – the committed couple who act as the nexus for *The L Word*'s circle of queer friends. At Bette and Tina's house, Jenny finds herself strongly attracted to a sultry coffeehouse owner, Marina. Locking gazes while discussing their nearly identical literary tastes, Jenny and Marina find themselves alone in a bathroom together where Marina frenziedly kisses Jenny. Spooked by Marina's aggressive advances, yet kissing back, Jenny breaks away, slaps Marina, and insists to Tim that they leave the party.

Jenny tries to make her relationship with Tim work; they get engaged but she cannot resist her attraction to Marina. When Tim catches Marina performing oral sex on her, Jenny does everything she can to repair their relationship. In a last-ditch effort to stay together, Tim and Jenny elope to Tahoe, but Tim angrily leaves Jenny asleep in the motel the morning after their wedding ceremony. Jenny hitch-hikes back to Los Angeles to find that neither Tim nor Marina wants anything to do with her. Portrayed intelligently on the producers' parts as an honorable man in an unfortunate situation, Tim allows Jenny to live in the backyard shed where she has set up her writing studio. The last six episodes of season one see Jenny, heartbroken, struggling with her sexual identity. She goes to girls' bars in West Hollywood and awkwardly tries to pick up women. She slowly builds friendships with the rest of the queer main characters of *The L Word*, evidenced when she accompanies the gang to the lesbian spring break party of Dinah Shore weekend. The season finale of *The L Word* leaves Jenny juggling a man, Gene, and a woman, Robin.

The beginning of season two sees a crucial transformation in Jenny's character. Gene breaks up with Jenny, declaring, "We don't have sex ... and I know why ... I'm sorry to break it to you, but you are a girl-loving, full-on lesbian." Jenny responds calmly, "I don't think that's for you to say." Unlike bisexual character Alice, who verbalizes her desire for both sexes and uses the term *bisexual* to describe herself, Jenny does not use any particular signifier of sexual identity to mark the nature of her desires, until midway into the show's second season, after, not insignificantly, another pool scene.

GETTING THE CAMERA WET

Early in season two, Shane walks over to the same backyard pool with Alice, two other friends, and a six-pack, delivering the same basic line that caught Jenny's attention in episode one: "Bette said that we can swim here whenever." Shane lifts a green T-shirt off nonchalantly and saunters over to the pool. The soundtrack ethereally repeats the word "wet," and then "get wet," as the four women pull off clothes and jump in while the camera submerges to water level. The splashes of the girls plunging in and doggie-paddling around create waves that rise to mid-level on the camera's lens. The girls' legs and arms are magnified under the water as Alice giggles in glee. Far from the bamboo fence, we spectators – travelers and locals alike – are "with" the lesbians; we are, briefly, *in the pool*.

After an interspersed scene, the camera returns to view Jenny walking toward the pool. Mark, season two's straight male character with a multi-episode arc (played by Eric Lively), and his friend, Gomey (a complete "rube" in Lesbian-Land), interrupt her path. Gomey looks over to the pool as the rippling light hits the trio's faces in the dark.

"That pool looks so fine, Jenny. Would it be cool if we join you?"

"We should probably ask them," Jenny says, separating herself from the group in the pool, even as Gomey has, with his "join you," obviously understood differently.

Gomey exits off-screen, as Jenny and Mark seat themselves in front of the bamboo fence that framed Jenny's initial voyeuristic gaze on the lesbian sex act in the pool. Mark's dialogue forces her to consider which side of the fence she is on now.

"Those girls, they're all gay, right? What about you? Are you gay?"

"No," Jenny starts, "I don't know…"

After waffling, she puts the responsibility of determining her sexual identity on Mark, asking, "What do you think?"

"If I saw you at a bar," Mark answers, "I would assume you're straight… Never know these days, do you?"

"No, you don't. Except, you knew they were, right? What do you think it is?" Jenny seems to be trying to measure both her difference from and sameness with the girls in the pool. The camera cuts to Shane and Alice laughing.

"I'd say it has something to do with their attitude," Mark ventures, in voiceover. The camera then returns to the two of them smoking in front of the bamboo fence. "It's not that they're masculine or anything, because actually some of them are pretty feminine… They have these very cool haircuts. It's obviously more than a haircut. It's… something that they exude that's… I'm gonna try and put my finger on it."

"Tell me when you do, Mark," Jenny says, meaning it honestly; she wants to know. Mark takes a final peer through the fence at the naked girls, and Jenny hits him, and insists: "Don't look!" Jenny shakes her finger at Mark, as if scolding a deviant child, "That's naughty."

Jenny's gesture to the straight male figure of season one (Tim) would be well represented by a finger beckoning come hither, an invitation to share an erotic "sight" with her. But Jenny's finger to Mark in season two now scolds, "shame, shame, don't look!" The concern – Jenny's and the series' – about straight "translation" has changed. If the first pool scene and its re-enactment acted as tutor texts, gently pointing the way for straight tourists, the second season's pool scene and accompanying poolside discussion seem more combative; all gloves are off.

Despite the erotic potential of a scene featuring skinny-dipping lesbians, this scene is expressly *not* a sex scene. Rather, it shows a group of friends having fun, delighting in and comfortable with their bodies. The "I could swim here whenever" from season one has shifted to "we could swim here whenever," singular to plural, sexual couple replaced by sexual community. Rather than briefly viewing the initial plunge from a bird's eye view – from the objective observer's standpoint, outside the action, as in the first season – we viewers are part of the group, reveling in the moment as "one of the gals." We too are beckoned to "get wet." "Getting wet," explicitly enunciated sonically and underlined visually, acts as a pun on erotic arousal and a textual urge to "join in." Season two thus reconfigures and recasts the first season's voyeuristic scheme. The lesbian couple is transformed into a lesbian community; a straight male, Mark, becomes the new tourist; and together, Jenny and Mark negotiate the pool scene with lesbian sensibility, not lesbian sex, as their joint subject. Juxtaposed, the figures of Jenny and Mark allow the show to explore larger questions of representing and understanding community from the inside and out.

Mark first enters Jenny and Shane's house (and the world of *The L Word*), video camera on and filming while the two friends are interviewing for a third roommate. The amateur filmmaker's entrance is obnoxious and presumptuous as he shoves his camera into the girls' faces and into their house, zooming in and narrating that they are "two dark-haired beauties with blue eyes." Desperate for rent money because Tim has moved out, Jenny and Shane take Mark's offer of first, last, and six month's rent in advance. Despite Shane's exasperation with Mark's intrusive introduction, Jenny warms to him. She gets his references to *Grey Gardens* and buys his line that the direct-to-video films like *World's Craziest Bachelor Parties* he makes for a living aren't his passion; he really wants to be a documentary filmmaker.

Tim's plot line over, the network specifically requested another straight male character in season two so that "the male audience … have a guy they [can] relate to," according to Showtime's senior executive Robert Greenblatt in *Entertainment Weekly*.[7] Yet Mark's character is a highly critical representation of a straight man: he has a pornographic interest in lesbians and their sex lives, expressed through crude flicks of his tongue. Rather than position Mark, like Tim, as a positive character for straight men to relate to and straight women and gay men to desire, the show utilizes Mark to address some viewers' criticisms of the show. Many queer viewers felt that the first season pandered too much to the voyeuristic proclivities of its straight male audience. Guinevere Turner, a member of *The L Word*'s writing team, was clear on this point in an interview: "Putting the voyeur into the show was the idea – acknowledging the concept of "I like to watch" and taking that man and turning it into a character. You know what everyone's criticizing and so you put it back into the show."[8] Representing Mark illicitly filming and spying on his unsuspecting roommates within the narrative, the producers effectively objectify and completely undercut his character, leading the ogling straight guy at the remote to feel less, not more, pleasure. By rendering Mark's behavior clearly despicable, *The L Word* also encourages male viewers to side with the girls against the guy, positively reinforcing male feminism.

Through a serial melodrama full of attractive females engaging in constant sex, *The L Word* articulates resistance through dominant culture's means,[9] performing "excessive lesbian sexuality and iconography that effectively counters the desexualization of the lesbian," to borrow Judith Butler's phrasing (23). The show not only anticipates its straight male viewer, it makes him central to the unspoken project at hand: the broad assimilation of queer difference. Critiquing the male voyeur through its narrative, *The L Word* urges straight male viewers to interrogate their own viewing practices. The show thereby coaches touristic viewers to problematize their own positionalities, and perhaps remold them.

While in the first season, Jenny asks Tim about the "otherness" of their neighbors – "the neighbors next door, are they a gay couple?" – Mark now solicits the other important, but missing, piece of information that complicates the initial voyeuristic configuration: "What about you? Are you gay?" Jenny first denies being gay, choosing the "straight" answer: "No." Next Jenny admits she's not sure, choosing the "in-between." And third, she answers enigmatically, offering a response that flirts with the identity but leaves it open to Mark's interpretation. By this cumulative effect, Jenny maintains all three answers. Without enunciating her claim to any of these identities – feminist straight woman, queer woman, lesbian woman – Jenny remains, for the text, a little of each. Not distinctively, now, a tourist, traveler, or local, a "confused" Jenny blurs these lines, becoming the catch-all vehicle. The "or, or, or" of these varied interpretations can be instead viewed as "and, and, and."

The night of her poolside conversation with Mark, Jenny later begs Shane to give her a haircut. Despite the fact that Mark characterizes the queer women's identifiable difference from Jenny as having to do with "more than a haircut," being rather "something that they exude," an "attitude," Jenny closes up the superficial gap between herself and the women in the pool. She ensures that if "very cool haircuts" have anything to do with it, she's seen as one of the girls. Yet Jenny weeps while Shane chops off her long black locks. The elusive "attitude" of the local, which the producers hint involves a certain degree of self-acceptance, is still to come for Jenny. The soundtrack, playing Iron and Wine's "Naked as We Came" over Shane's snips, hints at an initiation rite, a cutting off of excess layers, leaving Jenny exposed, vulnerable, figuratively nude. The wish for a haircut in order to mark her identity – obviously a painful rite for Jenny – reiterates her confusion about what lesbianism is and isn't. Is it (a) a style, (b) an attitude, (c) a desire, or (d) all of the above? While Mark cockily believes that he can "get it," that he can pinpoint what lesbianism is, Jenny, who may in fact be queer, still doesn't know. Through Jenny, *The L Word* again has it all ways, answering (d). The show positions lesbianism as a sensibility, not a sexuality. This is particularly important because, as a sensibility, lesbianism can potentially be co-opted by straight viewers.[10]

Thus, although newly shorn Jenny in the following episode delights in girls checking her out on the street, her full adoption of a local's sensibility has not yet solidified within the text. While queer viewers most likely consider Jenny a dynamic character who undergoes a transformation from a straight (tourist) and/or bi-curious woman (traveler) in season one into a queer who eschews labels (a local), in early season two, straight viewers continue to have, through Jenny, a vehicle that allows them to view the world of *The L Word* from a safely ambiguous place. The flexibility of Jenny's sexual identity is intentionally maintained by the show's producers. As Jenny increasingly becomes part of a lesbian community, the "conversion narrative" that takes her from looking on as a tourist to exploring as a traveler creates a simulated experience for viewers along with her. Even as

Jenny becomes ensconced in the local culture, her inauguration as an authentic "local" is put off; in fact, the question of her sexuality is intentionally deflected verbally up until the eighth episode of season two. Neither an outsider, nor quite yet a full insider, as an insider–outsider, Jenny is the perfect bearer of the tourist's removed, yet intermittently immersed, gaze.

DOCUMENTING "REAL" LESBIANS

After her haircut, however, Jenny no longer passes or intentionally presents herself as heterosexual. She first adopts the words "gay" and "lesbian" to describe herself in the following episode, when facing job discrimination. Incredulously, she asks a man who rescinds a job offer after learning of her girlfriend, "Are you firing me because I'm gay?" Recounting the exchange to her new girlfriend Carmen, she explains, "Mister Connor doesn't like the fact that I'm a lesbian."

"You told him that?" Carmen asks "How did that happen?"

"Guess it just sort of came out," Jenny says, pleased.

Now out, Jenny's new-found queer visibility has other unwanted results. Initially a poolside tourist of a different sort than Jenny, Mark is enticed to "travel" in the West Hollywood lesbian world, exploring as a social scientist. Observing lesbians through 24-hour surveillance, he engages in an omniscient perspective that he believes will help lead him to the "objective truth." The very idea of obtaining an omniscient perspective (Mark views from "above" and throughout the rooms of Jenny and Shane's house) is devalued by the text of *The L Word*, as Mark's notion that he can document a culture he is not a part of and come to know it is shown to be extremely problematic, if not outright wrong. *The L Word*, on the other hand, tutors via immersion mixed with the comfort of the distance the technology of television implies, offering its viewers multiple subjective viewpoints – stressing through visual and narrative cues a flexibility of identifications, rather than a documentarian's examination of the other from without. By surreptitiously video-recording Jenny as part of his dubious anthropological pursuit, Mark also answers his final take on the question of Jenny's sexuality. He views her as a lesbian. Not invited in by the locals in a way that allows him to indulge in erotic pleasure while maintaining his phallocentric privilege, Mark raids the local space by force, collecting information, then invoking the "science" of documentary filmmaking to absolve his invasion of privacy.

Mark's "documentary" project begs comparison to the exploitative "reality" videos produced by various corporations for late-night television of girls flashing or kissing for the camera. In these prevalent soft-core videos, a male cameraman often urges the women on, to "show tongue" as they kiss, and so forth, with saucy, suggestive commentary. The spectacle is in the "reality" of these displays, even as the verbal pressure of the cameraman seems to direct and even cause their performances. The "reality" of these filmed lesbian kisses is also called into question by the otherwise heterosexual display these mostly college-age young women on "spring break" offer. Jenny, Shane, and friends are lesbians who refuse to "go wild" for Mark, so he films them furtively. The films he thus produces bear resemblance to the many fly-on-the-wall-style pornos that claim to deliver "Real Lesbians."

Discovering that Mark has installed tiny surveillance cameras throughout her house, Jenny confronts him creatively. Stripping off her clothes and directly addressing one of the cameras installed in her bedroom, Jenny delivers a pornographic script: "My name is Mary. I'm fourteen years old, and I'm a virgin. My pussy's never been touched by a big cock before, and I want you to fuck me. Here's my pussy. I want you to take your big cock, and I want you to shove it up my ass. A boy has never seen my tits before…" She scrawls "Is this what you want?" over her chest in marker and stands before the camera until Mark responds, rushing into the house to make excuses for himself. Emphasizing herself as the sexualized object and visually raped victim of his gaze, shedding her clothing like the women in the pool, Jenny acknowledges both Mark's perpetration and his reading of her as a local. To some degree, the phrase written on her body, "Is this what you want?", asks Tim's prior line "Like this?" but facetiously, as if to say: "Am I getting your twisted construction right?" While the unselfconscious ethnographer believes he or she is reserved the power to define, Jenny revokes Mark's license to do so, pointing out the perverse nature of his gaze.

Mark's film project, which bends (and perhaps breaks) the definition of "documentary," centers on his two roommates and their lesbian friends, whom he pays twenty dollars an interview to speak on-camera about their sex lives. Sloppy attempts at ethnographic research are debilitated by Mark's leading, exploitative questions, which plainly lack objectivity. Through nine "strategically and respectfully placed" cameras (i.e. placed everywhere but the bathrooms) intended to further "capture" his subjects (without their consent), Mark becomes fixated particularly with Shane's bedroom practices, developing a form of non-penis envy.[11] Mark pays a woman to pose as a delivery girl and throw herself at Shane so he can get some "real" lesbian sex on film because "reality just needs a little help sometimes." While Jenny desired in season one to be fucked by someone like Shane, Mark desires in season two to fuck like Shane. Paralleling Tim's eagerness to fuck like the lesbian top in the pool (i.e. Shane) with Jenny in season one, season two once more portrays the straight male character as a "would-be," and ultimately inadequate, lesbian top.

By interspersing grainy black-and-white footage of lesbians as seen through the lenses of surveillance cameras among the normal, in-color shots of the show, the show makes its viewers doubly aware of their position as voyeurs. By offering a secondary camera lens "inside" the first (a meta-eye, if you will), *The L Word* reminds the viewer that the show itself is always mediated, reminding us that we are all tourists in "Lesbian-Land." This technique particularly solicits and critiques the straight male viewer watching for voyeuristic pleasure, even as it still provides him with the bedroom footage he is tuning in to see. Thematizing men's desire for women and for lesbians, we watch the prurience and duplicity of that gaze.

Mark's dishonest and perverse filmic attempt to capture the essence of (or, in more clearly pornographic terms, "put [his] finger on") whatever is specific to lesbianism draws attention to the differences between Mark's so-called documentary and *The L Word*'s own fiction. *The L Word* here slyly critiques the very notion of authentic representation and the perverse uses to which "scientific objectivity" and "ethnography" are often put. Through the exaggerated figure of Mark, the writers show that any representation of "the lesbian" – whether fictional or live – is constructed by and filtered through the author's subjectivity. Seeking pleasure through the pretense of knowledge, Mark is both ethnographer and pornographer. By affiliating these genres, the show exposes the fallacies of both, implicating and exonerating its own representations of "the lesbian" in the process.

The L Word does not offer a documentary on lesbians for the straight viewer's education, or make a claim to sate all lesbian viewers in search of "accurate" visions of themselves, although it plays to the tension of these desires. What *The L Word* does provide, the text implies, is the honesty of dishonesty – approaching the task of examining lesbian culture through fictional rather than social-scientific means.[12] Revealing its architecture, the show self-consciously owns up to and incorporates the fact that it offers more of a theme park version than the "real thing."[13]

HOW DO LOCALS DO IT?

Promoting the show as a follow-up to *Sex and the City*, the producers of *The L Word* faced the challenge of how to provide provocative images of lesbian sex that also come across as genuine to an audience with diverse sexualities. Offering multiple character couplings and representing alternative sex practices, the producers of *The L Word* organize a package tour they hope has enough variety to satisfy the visual appetites of tourists as well as the discerning curiosities of travelers, while providing a wide range of sexual practices in which locals can find "a taste of home." Strategically expanding upon the representations offered in season one, season two more sophisticatedly portrays the diversity that is queer sex. *The L Word* tries to answer, for its multiple viewing constituencies, the question, "What is 'authentic' queer sex?"

The show proceeds to answer this question in multiple ways, presenting numerous queer sexual representations, including casual sex, procreative sex, sex with love, sex talk, group sex, polyamory, sex with props or toys, fucking, verbal negotiations of sex roles and practices, and the trying on of various identities though role-playing during sex. Showing queer sex to encompass what heteronormative sex involves and more, *The L Word* portrays queer sex as ironically and freely playing with the gap between the actual and the real. Showing how heterosexuality takes itself for granted while its hegemonic power hinges on performances that must be constantly reiterated, *The L Word* puts heterosexuality and heterosexual sex into crisis. The pilot episode's first depiction of lesbian sex refashions and remotivates a highly stereotypical and "straight" pornographic scene that lacks personal intimacy. The camera duplicates this lack of intimacy formally through the use of long shots that also work to represent the distance of the voyeur, Jenny. This initial casual lesbian sex act, with its corresponding tourist within the scene, is followed directly by a second "private" sex act between *The L Word*'s central committed couple, Bette and Tina. The partners visit Tina's gynecologist with a sperm sample and intend to inseminate Tina. The doctor suggests that Bette might want to sexually stimulate Tina, as being aroused aids the process of insemination. She closes the door on the partners. Now that the couple are "alone," the camera offers viewers intimate close-ups. Shots from Tina's perspective reveal Bette's head moving under her gown as she orally pleasures her, and shots from Bette's perspective as she rises up to add conversational tidbits of Tina portray her waiting, frustrated, for Bette to go back under her gown. While not the "hot" sex of the first scene, this sex answers the question, "how do lesbians have babies?" While Bette and Tina's sex in the doctor's office, intermittent to begin with, soon gets interrupted with a polite knock on the door, this queer sex scene, *sans* orgasm, performs two important symbolic functions. First, it shows lesbian sexuality as medically endorsed and supported, rather than being pathologized as a psychiatric disorder as it has been historically. Second, it shows lesbian sex within this scenario as a procreative act. Thus, Bette and Tina are encoded by *The L Word*'s producers as a recognizable family unit and therefore an alternate form of the "normative."

While Jenny is depicted "queering" her sex with Tim by directing him to role-play lesbian sex, Bette and Tina's procreative sex act, serving a purpose often considered reserved for heterosexuals, "normalizes" their queer sex. Through intelligently switching meanings linked to "normal" and queer sex, *The L Word* shows both to be sites of performance. The queer always haunts the heterosexual, undermining the hegemony of heteronormativity and destabilizing the binary of normative and non-normative.[14] By actively destabilizing the categories of queer and straight sex, *The L Word* offers heterosexual tourists imaginative access to the possibilities precluded by heteronormativity even as it offers queer tourists access to envisaging lesbian sex as an empowered paradigm or measuring stick. This destabilization challenges the very idea of "measuring up" to any normative sexuality, and thus opens up a horizon of possibilities for pleasure.

Season two is rich with representations of lesbian sexuality that problematize phallocentric sex. Mark asks Jenny what the primary lesbian sex act is, claiming that "for straight people it's fucking … Everything we do, the kissing, the fondling, the foreplay, all of it, leads up to that one, ultimate, foregone conclusion."

"What makes you think lesbians don't fuck?" Jenny retorts.

"It's not possible," Mark argues, "unless we're talking dildos, which is cool, but it's not…"

"Are you fucking kidding?" Shane interrupts. "Where do you live, Mark? It's entirely possible," echoing a conversation from the equally conflicted lesbian filmic representation *Chasing Amy* (1997). Unlike the main character in that film, Shane suffers no fools, making a far more impassioned claim to the lesbian fuck. Here the dialogue underscores Mark's ignorance of lesbian sex, thereby delimiting his "alien" status in the "local" space. Shane's comments emphasize that even though he's "filming it" and it's right in front of him, he isn't "getting it." *The L Word* makes clear that fucking isn't reserved for penis and vagina; that lesbians can fuck with or without a dildo.

Within the same episode, viewers are offered a visual example, as best friends Alice and Dana, who have been resisting falling in love, have sex for the first time. Using their budding relationship, *The L Word* portrays sex as a learning curve that depends on complex negotiations based on trust. By turns playful, awkward, experimental, and passionate, Alice and Dana's sex acts involve visions of B&D, sex toy play, and role-playing. The show cleverly uses them, perhaps its most lovable and loving characters, to introduce all these elements of lesbian and alternative sex. The first time they have sex, Alice and Dana are so excited that they can't figure out how to get out of their clothes. Frenetically kissing, rolling on top of each other, fumbling, they lose any sense of the furniture. In a slapstick moment, Dana falls off the couch trying to get her pants off. Once they've gotten their bearings, we're offered a close-up of the two of them on the floor, Dana atop Alice, rocking her arm, face strained.

"I want more of you," Alice moans.

"Oh," Dana delights, kissing her romantically.

"Fingers!" Alice clarifies, sensing no shift in girth. "More fingers!"

A montage next advances us through their sex: Alice rides Dana on top of a chair, a close-in shot of Dana's head between Alice's legs suggests they are engaging in mutual oral sex, and the last scene finds Alice feeding a blindfolded and bound Dana whipped cream in front of the open refrigerator.[15]

Ending on a visual that emphasizes the many ways that queer erotic pleasure extends beyond genital stimulation, *The L Word*'s montage of Alice and Dana's sex foregrounds acts of lesbian penetration, engaged in vigorously. Through a montage sequence, the producers underscore the multiplicity of orgasms possible in succession between two women. Furthermore, *The L Word*'s portrayal of manual sex makes clear how a hand, as opposed to a penis, allows for the size of the vaginal penetration to change quickly on demand. This information (one hopes!) is not entirely new to straight viewers either. But *The L Word* explicitly dramatizes sex that does not centralize a penis, stressing how it allows for more participatory sex with varied possibilities and pleasures. Because it centralizes a penis as the primary tool for fucking, heteronormative (penis–vagina) sex – at least, the way Mark describes it – is shown to have more limitations than benefits.

As Alice and Dana begin their relationship together, *The L Word* also portrays the two new lovers as negotiating the particulars of their sex life by talking about sex, not just having it. The two are having a tiff on the couch, fully clothed, when Dana, ignoring their disagreement, starts to rub against Alice's crotch with her body.

"You're totally topping me again," says Alice, "have you always been a top?"

"I'm not a top," says Dana.

"Yeah you are," asserts Alice. "You know what I want you to do?," she asks in a barely audible whisper. "I want you to fuck me really hard with a strap-on."

"I don't know if I can do that," admits Dana.

"But you're doing it right now without even using one."

Dana, revealing a certain degree of sexual inexperience compared to Alice, is unsure if she can fuck, much less use a strap-on, but Alice assures her that she already knows how, that her grinding amounts to the same thing. Showing that queers can be sexually unsure, naive, or only comfortable with specific sex acts (just like straights), *The*

L Word directs its survey course on lesbian sexuality toward both straight and queer viewers.

Later, they discuss the idea again. "Is it a bisexual thing?" asks Dana as they lay in bed. "You trying to have your cake and eat your pussy too?"

"No," Alice says clearly. "It's not a bisexual thing."

"OK, good ... I mean, if you're trying to make me into a man because you think that there's something missing, then I want you to go ahead..."

Alice gets on top of Dana to explain further, "I think it would be really hot for you to fuck me like that. OK?"

In case audience members unfamiliar with queer sex haven't gotten it yet from Shane's explanation to Mark, or Alice and Dana's energetic penetrative sex, the producers spell it out again: neither a penis nor a dildo is necessary for fucking. Additionally, a strap-on does not signify a "stand in" for a penis. Sex toys of course, also have the ability to be utilized in straight sex, a fact *The L Word* drove home in its first season. In a witty sex scene between Alice and her lesbian-identified boyfriend, Lisa, he insists on using a dildo, rather than his penis.

The L Word readies its audience for the fact that it is going to show strap-on sex between two lesbians through two primer episodes. The couple first discuss that they are going to incorporate dildos into their sex life, and then they visit a sex shop to explore goodies together. One evening, Dana surprises Alice by coming out of the bathroom wearing a dildo. The camera pans down, stopping at the straps around Dana's waist and leaving the protruding length of the toy off-camera. Stopping short of showing a lesbian hard-on, just as they would not show an erect penis, the producers capture Dana's off-screen toy as it is hailed by Alice with her eyes.

The camera takes in Alice's expression as she responds to Dana's, "Don't laugh, OK?," with, "Fuck. Who's laughing?," before we cut away.

Since we can't see the dildo "in action," the producers depict the culprit in the following episode in a humorous light. Alice and Dana's strap-on is discovered at LAX by airport security and held up for inspection by the guards, Alice and Dana's friends, random strangers, and, similarly, the viewers of *The L Word*. Alice puts the dildo up to her crotch, mimicking how it's meant to work to her transfixed public in case anyone had any questions. Arriving at their destination, a port city where they will board an ocean liner teeming with lesbians, Alice and Dana's nipple clamps have been confiscated, but their dildo returned. The show thus riffs on the idea of sex toy play as a form of queer terrorism on heteronormative sex.

ALL ABOARD THE L BOAT

Devoting one whole episode to a voyage on board a ship run by Olivia Cruises, *The L Word* takes the show's previous symbol of the lesbian community, the pool, out to bigger waters. A large form of product placement, this "authentic" reference to the all-lesbian cruise company also acts as an insider's wink to queer viewers. Out to sea, on board a mobile queer utopia of sorts, Alice and Dana flex their sex-play, Jenny finally becomes a local, and the producers of *The L Word* chuckle to themselves at how far they've taken their joke on the lesbian–water association.[16]

Once within the privacy of their cabin, Alice and Dana play out a scenario from *The Love Boat* with Alice dressed as Julie and Dana as Captain Stubing. Interrupted and dragged to the dining hall in the middle of their role-playing, Dana sits down to dinner with her dildo strapped on underneath her captain's uniform. An on-board "sexpert," whose name, Phoebe Sparkle, evokes real-life sexpert Annie Sprinkle, remarks to a gentleman sitting next to her, "See, these girls are completely in their power, free to go wherever their libido takes them."

Also owning her libidinous desires aboard the Olivia ocean liner is Jenny, who, in a third significant swimming pool scene, finally jumps in. Dancing to a Sleater–Kinney song with a throng of queer women on the ship's poolside deck, Jenny removes a cap from her head, exposing her new short haircut. Lifting up her skirt and flashing a group of women, Jenny leaps into the pool – her skirt ballooning with air, as she finally swims, grinning, among lesbians – one of the group.

Although Jenny was utilized as a vehicle for straight tourists, her initial gaze comes finally, and retrospectively, to represent the queer spectator's gaze. Through the symbolic use of Jenny as both voyeur and object, *The L Word* displaces Laura Mulvey's model of "woman as image, man as bearer of the look," and concurs with suggestions made by queer theory about the queer spectator. Importantly, gay and lesbian scholars suggest the queer spectator is not required to choose between objectification and identification. Instead a dual experience can be sustained between desiring and inhabiting.[17] This experience – queer equivocation – need not be understood purely in Freud's narcissistic terms. If queer spectators are able to access such a slide of object and subject positions, we might consider that every spectator, through fantasy, can actively desire and imagine beyond the rigidity of sexuality and gender positionings. Through heteroflexibility, straight viewers are able to access the "local" imaginary, sharing in the queer sensibility. While texts suggest stable positions given carefully demarcated identities, viewers' identities, if only at the level of imagination, are a great deal more fluid than the positionalities proffered in texts. *The L Word* banks on heteroflexibility as well as queer equivocation, through its cultivation of the touristic gaze, a gaze which immersed, identifies with, and distanced, desires.

Themes of immersion and distance, authenticity and artifice, normativity and non-normativity flood *The L Word*'s narrative. These same insider and outsider tropes are reiterated in the show's marketing and pervade a contemporary media market characterized by heteroflexibility. Queer content is proving that it has pull for an audience broader than just the gay population. The straight crossover audience for gay- and lesbian-themed shows is large and easily tapped, as *The L Word*, along with other popularly rated shows, has demonstrated. In a 2004 *Hollywood Reporter* round-table discussion on "Gay Themes in Television," MTV's president Brian Graden explained this phenomenon as involving a queer "sensibility" that straights can enjoy and try on temporarily: "I think (that) post-Queer Eye, gay is more sensibility than it is specifically gay people and gay shows." Not only are heterosexual Americans becoming culturally equipped to decode gay and lesbian subcultural signifiers; gay and lesbian subculture is being consumed by, but also marketed to, straight culture.

Without reading *The L Word* as simply a commodification of lesbianism manufactured to sell to the masses, or applauding it uncritically as authentically lesbian representation, I see the show finally as both a capitalistic production and a sex-positive phenomenon. *The L Word* both intentionally rides a wave of co-optation and packaging – a straight appreciation and "trying on" of queer sensibility arguably ushered in by *Will and Grace* and *Queer Eye for the Straight Guy* – and increases the queer lexicon for everyone in positive, and increasingly sex-positive, ways.[18]

NOTES

1. Showtime Press Release, "Showtime Renews Critically-Acclaimed Series *The L Word* for Second Season," 29 January 2004.

2. The cable show's creator, Ilene Chaiken, called L.A.'s lesbian community "anthropologically specific" in an interview with PlanetOut.com. Beth Callaghan and Jenny Stewart "Ilene Chaiken Talks," PlanetOut.com, 5 April 2004.

3. My larger work on *The L Word*, coming from a distinctly *cultural media studies* perspective, analyzes *The L Word*'s cultures of consumption (the audience) as well as the cultures of production (*The L Word*'s production and writing team, Showtime Networks, and Viacom, the conglomerate that owns Showtime). Theorizing the agency of the spectator (through the terms *heteroflexibility* and *queer equivocation*), providing ethnographic audience research, and also providing industrial analysis, I show the many ways in which *The L Word*'s meanings are encoded and decoded.

4. Insofar as lesbian spectators are consuming mediated images of themselves, I argue that not only do straight audiences engage in a form of tourism when viewing *The L Word*, but lesbian audiences do too. Locals drawn to the latest "lesbian attraction," lesbian spectators enjoy *The L Word*'s eye candy along with straight "tourists." Like straight "travelers," they seek to identify the "authentic" within their grids of understanding. However, for the queer female viewer, the mediated "reality" of the show will never match up to reality. Expecting the show's queer viewers to compare notes as part of a deep desire to look and finally see themselves, *The L Word*'s producers knowingly offer recognizable "sights" and "experiences," gestures that try diligently to get lesbians "right." For the purposes of this essay, I will use "local" to designate the fantasy of the "authentic lesbian," both as she is imaged and articulated within the show and as he is implicitly idealized as the "expert" viewer. It is through the enticement of lesbian sex (a spectacle of attraction for straight and queer viewers alike) *and* through the wonderment of either "understanding" the other, or "recognizing" oneself (fantasy of authenticity), through both "watching from a remove" and "being there," that *The L Word* captivates its straight and queer tourists.

5. For more analysis of *The L Word*'s handling of butch and transgender representations, see my "Is She Man Enough: Female Masculinities in *The L Word*" co-authored with Kristen Schilt in the edited volume *Reading The L Word*.

6. The production of this T-shirt was not affiliated with Showtime Networks. Available on the Internet and advertised on fan sites, the shirt was mentioned in a *Los Angeles Times* article by Meghan Daum, "Making Straights Flush: *The L Word*'s Shane, Brought to Life by Katherine Moennig, Touches a Nerve."

7. See Fonseca.
8. Moore.
9. We can see *The L Word*'s general strategy as based in Michel Foucault's notions of resistance in *The History of Sexuality, Volume 1*. For Foucault, struggle, always inscribed within power, succeeds through becoming incorporated. While "revolutions" do occasionally happen, effective strategies of change, he suggests, act on the level of "points of resistance." These points of resistance are often transitory, "fracturing unities and effecting regroupings, furrowing across individuals themselves, cutting them up and remolding them, marking off irreducible regions in them, in their bodies and minds" (96).
10. Co-optation of queer sensibility may merely be one aspect of a television consumption characterized by "identity shapeshifting," as cable networks re-broaden and repurpose "narrowcast" niche programming through marketing and textual tactics. This co-optation should not necessarily be stamped "politically incorrect," nor lauded as unconditionally "freeing," without a thorough interrogation of both how it works and for what purposes.
11. Another way to put it is that the penis envies lesbian cock, always hard. See Sarah Smith's essay "A Cock of One's Own."
12. The fact that *The L Word* is a fiction, however, should not be used in any way to excuse it for representational faux pas, nor to say that as a TV soap opera it is politically or socially irrelevant. It is through processing fictional and "non-fictional" narratives, as well as through life experiences, that we form opinions of others and ourselves in society. As Baudrillard famously suggests of Disneyland in his article "Simulacra and Simulations," perhaps the fictional in fact serves to make us feel real or authentic: "Disneyland is presented as imaginary in order to make us believe that the rest is real, when in fact all of Los Angeles and the America surrounding it are no longer real, but of the order of the hyperreal and of simulation" (175).
13. Portions of "Mark's Documentary" were previously published on the online site AfterEllen.com as a critical commentary of the show, titled "Through Mark's Lenses."
14. See Wendy O'Brien's article "Qu(e)erying Pornography: Contesting Identity Politics in Feminism."
15. Perhaps a visual echo of the film *9½ Weeks* (dir. Adrian Lyne, 1986).
16. There has been a long-standing affiliation between women, water, and sexual awakening in women's literature, films, and art. The fate of "drowning" (in the freedom?) is also often presented as a possible threat. See e.g. Kate Chopin's *The Awakening* or Jane Campion's film *The Piano* (1993).
17. See Earl Jackson Jr.'s "Graphic Specularity: Pornography, Almodovar and the Gay Male Subject of Cinema"; Wendy O'Brien's "Qu(e)erying Pornography: Contesting Identity Politics in Feminism"; and Patricia White's *UnInvited: Classical Hollywood Cinema and Lesbian Representability*.
20. I would like to sincerely thank my mentor at UCLA, Kathleen Anne McHugh, for her incisive feedback during the drafting of this essay. Generous with her time, she not only helped me iron out semantics, she reminded me that being a confident female academic is always a political action. An earlier version of this essay won the 2006 Society for Cinema and Media Studies Student Essay Award and is forthcoming in *Cinema Journal*.

REFERENCES

Ang, Ien. *Living Room Wars: Rethinking Media Audiences for a Postmodern World.* London: Routledge, 1996.

Baudrillard, Jean. "Simulacra and Simulations." In *Jean Baudrillard, Selected Writings.* Ed. Mark Poster. Stanford: Stanford University Press, 1988. 166–84.

Boorstin, Daniel. *The Image: A Guide to Pseudo-Events in America.* New York: Atheneum, 1985.

Butler, Judith. "Critically Queer." *GLQ* 1, no. 1 (1993): 17–32.

Callaghan, Beth and Jenny Stewart. "Ilene Chaiken Talks." *PlanetOut.com.* 5 April 2004, www.planetout.com/entertainment/interview.html?sernum= 693&navpath=/entertainment/lword.

Daum, Meghan. "Making Straights Flush: *The L Word*'s Shane, Brought to Life by Katherine Moennig, Touches a Nerve." *Los Angeles Times,* 20 February 2005: E3.

Epstein, Jeffrey. "Gay Themes in Television." *Hollywood Reporter.* 26 March 2004.

Fonseca, Nicholas. "Return of the Pink Ladies." *Entertainment Weekly.* 18 February 2005: 38.

Foucault, Michel. *The History of Sexuality: An Introduction.* New York: Vintage, 1990.

Freud, Sigmund. *Three Essays on the Theory of Sexuality.* New York: Basic Books, 1962.

"Gay Themes in Television," *The Hollywood Reporter,* 26 March 2004.

Glock, Alison. "She Likes to Watch." *New York Times.* 6 February 2005: 26.

Halberstam, Judith. *Female Masculinity.* Durham NC: Duke University Press, 1998.

Halperin, David M. *Saint Foucault: Towards a Gay Hagiography.* New York: Oxford University Press, 1995.

Jackson, Earl. "Graphic Specularity: Pornography, Almodovar and the Gay Male Subject of Cinema." *Translations/Transformations: Gender and Culture in Film and Literature, East and West* 7 (1993): 63–81.

MacCannell, Dean. *The Tourist: A New Theory of the Leisure Class.* New York: Schocken, 1989.

Marech, Rona. "Nuances of Gay Identities Reflected in New Language." *San Francisco Chronicle.* 8 February 2004: A1.

Moore, Candace. Interview with Guinevere Turner. 10 April 2005.

Moore, Candace and Kristen Schilt. "Is She Man Enough: Female Masculinities in *The L Word*." In *Reading The L Word.* Ed. Kim Akass and Janet McCabe. London: I.B. Tauris, 2006.

O'Brien, Wendy "Qu(e)erying Pornography: Contesting Identity Politics in Feminism." In *Third Wave Feminism,* Ed. Stacy Gillis, Gillian Howie, and Rebecca Munford. London: Palgrave, 2004.

Rich, Adrienne "Compulsory Heterosexuality and Lesbian Existence." *Signs: Journal of Women in Culture and Society* 5, no. 4 (1980): 631–60.

Showtime Press Release, "Showtime Renews Critically-Acclaimed Series '*The L Word*' for Second Season," January 29, 2004.

Smith, Sarah. "A Cock of One's Own: Getting a Firm Grip on Feminist Sexual

Power." In *Jane Sexes It Up: True Confessions of Feminist Desire.* Ed. Merri Lisa Johnson. New York: Four Walls Eight Windows, 2002. 293–309.

Spigel, Lynn. "Installing the Television Set." *Private Screenings: Television and the Female Consumer.* Ed. Lynn Spigel and Denise Mann. Minneapolis: University of Minnesota Press, 1992. 3–38.

Strain, Ellen. *Public Places, Private Journeys: Ethnography, Entertainment, and the Tourist Gaze.* New Brunswick: Rutgers University Press, 2003.

Urry, John. *The Tourist Gaze.* 2nd edn. Thousand Oaks, CA: Sage, 2002.

White, Patricia. *UnInvited: Classical Hollywood Cinema and Lesbian Representability.* Bloomington: Indiana University Press, 1999.

Wolcott, James. "The Gay Divide." *Vanity Fair*, February 2005: 80.

Zeman, Ned. "Gay-Per-View TV." *Vanity Fair*, December 2003: 324.

5

QUEER AS BOX:

BOI SPECTATORS AND BOY CULTURE

ON SHOWTIME'S *QUEER AS FOLK*

BOBBY NOBLE

Despite its limited focus on mostly white gay cultures, leaving queers of color, lesbians, transsexuals, and transgendered characters marginal and underdeveloped, the *event* of Showtime's *Queer as Folk* – unfolding over the course of five seasons from 2000 to 2005 – remains historically significant for representing gay sexuality in graphic detail on American television.[1] There are in fact a number of easily anticipated ways in which *Queer as Folk* strikes certain segments of its audience as not queer enough. Lesbian-identified spectators in particular have formed ambivalent relationships with the series. As a former lesbian, however, and now female-to-male trans-boi, I can say that some of my most cherished pleasures in television culture have come from watching *Queer as Folk*. To be clear, *Queer as Folk* fails to represent the lives, loves, struggles, and realities of transsexual and transgendered people. Having said that, I invoke "trans" as a verb here, following the model by which various texts in mainstream culture are queered in order to fit lives organized outside of heteronormativity. By *transed* I mean to indicate a way of producing meaning and pleasure that works across – perhaps even against – stabilizations of gender through the sexed body within gay and lesbian popular culture. The intentional transition between these viewing positions – from lesbian to trans-boi – produces a very specific shift in my reading of the show's political implications.

"Boi" is a term emerging in genderqueer and trans cultures to mark spaces of embodiment outside of the binarized duality of the sexed body as either male or female. The incoherent boi body, replete with flat chest, facial hair, deepened voice, hormonally and sometimes surgically altered but not necessarily anatomically correct genitals, emerges as a new way of embodying gender outside of the rigid binaries of sexual difference. The deliberate incoherence of the trans-boi body, about which I will say more below, leads to a practice of reading not unlike the familiar strategy of gays and lesbians who read straight culture "gay," adapting hetero love songs and romantic scripts for gay purposes. In the "transed" reading, the transsexual audience member reads for the incoherence beneath the surface of seemingly unbroken gay, lesbian, or even queer narratives, reaching beneath the dress of a character or television show to locate evidence of incoherent desire, moments in which body parts, gender scripts, and narratives of desire do not add up neatly as heterosexual or homosexual. It is the accidental production of such ruptures that make *Queer as Folk* a productive moment for developing post-queer third wave feminist media practice of what I will call *transed* gender incoherence rather than queerness. Indeed, I court the term "post-queer incoherence" to mark a relation to queerness that deepens the work of queer theory toward destabilizing the relationship between bodies, orientations, desires, object choices, and sexual positions. The most productive viewing moments might be said to *trans* the text by decoding it from a viewing position that crosses the gender lines conservatively drawn around predictably sexed bodies in the plots, a technique to which I return in the second half of this chapter.

PLAYING LESBIANISM STRAIGHT

The primary lesbian characters – Lindsay and Mel – are white upper-middle-class professionals, coupled, monogamous, politically sensitive, and as such are constructed as the background against which gay male cultures are screened. Each season has shown development in their characters individually and also as committed life partners. Having been together for ten years, Lindsay and Mel have met many familiar challenges of long-term couples: managing to keep their sex life active and spontaneous, balancing split obligations between family and profession, and facing the rejection of extended family. They are, in a context of an almost exclusively male gay subculture, increasingly the figures of stability, monogamy, commitment, and support to their many gay male friends. Given the success of *Queer as Folk*, these representations engage in the hegemonic work of consolidating a particular set of meanings around the lesbian identity, both within the GLBTQ community and in the anti-homophobic non-lesbian viewing audience. It is that work – the work of rendering certain kinds of queer desires stable and conservative while others are groundbreaking – which this section seeks to elaborate.

At the end of season four, one-half of our token lesbian couple, Lindsay, experiences a tortured and, in her mind, incoherent attraction to the artist Sam Auerbach. At the beginning of this particular plot line, Lindsay attempts to bring Auerbach's work to her gallery but discovers that he is an offensive womanizer who treats his female assistants and staff as objects for sexual sport. He has no time for casually dressed dykes with no make-up. Lindsay struggles to reconcile her admiration for Auerbach's paintings with her repulsion at his personality, and she strategizes, at Mel's suggestion, to convince him to let her show his work at her gallery by flirting with him. Her blonde hair more attractively coifed, her lips reddened and moist, she quickly accomplishes her goal, but once she and Sam begin to work together, Lindsay's attraction to him turns from pretense to provocative taboo. He encourages her to return to her own painting, an artistic side of Lindsay that has been subordinated thus far in the plot to her home life with Mel. In stimulating her creatively – not to mention in posing nude for her new work – Sam rekindles Lindsay's longing for straight sex, which is strikingly coded as a more creative activity than lesbian sex, demonstrating either a backlash logic of reversal (straights as the new marginalized sexuality) or else the queering of queer culture (straight as the new queer).

Moreover, Lindsay's attraction to Sam keeps her at work and away from home where Mel, struggling with her pregnancy, remains unaware of this new suitor. During one particularly steamy sex scene between Lindsay and Mel, Lindsay makes her dissatisfaction with Mel's oral ministrations quite apparent. What Lindsay craves instead is fucking – that is, penetration – an especially new desire for her, clearly borrowing from her attraction to the brutish hyper-heterosexual

Sam. Mel, in a gesture of loving accommodation, digs out what looks to be a 25-year-old plastic, battery-operated vibrator, the kind labeled and sold as personal massage devices, ancient relics of the sex toy economy in lesbian subcultures. "We haven't used this for years," says the unwitting Mel. In this scene, Lindsay's most unspeakable lesbian desires emerge – that is, her desire for phallic masculinity and its very active penis. What remains in excess, strange and queer, is not the affectionate attention of a monogamous lesbian partner with a dildo but the illicit, taboo, and politically quite inexcusable attraction to a womanizing man. Given how much work has gone into lesbian explanations to straight culture that two women with a dildo are not making do with a faux cock, it registers as odd, retrograde even, that *Queer as Folk* would depict the lesbian dildo as an inadequate replacement for Sam's penis. Lindsay eventually gives in to her desires, hiking up her skirt for a bit of rough and spirited sex against a blank wall in the gallery. The location against an art gallery wall is significant; not only is this very much a public space outside of Mel and Lindsay's domestic, warm, comfortable middle-class bedroom, but it is also a space of blankness, inviting the procreative act as impromptu art. Indeed the desire that has no name is, in this subplot, heterosexuality. The show has come full circle, then, queering heterosexuality and normalizing lesbian sex, with or without dildo, as passé.

In an effort to contain the damage this affair could have on her relationship, Lindsay does not confide in Mel and rejects all further sexual advances from Sam. Unable to fully walk away from Lindsay, Sam, on the other hand, shows up at Lindsay and Mel's home in the suburbs to make one final plea to Lindsay, imploring her to abandon her current life to follow both her own artistic impulses and her newfound attraction to him. They exchange the following words outside of Lindsay's home with Mel:

Lindsay   It can't happen again Sam; there are lines.
Sam   As a kid, I crossed over all the lines, colored outside of them
        on purpose.
Lindsay   That's fine as an artist, but inside there, right on the other
        side of that door, I have a family.
Sam   But that's not all you are.
Lindsay   I'm choosing them.

In choosing to remain in her current lesbian life, Lindsay inadvertently codes "lesbian" as domestic and thus traditionally feminine, preferring nesting to role-play and electing clear sexual identities over free-floating desire. The fact that Mel is pregnant during this lovemaking further diminishes whatever mild hints of gender play might otherwise linger in Lindsay and Mel's bed. There is no power exchange, no top/bottom or BDSM play, no lesbian cock play. Whereas their dildo strains ineffectually to spice up the lesbian marriage bed, Sam's insistent penis and aggressive heterosexuality connote transgressive desire coloring queerly outside the lines. Sam unexpectedly calls into question the limiting boxes of sexuality and gender while Lindsay's lesbian life is positioned as "less than" heterosexual – less perverse, less free, less creative. Is that "*all* you are"? – the question lingers in the lesbian spectator's mind, troubling any easy fanhood of *Queer as Folk*.

Queer as Folk thus constructs lesbian desire in epistemologically predictable ways: as non-phallic, anti-penetration, morally self-righteous, and remarkably un- and even anti-queer. Lesbian sexual practice is conceptually constrained by conservative gender-based knowledges of feminine sexual bodies, precluding the possibility of representing that body as queer. "Lesbian" is overdetermined as a conservative "choice" to stay within the limits of boxes, lines, and categories. Such constructions of lesbian desire as what Eve Kosofsky Sedgwick would call gender-separatist – as attraction to gender similarities, not difference – fold the lesbian body back inside the contours of the essentialized female body, containing both aggressively within constructions of female desire as anything but queer. That female body, to return the cliché back to its literal referent, encases lesbian desire within the physical limits of the "box" – as passive pussy, as hole, as container. Mel and Lindsay are always already ensnared by the limits of their gender difference, not only boxed in by their lesbian desires but quite literally by childbirth, pregnancy and babies, so much so that Mel, pregnant, is confined to bed rest until reproduction is finished with her body. Lindsay attempts to step outside of her box but chooses its limits instead. Any notion of *elsewhere* remains invisible, either outside of the camera's range, or outside of what's intelligible within these "queer" paradigms.

More significant than a shift in epistemological tropes on *Queer as Folk* – from queer liminality to lesbian separatism – are the ways that this shift is mapped, throughout the series and in this episode in particular, on to conservative gender affiliations *based on sexed bodies*. On *Queer as Folk*, all the men are sexually voracious, thus grouping men conservatively under a separatist mark of gender difference – that is, all men have a sex drive qualitatively different from women's. Under these terms, we are asked to accept that there are few differences between the sexually rapacious Brian and the equally rapacious Sam, other than *mere* object choice. They both engage in a constant search for sex, and both are constructed as stone – that is, emotionally and sexually impenetrable to their sexual partners. Each is driven, in other words, by his cock. Similar lines of affiliation are drawn around women in the show, especially evident when, in her efforts to acquire Sam's art for her gallery, Lindsay adopts the persona of flirtatious, admiring, heterosexual femininity to win him over. One of the effects of the Sam–Lindsay subplot is a shift in focus on the show from the hetero/homo to the male/female binary, where men are reified as excessive in their physical appetites, and women are returned to their stereotypical focus on emotional lives over sex drives. These lines of affiliation are quite gender normative in their ideological work.

At the same time, though, this shift creates a curious moment. For Lindsay and Mel, the gender persona of flirtatious, admiring, heterosexual femininity is, at least for a short time, a powerful and very queer drag performance. In the beginning, and without knowledge of Lindsay's growing attraction for Sam, Mel encourages Lindsay's strategic deployment of femininity. There is, in this complicity between them, a parodic and controlled orchestration of something resembling the heteronormative traffic in women. In her essay "The Traffic in Women: Notes on the Political Economy of Sex," Gayle Rubin argues that within patriarchal kinship systems, women are exchanged as a commodity between, for instance, fathers and husbands, leaving women both valued as objects but powerless to refuse the value or man to whom they are assigned. In a queering of that economy, Lindsay traffics in her own valued sexuality to ensnare Sam's work for her gallery. In fact, this is a moment where masculinity's desire for a semblance of femininity is the commodity exchanged between knowing lesbians. Mel encourages Lindsay and the moment is ripe as the political economy of sexual and gender both overlap but are resisted through queer parody. This is also a powerful queer rupture for spectators, one which hails a queer audience while simultaneously conscious of a heterosexual gaze. The pleasures of this spectacle are very queer; as in any drag performance, pleasure is produced by contradiction when the lie (Lindsay playing straight femininity straight, to borrow Biddy Martin's phrase) is staged to be misrecognized by an unknowing player as the truth, all under the watchful gaze of a queer audience enjoying the spectacle. However, the fruitfulness of this rupture is thwarted by Lindsay's own seduction in these terms of exchange. In other words, her supposedly "real" desires as a lesbian are undone by the "performance" of essentialized heterosexuality. In *Femininity Played Straight*, Martin predicted these limited deployments of femininity within such androcentric queer imaginaries. Femininity will always "constitute a capitulation, a swamp, something material, ensnared and ensnaring" and cannot, because of its overly powerful materiality, sustain queer ruptures (73).

The truth is, though, that I am not primarily interested in scrutinizing the investments that the writers of *Queer as Folk* may or may not have in constructions of lesbian sex. There has always been disinformation in the gay imaginary about lesbian sex cultures, and *Queer as Folk* is no exception. That said, I am nevertheless concerned about the degree to which these limited depictions of lesbian desire and bodies accomplish particular *kinds* of hegemonic work. Whereas most lesbian critical focus in television studies has been trained on the question of whether television lesbians are queer enough (e.g. the "lipstick" lesbian debates surrounding *The L Word*), my interest as an FtM spectator focuses on the question of whether television reading (reception) practices are restricted to the traditional gendered subject positions, like "lesbian," or whether they can be represented as participating in transsexuality. In this focus, I am not just flagging Judith Halberstam's inquiries into female masculinity. Where Halberstam rightly argues that female masculinity is a non-derivative site of masculinity, I push that argument beyond its own limitations by suggesting that what *Queer as Folk* offers is the ability, on the site of reception, to reconfigure the limits of how bodies themselves are defined, as much as how genders are mapped on to those bodies. That is, Halberstam's argument requires that the ground of female masculinity – the female body – remain stable as that foundation upon which the figure of the masculine can be written. I am arguing instead that the identifications enabled by *Queer as Folk* offer the spectator the ability to transcend the binarized limits of embodiment, enabled as much by anti-normative pleasure as by anti-normative genders. Within the lesbian community as represented on *Queer as Folk*, the presence of masculinity – even lesbian masculinity – has been fraught with political conflict. In the characters of Lindsey and Mel, *Queer as Folk* seems to reiterate this investment in coding "lesbian" as synonymous with "uber-female." These essentialist depictions of female nature as nurturing, egalitarian, and non-genital leave the masculine lesbian, not to mention us tranny bois, out of the picture entirely.

QUEER AS BOI

The first key to sifting through the various kinds of queer content available to audiences of *Queer as Folk* comes from the ambiguous irony that, according to Romy Shiller, many of the most ardent viewers of this show are heterosexual women:

> Like many women across the country who watch the show – fifty-two percent according to the Nielsen ratings in 2001, and growing – I'm addicted. I am not alone. "At the beginning it really surprised me," says *Queer as Folk* producer Sheila Hockin. "All of us working on the show, Showtime in the States and Showcase in Canada, expected to have predominantly a gay male audience." Because most of the lead characters are male, the assumption was that "the group of people portrayed would likely be the people watching the show. It startled us in the beginning and at first we thought that maybe we're drawing gay women." After reviewing fan mail and Web sites about the show they realized it was a lot of straight women.

In other words, heterosexual women constitute a powerful emerging demographic as consumers of sexualized images of men – even, or perhaps especially, queer men – in popular culture. Enacting the claim of sex radical feminist Lynne Segal, that "it is all too easy to see why in fantasy women may choose male figures for erotic identification, as well as for objects of desire" (238), the "genderbent" allure of *Queer as Folk* comes from the degree to which its depictions of masculinity appeal to heterosexual women, not only as sexy boys to ogle but also as projections of themselves (e.g. subjects of cross-gendered sexual identification). Shiller in fact characterizes these straight women in the audience as "the ultimate queer quotient":

> Femininity and masculinity, associated with "appropriate" sexual identification and desire, is suddenly attached to culturally inappropriate male and female bodies. There is an explosion of identification: girls desiring straight boys playing gay boys. Girls wanting to be a feminine boy kissing a butch boy. Girls wanting to be taken by or wanting to take a gay/straight boy. Girls romanticizing gay desire and freedom of sexual play. What we are experiencing now is Gender Meltdown.

That *Queer as Folk* creates multiple viewing positions for queerly affiliated female viewing subjects – if only for the purpose of watching the show – is absolutely worth feminist extrapolation, especially when it comes to theorizing the possibilities of a third wave sex radical spectatorship. This attraction of straight female audience members to queer representations substantially and, one hopes, irreversibly transforms their relationship to television's constructions of female sexuality, so that new and queerer kinds of identifications emerge that have not historically been available in traditional (straight) television forms.

One site of those new identifications is signaled in Shiller's repeated use of the term "boy," as the culture of boyhood indeed features prominently in *Queer as Folk*: from Justin's literal youthfulness (he's 17 when he and Brian meet) to Michael's lingering status as *not quite grown-up man* owning a comic book store and eventually making his own comic books. The question – why so many boys in *Queer as Folk*? – opens a virtual Pandora's box of related questions: Is there something particularly queer about the boy? What it is that makes a boy a boy and not a man in the first place? Is boyhood confined to a particular chronological age? In "Why Boys Are Not Men," Steven Cohan searches for answers to these questions by looking at the history of boys and men in Hollywood, asserting that the boy first appeared in the films and film cultures surrounding the new 1950s boys of Hollywood. Tracing the emergence through the postwar era of what tough-guy John Wayne dubbed the "trembling, torn T-shirt types" – Marlon Brando, Montgomery Clift, James Dean, Sal Mineo, the young Paul Newman, and so on – Cohan posits that Hollywood crystallized a new visual subjectivity, the boy-man. "One has only to recall," argues Cohan, "the galvanizing early screen appearances of the young Clift and Brando to see how readily imagery of a youthful male body, not only beautiful to behold but also highly theatricalized, marked out the erotic appeal of these new young actors within the star system, underscoring their alienation from the screen's more traditional representations of masculinity" (103). What appealed to mainstream American culture then was precisely this notion of boy-ishness. Such a new look challenged the conflation of sexuality and gender that supported a symbolic economy in which "boys" were made legible and thinkable opposites of "men." The result of this open rejection of the imperatives of masculinity (e.g. grow up and be a "real" man) was an erotic performance or impersonation that productively always fell short of the original. In falling short – that is, in refusing to be all that a man was supposed to be – the boy becomes a viable male subject.

Moreover, what was particularly compelling about the boy was signaled by Wayne's adjective "trembling." The term rightly associates the new look with emotion and vulnerability. Whereas old-guard actors like John Wayne wore masculinity on the outside as action, toughness, and phallic power, the Brando and Dean types interiorized masculinity, converting social nonconformity and rebelliousness into inner torment and emotional excess, and adopting a look synonymous with failed manhood: perpetual boyhood. Boyishness then consti-tuted a gender-conflicted performance that signified at once failed masculinity and an excess of masculinity. The "highly theatricalized" boy body is, thus, a queer body, anti-normative in orientation to the imperatives of masculinity, always already stylized – even, I propose, transgendered. In this light, Justin's performance of "boy subjectivity" on *Queer as Folk* is arguably a trans performance as he works against the expectations overdetermined by his biologically male body. Isn't part of the appeal of boyishness precisely masculine feminization? The concept of "masculine feminization" overlaps with Judith Halberstam's landmark discussion of female masculinity but remains in excess of this schema, and this space of excess marks the interpretive site at which gay boys in media culture slide in interesting ways into positions that the trans-boi spectator can begin to identify with.

Noted in both the Canadian and American queer press, boi is emerging as a complex embodiment of masculinity. The emergence of this boi – the lesbian boi, for instance, or the trannyboi – is unfolding in conversation with queer, trans, and mainstream categories of masculinity alike and is defined not by the sexed body but by performative effect. The boi is, in Sarah Trimble's words, "playing Peter Pan," negotiating between relations of proximity to and deferral of conventional masculinity. This cross-sexual identification has not been sufficiently taken into account by existing feminist theories of spectatorship. The "female" viewing subject who desires – and desires to be – the gay men on *Queer as Folk* is not John Berger's woman "watching herself be watched." Berger's famous treatise on the gendered relations of the gaze, *Ways of Seeing*, argues that ways of looking are gendered. "Men watch," he notes in his study of both classical art and contemporary representational practices, while "women watch themselves be watched" (47). By maintaining this split in looking between active/male and passive/female, Berger shares much with film critic Laura Mulvey. In "Visual Pleasure and Narrative Cinema," Mulvey uses psychoanalysis to analyze how social structures external to film determine not just how a film will be read but also how sexual difference controls interpretive practices. For the female viewer, pleasure is always already passive (she is "to-be-looked-at-ness") and can only be organized around an iden-tification with an active male gaze, which is put on and worn like a costume, turning the female viewer, following Mary Ann Doane's metaphor in "Film and the Masquerade," into a transvestite (24). In other words, the female viewer must watch the passive heroine with – and like – the male viewer, borrowing his objectifying gaze and limiting her interaction with the screen to these preordained sexist and heterosexist dynamics. In contrast, pleasure for the boi viewer of *Queer as Folk* is constituted around an active gaze: perhaps the straight female gaze taking pleasure in gay male bodies (like bachelorettes at a Chippendale's strip show, willfully refusing to "see" the men's sexual orientation) or, more subversively, the homosexual male gaze taking pleasure in the objectified male body. The boi viewer identifies ambiguously, in the latter case, with the stone top and/or the gay male bottom. For such a viewer, this is a potent and unwittingly incoherent circuit of gendered desire not located within the essentialized contours of the body but emerging performatively within transient identification.

There is something thrilling about disconnecting the biological body from the desiring gaze, but another critic, Leah Rumach, unknowingly performs the bargain struck to accomplish such genderbendings:

> *Queer as Folk*'s graphic boinking and General Hospitalesque story-lines – at least one overdose, 213 jolly rogerings, 107 ingestions of illicit drugs, one sperm donation, one gay bashing *and (oh, yes) two lesbians who are married and have a kid and careers and um, OK, that's enough about them* – have created a rabidly devoted fan base of queer folk and a contingent of perhaps slightly unhinged straight women. (*Yeah, us!*). (my emphasis)

Rumach's parting "Yeah, us!," following on the heels of her dismissive "that's enough about them" (the boring lesbian characters), performs the hegemonic bargain her enthusiastic heteronormativity won't let her know. The important work of expanding a straight feminist sexual repertoire is accomplished at the willful boxing in of lesbian sexual practice. But what we might call the circuit of culture – that is, culture as the effect of production, consumption, but also, in Stuart Hall's terms, use-value – functions differently for these two viewers. Hall reminds us that the successful communicative event is not simply the ingestion or decoding of text. It is also measured by the degree to which encoding and decoding practices enable meaning-making, or, what I am calling consolidation of hegemonic ideas. Hall puts it this way: "if the meaning is not articulated in practice, it has no effect. If no meaning is taken, there can be no consumption" (167–8). He goes on to suggest that "meaning" itself should be understood as an encoding practice that is able to satisfy a need, be put to use, or able to influence, entertain, instruct or persuade with consequences (168). Where, for Shiller, *Queer as Folk* enables queer identifications that quite literally unmoor sexual and gendered subjectivities from bodies, in Rumach's formulation these same queer identifications consolidate heteronormativity. Heterosexuality is perceived as queer (as in disruptive or anti-normative) on *Queer as Folk*, so long as it runs along the gay male/straight female (or straight male [Sam]/gay female [Lindsay]) axis of affiliation, but heterosexuality functions conservatively if, like Lindsay and Mel's dildo, it runs along a lesbian axis.

It is necessary, therefore, to construct some alternative bargain for the trans-boi viewer, whose flirtation with heterosexuality constitutes a dramatically disruptive and anti-normative identification. While in both production and reception, *lesbian* tends to mean *female by nature*, and masculine means *queer by choice*, the following reading of *Queer as Folk* seeks to change these lines of identification, developing a trans spectator position from which "lesbian" might be more continuously connected to "queer" and "masculine" and "boi" all at the same moment. Where Rumach and Shiller find pleasure through a queer cross-identification – that is, as heterosexual female subjects – *Queer as Folk* at the same time provides a plurality of ways to materialize trans genders and boi-ish desires through identification. I want to add another narrative of consumption to those by Rumach and Shiller, which returns me to the question of a trans viewing position, to be distinguished from the female spectator as Mulvey's masochist or Doane's transvestite, delineated above.

RECASTING TELEVISUAL RECEPTIVITY

It took a while before I was able to discern the details of my drive to watch *Queer as Folk*, or the orientation and politics of my pleasures in the show. Repeatedly, what I found myself looking for in each episode, especially those featuring group sex or bathhouses or the back room of Babylon, have been scenes of male penetration. While Brian remains an interesting character as a top, it was in fact the voracious bottoms that invited me back to the show each week. One of the complexities of bio-male as well as boi bottoming – either for other men or for women – is its incoherency within heteronormativity. While one could argue that there are no shortages of heterosexual fetish fantasies that involve female dominatrixes, they usually do not involve male penetration, straight men typically preferring to submit rather than to bottom. But what I have been drawn to in *Queer as Folk*, week after week, is its unabashed depiction of top–bottom relationships between men. For Brian and Justin, the choreography of top–bottom plays out literally across age lines. For Ben and Michael, the differences between them sexually are mapped onto not only physical differences in size but also career choices – professor and comic book collector/maker – indicating a different kind of age difference (daddy–boy). Differences in sexual appetites for Teddy and Emmett are articulated through a kind of queer visibility that positions Emmett as effeminate to Teddy's conventional (though gay) masculinity. But Brian and Justin in particular offer a fruitful site of crossover gender and sexual identifications.

Many of the plot's tensions throughout the show derive from the relationship between Brian and Justin. In episodes 1 and 2, the *Queer as Folk* story begins inside what we later discover to be Babylon. The scene is typical: hundreds of half-naked men are dancing to loud music in the very crowded gay bar. A voiceover that we later discover to be Michael guides the viewer through the sea of beautiful, buffed, beefcake boys. Eventually we meet Michael, Emmett, and Ted, who are all waiting for the stud among them – Brian – to finish with his bottom of the moment in the back room. As they all converge outside ready to climb aboard Brian's jeep, we watch as Brian sees Justin for the first time. Just prior to this moment, we've watched the young, white, blonde, high-school student Justin as he enters the gay village for the first time. Seemingly overwhelmed by the sights and sounds and options around him, Justin is depicted as leaning against a streetlamp to rest. The scene is filmed in slow motion as we watch Brian first spot, then pick up, the beautiful young Justin. Brian abandons his friends as he takes Justin back to his loft.

Upon their arrival, Brian unabashedly disrobes. Once naked, we see him from the back as he opens his arms wide to Justin. The camera pans around to capture Brian from the front – from what would be Justin's view – and Brian invites Justin, as well as the viewer, to actually *see* him, to visually consume his body from the position of the anticipatory bottom. Again, this is no longer Berger's "men watch; women watch themselves be watched" economy. Instead, there is a "misunderstanding" in this moment where gay masculinity, not femininity, watches itself being watched. Hall suggests that misunderstandings arise from the disjunctures between dominant encodings (Brian's invitation to look at him as a refusal of heteronormative shame and an inversion of the heteronormative gaze) and the viewer's decoding (which will vary, depending on who that viewer is within the larger heteronormative context: a returned look; a look away; a desiring look through Justin's eyes). Justin not only looks at

Brian; he steps forward into a sexual embrace with him that takes them and the looking audience directly to Brian's bed.

Several other events occur in this episode to delay what occurs in that bed. As we discover, Brian has provided sperm to Lindsay and Mel, who, as it turns out, goes into labor while Brian has been seducing Justin. After picking up Michael (who is clearly unhappy about Brian's attraction to Justin) and visiting Mel, Lindsay, the new baby Gus and a crowd of dykes in the maternity ward, Brian and Justin return to Brian's loft where we watch as he initiates Justin into the culture of queer sex. That initiation is one in which Justin learns to make queer sense of his body in an entirely new way. Brian tops Justin, and Justin receives Brian and his instructions for bottoming. As Brian mounts Justin, just at the moment before penetrating him, Brian instructs Justin to position his legs on Brian's shoulders. At that point, Brian leans forward and enters him, forcing Justin's legs almost directly over his own head. The sight is shocking at first for the viewer, and clearly is a bit shocking for Justin as well. "Now just relax," Brian tells Justin (and us), and they fuck as the camera cuts away.

It's all too easy to construct penetration in any context as reducible to passivity. But that would be a misreading of the potential of receptivity. In her essay "Recasting Receptivity: Femme Sexualities," Ann Cvetkovich reads the narratives of butch–femme and gender queer cultures to reconfigure sexual receptivity – what she calls "being fucked" – as an active and engaged process that takes place with bodies but also transcends the limits of the biological. "Different kinds of penetration mean different things," she argues, providing a way of thinking about bottoming as "a complexity sometimes effaced in a phallocentric culture that assumes only penises do the penetrating and that vaginas are meant to be penetrated ... [P]enetration, however, [functions] as a metaphor that signifies not domination but something else" (136–7). Indeed, before Brian fucks Justin with his cock, he gives him a lesson in rimming. In both instances, Justin is hailed into sexual experience by Brian, but he is also very actively pursuing his own desires as a bottom to Brian's top, despite the obstacles to coming out as a gay adolescent. In this way, bottoming – that is, being penetrated – provides access to power, and, as Cvetkovich puts it, not just sexual power but social power as well

(129). This is, then, precisely what Hall describes as meaning-making, where meaningful consumption means decoding, receiving but also actively engaging in the labor of reception in ways that "have an effect, influence, entertain, instruct or persuade, with very complex perceptual, cognitive, emotional, ideological or behavourial consequences" (167–8). Everything in Justin's world is meaningful now in a way it wasn't before; he has access to a sexual and social power with which he engages Brian – otherwise every bit the stone top, both physically and emotionally – in a relationship. He negotiates through violent homophobia, parental obligations, peer pressures, social networks, creative enterprises with Michael, and so on. Indeed, he now understands his own body as part of that "something else" in ways that transcend the cultural imperatives imposed on that supposedly self-evident biology.

With receptivity reconfigured outside of the sexual imperatives of biological determinism, the possibilities for spectator crossover become reconfigured as well. In fact, this may well be one of the reasons for Shiller's thrilling and eager consumption of *Queer as Folk* on such a regular basis as a heterosexual woman. Instead of identifying with a passive image of self, the previously objectified woman-as-hole-as-box takes on the active receptivity of the gay bottom. Then again, the sexually rapacious woman might become the unapologetic gay top. But what really interests me are the ways that such complex depictions of top–bottom, active–receptive sexual subjectivities provide that "something else" by way of several identificatory possibilities for the FtM trans man too. Living in an FtM transsexual body is, of course, living in, with, and through corporeal incoherence. That is, very few FtMs can afford successful lower surgery as most phalloplasties remain simply cost-prohibitive. But many more, like myself, simply do not desire the procedure. Many of the FtM bodies depicted, for instance, in the photographs of Del La Grace Volcano are transed and incoherent within current sex/gender economies.

In other words, regardless of whether or not trans men have bottom surgery, most of us, if not all, continue to live our lives as bois with, dare I say it, boy-pussies. As such, the bigger question at stake about living incoherently, even for those trans men who do have bottom surgery, is this: What representational elements of television

culture can we connect to the physical site that is quietly and euphe-
mistically identified among FtM men as "the tranny bonus hole"? In
his interviews with FtM tranny bois as well as with intersexed folks,
Colin Thomas teases out the way that trans folk rearticulate gender
possibilities based on a decoding of the binary gender system even
as it, like television, attempts to box subjects in. "Hanging out with
gender-variant people," Thomas writes, "can quickly dislodge one's
concepts of what it means to be male or female, gay or straight" (3).
In fact, one of his interview subjects notes these boxes of language
mirror the limits of bodies when "he" says: "If there was a tranny
pronoun, I'd use it … I'm male, but I'm not suddenly this bio-dude
either … I do plan on keeping my tranny bonus hole [though].
That's staying" (1). This is not the same hole that defines femininity
(the vagina-as-sheath-for-penis) and by implication lesbianism (the
for-women-only vagina); this is the hole that defies existing gender
taxonomies. It exists as radical sexual potentiality.

Because popular cultural images of transsexual and transgendered
people often traffic in depictions of permanently damaged relationships with bodies of origin as well as with sexual pleasure (think *The
Crying Game* or *Silence of the Lambs*), trans folk must look elsewhere
for exuberant images of gender and sexual incoherence. We must,
in fact, produce transed readings of gay culture. To wit: the visual
spectacle in *Queer as Folk* of a man on his back with his legs in the
air being fucked provides a powerful site of identification for trans
bois. My own trans identifications occur as the product of active
labor. But as a heterosexual boi with a long lesbian history, my
active identifications are with gay male bottoms who demonstrate
little conflict around penetration and masculinity. Part of what *Queer
as Folk* offers is the opportunity to reconfigure sexual subject positions through such active decoding, so that the gay male bottom is
available to straight women, trans men, and bois of any gender as
an empowering reflection of active receptivity. In this case, identification and spectatorship are not conditioned or enabled by the sexed
body; that is, viewing as a woman or a man would not preordain the
characters with whom one might identify. Trans people, for at least
some length of time, live incoherence. Many stay committed to it
as a radical and embodied sexual politics long after transition. For
FtMs, "transition" is often a permanent state given the deficiencies of

surgical procedures. *Queer as Folk* is the one television text that puts a picture in my head of the radical possibilities of sex – dislocating the active–passive, male–female dichotomies as well as the active male/passive female continuities of heteronormative sexual culture – thereby allowing me to transform my own practice as a queerly identified heterosexual trans man. And this is the most interesting irony of all: these images provide ways for those of us with such bonus holes to enjoy them still and to do so within the limits of what it means to be manly, not in the hegemonic sense, but quite queerly. These are precisely the moments where *Queer as Folk* pushes beyond even its own imagined queerness into what I have been identifying as a post-queer incoherence. The show lends itself to libidinous cross-gendered identifications that defy both passive voyeurism and limited sexual taxonomies, or, I should say, the show's viewers raid its contents, lifting queer images and recoding them trans.

NOTES

1. Although the analysis of race on this series is beyond the scope of this chapter, *Queer as Folk* should be noted as a textbook case study in the five strategies of whitewashing identified by Allan Bérubé in his essay "How Gay Stays White and What Kind of White it Stays": the deployment of race analogies; the mirroring of white normativity as a tactic of winning credibility; excluding people of color from controlling images or representations; the marketing of gay as white and middle class within commodity capitalism; and the assumption of the white shield that camouflages unearned and unmarked privilege.

REFERENCES

Berger, John. *Ways of Seeing*. New York: Penguin, 1972.

Bérubé, Allan. "How Gay Stays White and What Kind of White It Stays." In *The Making and Unmaking of Whiteness*. Ed. Birgit Brander Rasmussen, Eric Klinenberg, Irene J. Nexica, and Matt Wray. Durham NC: Duke University Press, 2001. 234–65.

Cvetkovich, Ann. "Recasting Receptivity: Femme Sexualities." In *Lesbian Erotics*. Ed. Karla Jay. New York: New York University Press, 1995. 125–46.

Doane, Mary Ann. "Film and the Masquerade: Theorizing the Female Spectator." In *The Sexual Subject: A "Screen" Reader in Sexuality*. London: Routledge, 1992. 227–43.

Halberstam, Judith. *Female Masculinity*. Durham NC: Duke University Press, 1998.

Hall, Stuart. "Encoding, Decoding." In *Media and Cultural Studies. Keyworks.* Ed. Meenakshi Gigi Durham and Douglas M. Kellner. Oxford: Blackwell, 2001. 166–176.

Martin, Biddy. *Femininity Played Straight: The Significance of Being Lesbian.* New York: Routledge, 1996.

Mulvey, Laura. "Visual Pleasure and Narrative Cinema." In *A Cultural Studies Reader.* Ed. Jessica Munns and Gita Rajan. New York: Longman, 1995. 322–32.

Rubin, Gayle. "The Traffic in Women: Notes on the 'Political Economy' of Sex." In *Toward an Anthropology of Women.* Ed. Rayna Reiter. New York: Monthly Review Press, 1975. 157–210.

Rumach, Leah. "Tailing Tighty Whities: Straight Girls Swoon over Boys of *Queer as Folk.*" *NOW Magazine,* 22, no. 31 (2003), online edition.

Shiller, Romy. "The Show Has Never Been Written for Straight Women: So Why is *Queer as Folk* Making Women Wet?" *Fab Magazine* 260. 2004.

Sedgwick, Eve Kosofsky. *Epistemology of the Closet.* Berkeley: University of California Press, 1990.

Thomas, Colin. "Beyond the Binary: Adventures in Gender." www.straight.com (accessed 31 July 2005).

Trimble, Sarah. "Playing Peter Pan: Conceptualizing 'Bois' in Contemporary Queer Theory." *Canadian Woman Studies/Les Cahiers de la Femme* 24, nos. 2–3 (2005): 75–9.

6

HBO'S OZ AND THE

FIGHT AGAINST PRISONER RAPE:

CHRONICLES FROM THE FRONT LINE

LARA STEMPLE

We are living in a frank and realistic age, yet the subject of sex in prison – so provocative, so vital, so timely … is shrouded in dread silence.

Joseph Fishman, 1934 (quoted in Struckman-Johnson)

[OZ is a] pain-provoking, barely watchable prison drama that revels in nudity, rape, masturbation and multiple bloodlettings – and that's just in the opening credits.

Robert Blanco, USA Today, 1998

I spent four years of my life obsessed with the topic of sexual violence behind bars. Until last year I was the executive director of Stop Prisoner Rape (SPR), a national human rights organization working to end the sexual abuse of men, women, and youth behind bars. As funeral directors and White House staffers can surely attest, a single television program has the power to shape the cultural lens through which others view our work. In my case, that show was OZ.

Until OZ, prisoner rape had barely registered on the television landscape outside of tasteless jokes on late-night TV. And while HBO's six seasons of OZ explore many powerful themes – racial and ethic tribalism, the inexplicability of human evil, religious redemption – the theme of male-on-male rape resounded strongest.

To hear the critics tell it, OZ is *real*. They claim that the show, which is set in a "realistic prison," is "chock full of reality," sets the "standard for realism," "doesn't get any more real," shows the "cruel reality of the Big House," and contains "realism so gritty that you sometimes feel bruised."[1] Either these critics learned everything they know about prisons from fiction, or "realism" is just a term which means life in OZ is really, really bad.

Make no mistake about it: OZ is not real. Often it's not even close. Among the items the inmates in OZ have access to: ten-inch kitchen knives, ballgowns, rat poison, a hospital medicine cabinet evidently run on the honor system, a video camera, straight razors, a gun, fishnet stockings, bomb-making supplies, and a personal cappuccino machine. This television series is fiction, and yet OZ, like no show before it, takes on and busts wide open the very real problem of prisoner rape. With unflinching persistence, OZ exposes this sad aspect of life in America and tells us something about what it means when men rape other men. While OZ sometimes gets prisoner rape wrong, it gets important parts as right as any work of fiction could.

Augustus Hill, the wheelchair-bound inmate whose introductions anchor each episode, sees it this way: "They call this the penal system. But it's really the penis system. It's about how big, it's about how long, it's about how hard. Life in OZ is all about the size of your dick and anyone who tells you different ain't got one." With that, Hill points out the simplistic privileging of masculinity in prison culture, reinforcing it with the ultimate jab – being dickless, or not really a man at all.

Despite my exposure to the world of prisons and the violent things that happen within them (granted, not as an inmate), I find myself utterly stunned by the gloves-off nature of OZ. The show displays prison life in its rawest conceivable form. It's about men and violence and sex. "No fighting, no fucking" are the rote instructions given to new arrivals at Emerald or "Em" City, the show's experimental housing unit within the Oswald Maximum Security Penitentiary.

As I watch, I can't help but draw comparisons to some of the real stories of prison life from my work. Against this backdrop, I find OZ to be both too terrible and sometimes not terrible enough. I sit bolt upright one minute and roll my eyes the next. It's too terrible in that we see disgusting images, seemingly designed to shock. We watch as an inmate carves out the eyeballs of a guard. Another chews off hunks of his own flesh until he bleeds to death. One takes his feces from the toilet and smears himself and his cell walls. One receives his child's dismembered hand in the mail. One drinks his own urine.

While HBO's original programming deserves its many accolades, watching it is sometimes like watching a fifth-grade boy on the playground, a safe distance from parents and teachers. He runs around and swears and kicks kids because he can. The exhilaration he gets from this freedom almost compels the "motherfuckers" from his lips and sends his middle finger skyward. And like the fifth grader, HBO sometimes seems childish for mistaking vulgarity for being grown up, for sophistication.

On *OZ*, revolting images often seem designed just to revolt us. They certainly give those who know about prisons reason to dismiss the show. I can almost hear Jim Gondoles, the cantankerous head of the American Correctional Association, sighing "Oh, come *on*" while watching it. In fact, during Stop Prisoner Rape's efforts to move the first-ever federal legislation to address prisoner rape through Congress, opponents nicknamed it "the *OZ* bill" (Martin) to make the point that the premiss on which our bill was based was preposterous. Fictional.

In its rush to move from one extreme, testosterone-fueled scene to the next, *OZ* often misses the details, which, to me, reveal the more painful implications of prisoner rape. I'm thinking of Tom Cahill, who in the 1960s was held in jail for peace protesting and was gang raped for twenty-four hours. A detail that never left him, and also stuck with me, was the pathetically insignificant reward the guards offered for any inmate who would rape or "take care of him": an extra ration of Jell-O. Marilyn Shirley, who was raped by a corrections officer as another stood watch, is now in her fifties, living with her husband of thirty years. She never fully recovered from the trauma, and, she tells people bravely, she still wets the bed at night in fear. Rodney Hulin hanged himself at the age of seventeen because he could no longer endure the repeated rape he faced in an adult prison. His mother, Linda, is still haunted by the memory of Rodney's inconsolably bereft sister clawing at the soil of her young brother's grave.

When the public snickers at jokes about prison rape, I doubt their vision includes peace activists, women, or adolescents. Our generalization of "prisoners" as a faceless, monolithic other has dehumanized those behind bars so thoroughly that personal details are essential to bringing each individual to life in the public mind.

THE TRUTH ABOUT PRISONER RAPE

Tobias Beecher, one of the central characters in *OZ*, is a Harvard-trained lawyer who finds himself serving time for committing vehicular homicide while intoxicated. Bespectacled and clean-shaven, he arrives in OZ, standing in the receiving room in worrisome contrast to the thuggish, streetwise men who make up the population of Em City, where Beecher has been assigned to live. "What are you in for, shaving points off your golf score?" he's asked.

Not long into the first episode, "The Routine," prisoner rape presents itself as part of this routine. Beecher is assigned to share a cell with Simon Adebisi, a muscular African inmate who openly flaunts his status as a sexual predator. As they share their first night in the cell, Adebisi approaches Beecher in his bunk as Beecher scoots away. "I won't be fucking you – at least not tonight," Adebisi purrs in his Nigerian accent.

The next day, Beecher appears to be rescued from Adebisi by an older white (read: less sexual) inmate, Vern Schillinger. Before long, however, Schillinger makes it clear that he has simply taken Adebisi's place. Pointing out his own white supremacist tattoos, Schillinger promises to brand Beecher with one, calling him "my livestock." "Because now, Tobias," he explains, "your ass belongs to me." Soon Schillinger has raped Beecher and subjugated him into sexual slavery.

In one of the audio commentaries provided with the *OZ* DVD sets, series creator Tom Fontana attempts to convey the wonderful open-mindedness of actor Lee Tergesen, who plays the unfortunate Beecher. He tells a story about driving with him to Canada for an awards ceremony. They are stopped by a Canadian passport official, who asks Tergesen, "Are you the one that gets fucked up the ass all the time?" Fontana loves Tergesen's response: "Only when I ask for it." In other words, doesn't this straight actor demonstrate impressive nonchalance in the face of being seen as the inmate who takes it up the ass? It's certainly a braver reply than "you must have me confused with someone else."

But Tergesen's answer is a lie. Beecher goes on to have consensual sex with other inmates, but he is also raped. Repeatedly. He takes it up the ass *even when he doesn't ask for it*. The actor, Lee Tergesen, cannot speak the truth about his fictional character, Tobias Beecher. More puzzlingly, Fontana applauds it as a gutsy statement. Their denial about fictional characters makes the likelihood of openness from real male rape victims seem vanishingly small.

How can we possibly move away from prisoner rape's status as an unspeakable subject? It's a problem shrouded in shame and secrecy like no other in the U.S. today. Few people realize, as Cindy and David Struckman-Johnson report in "Sexual Coercion Rates in Seven Midwestern Prisons for Men," that one in five male inmates has experienced a pressured or forced sex incident (379). They have also discovered that women inmates, who tend to be assaulted by male staff members, experience rates of abuse ranging from 8 to 27 percent (222). Juveniles held in adult prisons, as is increasingly the case, are five times as likely to be sexually assaulted as youth in juvenile detention (Fagen, Forst, and Vivona 9). Many survivors of prisoner rape never tell anyone about their abuse, and fewer still make official reports. When the real-life men associated with *OZ* can't talk about it, it's at least some consolation that we can look to the characters they created in *OZ* for a bit more truth-telling. Maybe fiction makes it easier.

In OZ, as in reality, prisoner rapists like Adebisi and Schillinger are at the top of the prison hierarchy. They maintain their dominant position by subjugating others. Despite the fact that the predators are, by definition, the ones initiating the same-sex sexual contact, they remain heterosexual in their social roles and in their self-perception. *OZ*, unlike the movie *Shawshank Redemption*, gets this right. In *Shawshank*, the perpetrators are depicted as a band of tough but overtly gay rapists, who call themselves "the Sisters." Not only does this smack of the gay-predation paranoia propagated by Christian fundamentalists, but it gets it exactly wrong. In prison the rapists are straight guys. The victims are feminine (small, weak, or gay) and feminized (called "my bitch" or "my woman" and made to clean cells, provide back rubs, and give blowjobs).

But why does it matter whether *OZ* gets it right in terms of predators and prisoner rape? Does it really make a difference whether this sometimes preposterous work of fiction is also sometimes accurate? *OZ* undertakes a dialogue about prisoner rape that was glaringly absent from the cultural conversation, given the scope and seriousness of the problem. It matters whether *OZ* gets it right because television shapes our understanding of this widespread crisis, influences our culture and, potentially, society's response to the problem. It even speaks to survivors of rape behind bars themselves, framing their understanding of the painful incidents they may have otherwise tried to forget. As Sarah Projansky explores in *Watching Rape*, the media's frequent use of rape images shapes cultural understandings about sexual violence in ways that can be enlightening or problematic. Similarly, in *Reading Rape*, Sabine Sielke writes of "the prominent status of rape as a central trope within the American cultural imaginary" (4). She refers to texts that "translate pain into art" and "transform the unspeakable into figures of speech.... They tell stories and translate tales of violation into nationally specific cultural symbologies and conclusive narratives. As such, they both form and interfere with the cultural imaginary. Like news about crimes, they may even offer a lesson, some high concept" (5–6).

OZ itself blurs fiction and reality by providing real-life facts about the U.S. prison system. Playing the wise Greek chorus, Augustus Hill routinely opens episodes with a tidy lesson in prison policy. We learn, for example, that the U.S. makes up 5 percent of the world's population, but holds 25 percent of the world's prisoners. We're given Department of Justice statistics on inmate education levels and told that California spends more money on prisons than on higher education. Hill uses the activist-friendly term "the prison industrial complex"[2] and lectures on the fifth and fourth amendments to the U.S. Constitution. A few of his lessons are simplistic to the point of being inane: "People do terrible things to people. That's why we have so many prisons in the world." Hill holds forth on the impact of healthcare privatization on inmate health, and of course he doesn't forget the death penalty.

The topics touched upon in these introductions throughout the show's six seasons represent a fairly thorough recounting of contemporary American prison issues. But prisoner rape is never one of those issues. We learn that census counters count prisoners in the town where they're held and not the town where they're from, but we're never told that one in ten men in prison have been raped (Struckman-Johnson 379). Instead, prisoner rape functions as a central plot device and creates an environment in which our darkest suspicions about life in prison are confirmed.

NOT BITCH, EXACTLY

Tobias Beecher, who entered OZ a lifelong heterosexual with a wife and two kids, finds himself transformed sexually over the course of his prison sentence. After he sheds his victim status by biting the tip off of one man's penis and shitting in the face of Vern Schillinger, he goes on to have multiple consensual sexual encounters with other men. He even falls in love with one of them, Christopher Keller. Keller was also married on the outside, but he picked up men at bars for sex (and, in a typical aside about an OZ character: he occasionally murdered them). In one of their first conversations, they talk tentatively about their sexuality. Keller to Beecher: "Are you a faggot?" Beecher, quickly, "No. Are you?" Keller replies confidently, "I do what I have to." Their mutual attraction is palpable, and we're hopeful that Beecher might find solace in a real relationship, even with this damaged man.

Unfortunately, Keller is a just lackey for Schillinger and his seduction of Beecher is part of a revenge set-up. Keller does Schillinger's bidding as part of an arrangement they developed a decade earlier. Schillinger saved him from rape at the hands of another inmate at the age of seventeen, virtually owning him ever since. This reflects a common phenomenon in the prison subculture known as "protective pairing." A weaker, often younger inmate "hooks up" with a stronger inmate to exchange sex for protection. The weaker inmate must submit sexually and socially, and in return the dominant inmate protects him from rape and abuse at the hands of others.

In the process of orchestrating the set-up, however, Keller actually develops feelings for Beecher. Unlike most real-life "punks" who are forced to hook up for protection, Keller is powerful enough to disengage from Schillinger. Once he does so, a genuine relationship, with all its missteps and occasional cruelties, emerges between Beecher and Keller. Their relationship spans multiple seasons, allowing the characters to explore many complexities of sex and gender dominance. Neither is the consistent holder of power in the relationship, but Keller is the sexual top. While conducting an interrogation, an FBI investigator prompts Keller, "You suck Beecher's dick."

"He sucks mine," Keller corrects him.

The exchange accurately reflects a powerful sexual norm in American prisons. It's never shameful to get a blowjob, only to give one. In a later episode, Keller struggles with the intensity of his feelings for Beecher and says to him, "I'm trying to figure out a way to tell you I love you." "How about I fuck you in the ass?" is Beecher's reply, revealing something about their unspoken sexual rules. To submit oneself to penetration is to show love, to do a favor – apparently something Keller doesn't often do. As Beecher and Keller continue to develop their relationship, each grappling with his sexual identity in different ways, Augustus Hill offers a too-tidy summation. "People are defined by three things. Their heads: what they think. Their hearts: what they feel. Their dicks: who they fuck. At the end of the day each of us has to answer one question: who am I?"

Later, deep into the fourth season, Beecher comes up for parole and begins to brace himself for life on the outside. For the first time in years he flirts with a woman, his lawyer, whose contagious optimism about her early release adds to her appeal. During this time, a tough-nosed former colonel of the U.S. Army, convicted of raping a woman, arrives in OZ and is assigned to a cell with Beecher. "I hear you're a faggot," he confronts Beecher, forcing him to answer the same question Keller had posed a few seasons back. Beecher has been through a lot since then, and the audience wonders, well, *is* he?

"What's the difference," Beecher rather profoundly sighs. In tightly edited back-to-back scenes, we first feel the heartache as Beecher and Keller prepare to say goodbye; in the next, Beecher asks his lawyer out to dinner.

Grappling with the disorientation, he asks the prison nun, "If I get out, what will I be?"

I have seen this struggle many times. Men who identified as straight on the outside and who are raped – notably known as being "turned out" in prison jargon – grapple with who they've become. And it's not just the assault to their "manhood" that can accompany the failure to defend themselves. Some men become aroused during an assault. Some even ejaculate. Some form relationships with the men who abuse them. And some learn to turn the tables on the sexual power dynamic. A survivor I know named Steve Babbert identified as heterosexual when sent to prison for the first time. His small stature quickly landed him the status of repeat rape victim. Stripped of all sense of control, he soon realized that becoming more desirable was his only way to access power. He began to adopt a female persona, feminizing himself with the few means at his disposal, like purple Kool-Aid for eye shadow. Steve soon became Stephanie and became sought after enough that he could, to a certain extent, negotiate his relationships. Like Beecher, he began as a victim, and he adapted as best he could. Now on the outside and struggling to cope with anxiety and post-traumatic stress disorder, Steve still cross-dresses sometimes, and Stop Prisoner Rape gets the occasional email from him signed Stephanie. Certainly prisoner rape changed him.

So what are we to tell a previously self-defined heterosexual survivor of prisoner rape who worries that he might now be gay? The luxury of fiction allows *OZ* to present this dilemma, look at it, and not resolve it. But when a nineteen year-old from Watts with an eighth-grade education is raped and wants reassurance, "The factors that influence one's sexuality are complicated and the subject of much debate" is not the right answer. Neither is, "What's so wrong with being gay?" Ultimately, "Being raped does not *make* you gay" is the best we can offer.

In contrast, Beecher and Keller take on the confusing mess of sexuality pretty well. In season four, a journalist asks Keller about homosexual activity in OZ, and he illuminates these complexities: "By homosexual activity, do you mean the abiding love of one man for another, or butt fucking?" Gay or straight, true love or just sex – *OZ* asks but doesn't answer.

Its characters squirm within the confining prison walls and the limiting prison subculture, struggling to adapt. Some might argue that *OZ* is too amoral in this regard, failing to challenge the political and historical context leading to the characters' oppression and offering them little more than a range of unsatisfying alternatives. In her critique of *Thelma and Louise*, Projansky notes, "None of the responses offered in the film ultimately is effective in preventing further rapes, however. Instead they function as a series of options (rather than solutions) for dealing with a continuously assaultive world" (127). Susan Bordo derides the "postmodern conversation" occurring on television in which "[a]ll sense of history and all ability (or inclination) to sustain cultural criticism, to make the distinctions and discriminations that would permit such criticism, have disappeared" (248). It's hard to imagine OZ offering real solutions to prevent prisoner rape or presenting a sustained, historically contextualized critique (though Hill's intro segments provide some attempt at the latter). Besides, the limited options are largely the point. OZ does well enough to display the chilling scenario faced by men who are stuck with the ignorance, hatred, and violence of daily prison life.

When Adam Guenzel, a young frat guy whom Beecher knew on the outside, arrives in OZ to serve time for raping a woman with a buddy, Beecher is once again confronted about his sexuality. "Were you a fag before you came to OZ or did you start here?" Guenzel asks in disgust.

"Depends on what you heard."

"That when you first arrived you were Schillinger's bitch."

"Yes."

"Then some guy named Keller's bitch."

"Not bitch, exactly."

"Then what, his girlfriend?"

"People like to reduce things to their most basic form."

"You're either a fag, or you're not."

Guenzel's aggression escalates, and he comes to blows with Beecher. Guenzel ends up detained in a separate cage, where he screams "faggot" with all the vitriol he can muster. Guenzel is the simpleton who understands neither Beecher nor the realities of prison life. Not only does Beecher realize that he has coped as best he can under limiting circumstances, the viewer realizes this, too. The audience is set up to reject Guenzel, and with him the notion that you're either a fag, or you're not.

The exploration of adaptive relationships in OZ is subtly illustrated in another small subplot. Perhaps fearing that the exclusively male–male dynamic was too unrelenting for audiences to take, Fontana introduces a female inmate by inventing a co-ed death row. Shirley

Bellinger, scheduled for execution for drowning her daughter, is single-celled across from several men on death row. Through her cell bars she comes on to gay inmate, Richie Hanlon. Just as straight men in OZ adapt to their limited options by forming same-sex relationships, Hanlon settles into a relationship of sorts with Bellinger. Their dynamic is that of a traditional, long-time married couple – quietly domestic and basically asexual. They sit in their cells opposite from one another inattentively chatting, only half-listening to each other in a sweet, comfortable way. She's made him into a husband. "Richie, hon," she calls to him and has him hold out his arm so that she can look across the hall and estimate the proper length for the sweater sleeve she's knitting him. Adaptive relationships like Hanlon and Bellinger's are formed within the context of prison's limits, and identity proves sufficiently fluid to accommodate these limits.

EXPLOITATION OR EDUCATION?

Toward the end of my time at SPR, one of the most powerful stories of prisoner rape that our organization had encountered emerged. Kerry Max Cook, a prisoner rape survivor, spent more than two decades on death row before being exonerated. He served twenty-two years for a crime he didn't commit. Now *this* is a story it would seem the media could get behind. But the details are too terrible for news, for reality. The *New York Times* promises "All the news that's fit to print," and the most poignant details of Kerry's story would hardly make the cut. After suffering repeat assault for years and experiencing a state of gender confusion and emotional trauma, Kerry cut off his penis as instructed by his abusers. He also cut open his scrotum and removed his testes. He was forced to go by "Cindy," the name tattooed on his body alongside images of fairies. One of his rapists carved the words "good pussy" across his backside with a knife. The *New York Times* would never publish these words, but HBO would show them.

This is a familiar tension when working to make change on issues that have a salacious appeal. On the one hand, we seek to bring attention – including media attention – to the problem. On the other, it's easy for certain issues to be sensationalized. In the SPR office we sometimes worry aloud whether a particular description of prisoner rape is "too *Hard Copy*." On one occasion a reporter with the *Los Angeles Times Magazine* asked me if he could quote me as saying something along the lines of "The next time you're in the grocery store, the person in line behind you could be a prisoner rape survivor just waiting to take revenge." Aside from the dubiousness of suggesting quotes in terms of journalistic ethics, the reporter clearly missed our message. We're trying to humanize prisoner rape survivors, I explained, declining the offer.

Does *OZ* sensationalize prisoner rape? T.J. Parsell, a survivor who serves on SPR's board of directors, thinks so. One of the things that prompted him to reach out to SPR was an experience he had with *OZ*. Before he had begun to work on this issue, he was out one evening to rent a movie, and the video store clerks were watching the first season of *OZ* on the overhead TVs. In the episode playing, Schillinger has just forced Beecher to dress in drag, complete with eye make-up and Revlon lipstick. As the other inmates laugh at Beecher, the male clerks joined in the laughter, and T.J. froze beneath the crushing weight of seeing others make light of something that had nearly destroyed him. Enough was enough, he decided, and he contacted SPR shortly after. I believe I would have had the same reaction if I had been T.J. in the video store. And there are certainly countless examples of sensationalism in *OZ*. But when I watched the same scene at home alone, I was moved by it. I had heard stories like Beecher's time and again, but seeing it depicted visually was powerful for me. I heard the laughter from the other inmates as maniacal, and I felt *OZ* feeling Beecher's pain.

With viewers as different as T.J. and me and with viewing contexts as different as a public video store and a private living room, different perspectives are inevitable. In my view, *OZ* didn't use rape to tantalize viewers, to glorify sexual violence or to make people laugh. The depictions of rape scenes were not particularly graphic (unlike many of the scenes of non-sexual violence) and they certainly weren't sexy. Maybe men can't manage to glamorize rape when other men are the victims.

Conflicting interpretations of depictions of rape are not unique to *OZ*. One of the films best known for addressing rape, *The Accused* (1988), was criticized for the intensity of its gang rape scene, despite its popular perception as an anti-rape film. Discussing this controversy Projansky writes: "the graphic rape scene functions, paradoxically, both to challenge rape myths from a feminist perspective and to contribute to the existence of violence against women in media culture" (96).

T.J. was not alone in his belief that *OZ* went too far, and Tom Fontana attempted to respond to complaints about *OZ*'s gratuitous "unwatchability" in an audio commentary.[3] He argued that people who bemoan the violence in *OZ* are simply refusing to look past it to understand that he is, in fact, condemning the violent things inmates do to one another in OZ. In a press interview, he explained: "I think I have a responsibility that if I am going to do violence, then that violence should be terrifying and everybody watching goes, 'Oh my God, I don't ever want to be close to that.' I want to be shocking, but I don't want it to have a half-life. I want it to be something repulsive" (Sullivan).

So who's right? I agree with Projansky's paradox: depictions of rape have the potential to challenge norms *and* reinforce violence. But it's worth noting that male rape in prison is not at the same moment in its cultural timeline as sexual violence against women. The same program about father–daughter incest that seemed transformative in the 1970s might seem exploitative today. Right now, our society seems largely incapable of talking about prisoner rape outside of don't-drop-the-soap jokes, so the serious treatment that *OZ* offers serves as a welcome addition. We might someday reach a point of cultural saturation after which prisoner rape stories no longer inform and only entertain, but we're not there yet.

In another audio commentary, Fontana flirts with actress Rita Moreno and reveals a different motive for *OZ*'s raw approach. Fontana is telling Moreno how attractive she is to the other cast members (the unspoken undercurrent being that this is noteworthy only because she is no longer young). When describing the cast's lust, Fontana starts by saying that "Every guy on this show…"

Moreno interrupts him, cautioning, "Watch your tongue now."

He edits himself, "…wanted to take you in the dressing room and *ravish* you."

"Well you did that rather well," she congratulates him. "Why couldn't you have used that language more often on the show is what I want to know," Moreno inquires, offering a glimpse of her perspective on the show's explicit nature.

"'Cause nobody would have watched," Fontana retorts.

"You're right," Moreno agrees, surrendering to the ostensible demands of the public.

Critiques about today's graphic media culture fall along two related but different lines. Some argue that showing violence coarsens society, that the sheer volume of these depictions has changed our culture for the worse. If Fontana and Moreno are correct, we've reached the point where today's public will turn elsewhere for entertainment if a certain threshold of crassness is not met. A different critique concerns the impact of watching violence (or playing violent videogames or consuming pornography) on the viewer's attitude and behavior. To the ongoing debate amongst both theorists and behavioral psychologists about whether and to what extent this occurs, I add my own anecdotal experience. Repeat exposure to stories of prisoner rape has numbed me.

In the same way a trusted friend will pull you aside and whisper in your ear that you have something in your teeth, my husband recently had a chat with me about my dinner party manners. "During dessert," he started gently, "you launched into some pretty graphic details about that Kerry Max Cook case. We weren't ready for it. You have to remember that it's too much for other people, we're not there yet."

But *OZ* is there. Like me, *OZ* doesn't flinch. I was the smallest girl in my grade school class, too afraid to climb trees or roller-skate backwards. Now I'm part of the world of prisoner rape and I watch unwatchable *OZ* without recoiling. Like the character Tobias Beecher, I went to Harvard Law School, a credential cliché, overused in fiction to signify wealth, status, and access to power. And, like Beecher, I've instead landed in the world of prisoner rape, with its landscape of shame and pain. Survivors of rape behind bars have become my colleagues and my heroes. Together, we made the Bureau of Justice Statistics use the word "blowjob" instead of "fellatio" in their prison survey so that inmates would understand the question. Stories like this made up my response to "how's work going?" for four hard-to-believe years. I am changed, and like the characters on *OZ* and the survivors I work with, it is prisoner rape that changed me.

Much like veterans of the same combat battalion, SPR staff members share stories about how those who haven't been in our shoes just don't seem to get it. When the office is abuzz with press calls or questions from survivors preparing to testify, our work feels so vital, so urgent. But to outsiders, the issue can seem trivial or uncomfortable. We commiserate over awkward moments, like Thanksgiving dinner conversations along these lines: "You're working for Stop Prisoner *who*?" "Stop Prisoner *Rape*, Grandma." We share tips for talking to someone for the first time who quizzes us about our work.

First: "Me? Oh, I do human rights."

Then: "Mmm hmm. I focus on sexual violence issues."

Next: "Well, I work on sexual violence as it affects people in prison, jail, immigration detention."

Finally: "It's called Stop Prisoner Rape."

Only the most persistent will reach the fourth answer, allowing a dodge in the majority of small-talk scenarios. It's not that we're ashamed – to the contrary, I think we're proud. Some of us are exhilarated by the pace of the change we're creating in contrast to other advocacy experiences we've had. We avoid the subject because we're tired of the awkward reactions or we're just happy to be away from work, not facing prisoner rape.

THE HEALING PROCESS

Most SPR staff members are non-profit liberal types with sexual harassment sensitivities, making the gritty sex talk that comes with the territory all the more surreal. Young staff members who start out weak-kneed and queasy the first time they interview a prisoner rape survivor must learn to speak comfortably about the graphic details of a case. An unembarrassed approach is essential to illustrating that this is a valid topic for public discussion and government action. At other times, though, a gentle approach is needed. We have to tread gingerly with survivors who have certain needs, like Steve Babbert, who, since his time in prison as Stephanie, doesn't like to speak with men.

One of the few scenes in *OZ* to deal gently with prisoner rape comes when Cyril O'Reily, a developmentally disabled inmate who was also raped by Schillinger, talks with Gloria Nathan, the prison doctor. After a rapist attacks Nathan in her car, she takes a leave of absence from work to recover. Her co-workers rally around her, offering support and encouraging her to return to work only when she's ready. The warden gently reminds her that "healing is a process, a slow process" – an unintentionally ironic display of sensitivity from a man wholly unfazed by the abundant inmate rape occurring on his watch. Cyril's diminished capacity allows him to innocently ask Nathan if she was on vacation because she was raped. Yes, she replies, she was. Cyril says quietly, "I wish I could have," he pauses, "taken a vacation after I got raped."

In this moment we see, importantly, a male rape victim who is hurting just like the female rape victim. They're not really that different, after all. At the same time, we're reminded of the cruel reality of prison life: there is no escape. In his book *Prison Madness*, psychiatrist Terry Kupers states that a prisoner must have a sense of safety before he can begin to process a traumatic event like rape. The symptoms of post-traumatic stress disorder can be exacerbated when the victim does not have control of his boundaries or when he is subject to repeat abuse (147–9). Oftentimes prisoner rape survivors cannot escape from the perpetrator or from the surroundings where the assault occurred. Someone mugged on a street corner might avoid that intersection for the rest of his life, but a prisoner cannot retreat – even for a day – in order to heal.

The healing process is something that has long been denied prisoner rape survivors in the U.S., but the prisoners in OZ fair a little better than most. The prison nun, Sister Peter Marie Reimondo, begins to take on this issue in the fifth season. She gently asks rape survivors about their experiences, and even attempts to lead Schillinger and Beecher through a reconciliation that includes a discussion about how Schillinger's abuse affected Beecher.

Sister Pete also reaches out to Peter Ciabetta, the son of a powerful mafia leader. The younger Ciabetta is raped by Adebisi after Ciabetta's father is killed. Like real-life prisoner rape survivors, the stigma never leaves Ciabetta and he's perpetually known as "Adebisi's bitch." The other Italians lose respect for him, and he's eventually raped again, this time by Schillinger. Like other victims, Ciabetta experiences flashbacks to the rape experience and has difficulty talking about what happened. Sister Pete suggests that they schedule a counseling session with his wife but he's "not ready to face her yet." And, illustrating one of the biggest barriers to addressing rape, Schillinger warns Ciabetta against revealing any incriminating details about the rape. The relative power of the rapist over the victim and their close proximity to one another present formidable obstacles even to those corrections employees who, like Sister Pete, want to help.

In most prisons throughout the U.S., services like those provided by Sister Pete are rare. Busy coping with suicidality, schizophrenia and the like, mental healthcare providers in prisons don't prioritize treatment like post-rape counseling. And even outside of prison, rape crisis centers have only just begun to open their doors to prisoner rape survivors who are coping with the abuse they endured while inside prison. In the last few years, SPR has persuaded hundreds of rape crisis groups to begin to offer counseling to this enormous population of victims once they're released. A new SPR program will bring rape crisis counselors directly into select California prisons, potentially altering the mental healthcare landscape dramatically.

In the sixth and final season, *OZ* introduces another mental health innovation, a prisoner rape survivor support group. I have never heard of such an effort in any prison in the United States (though they are used in South Africa). In the *OZ* version, James Robson, a former Aryan thug who is repeatedly raped as part of a protective pairing relationship, first discusses his abuse in private counseling sessions with Sister Pete. He admits that his father sexually abused him as a child, a history not uncommon for prisoners in real life. He cries over the ramifications of the abuse he has experienced in prison, including his mistreatment of his wife during a recent prison visit. "I was raped and that's why I'm a fucking fuck-up."

In group therapy, Robson is joined by a handful of others, but he is the only regular character on the show. The anonymity of the characters detaches their dialogue from any plotline, making the scene entirely about rape itself. Robson doesn't even speak until the end. One line is spliced on top of another line, on top of another – each a fragment of the pain caused by rape.

One of the lengthier descriptions opens the scene. "I came to OZ nine months ago. I was a virgin, so right away I was targeted. So I kept breaking the rules, refusing to go to work or take a shower, shit like that. They put me on special restrictions. I figured I'd be safe, locked in my cell all day. But they put this lowlife in my cell and he, he beat me until I said yes. As he was doing it I could hear the TV in the CO's office. They were watching *I Love Lucy*."

Four other inmates give briefer excerpts. "Thanksgiving day, six guys come into my cell while I'm asleep. They held me down and they put a razor to my throat."

"I asked for a kit to collect evidence to prove what happened. The CO waited two days to take me to the infirmary."

"He said he bought me for two cartons of Cools."

The inmate who'd asked for a rape kit continues, "By the time the nurse examined me there was nothing left to find."

"I, I tried to ride, but I ran outta money."

Returning to the Thanksgiving Day gang rape, "They took turns anally or orally penetrating me."

Three inmates continue to speak, with fractions of their lines overlapping with one another in a tightly edited and powerful mosaic.

"Someone wrote my mother. She wrote the warden…"

"I was rented out…"

"…please help my son."

"…three dollars for a blowjob…"

"The hack told me…"

"…five dollars for anal sex."

"…quit whining. To stand up and fight."

Next we return to the inmate who heard *I Love Lucy* in the background during his rape. "I saved the sleeping medications the sister was giving me. Ten days' worth, a thousand milligrams. One night after… I took 'em all. I had no choice."

With different inflections, each prisoner echoes, "I had no choice."

"I had no choice."

"I had no choice."

"I had no choice."

Robson is last, "I had no choice."

This is easily the most accurate and riveting fictional treatment of prisoner rape I've seen, read or heard. SPR couldn't have done it any better, and I wouldn't be surprised if the research for this scene included the letters from survivors that SPR posts on its website.[4] It touches on many of the advocacy points SPR routinely presses for:

sensible cellmate pairing, prompt medical attention, the provision of rape kits, and staff responsiveness.

Another component important to the rape victim's healing process is the acknowledgement of the abuse as a real social problem. A key moment in all movements for social change comes when the issue transitions from obscurity into the main of public discussion. This public dialogue fuels change, and in the case of issues with a "shame" component the public dialogue is part of the change itself. In the 1970s, Phil Donahue and others helped break the taboo against talking about incest. By the 1980s the term "date rape" had become commonplace on college campuses across the country. If the dialogue about prisoner rape continues on its current trajectory, the 2000s will be cited as the decade this issue came out of the shadows.

One sticking point will always be the prisoner who "deserves" to be raped. Since, in contrast to global trends, Americans are comfortable sentencing people to death, surely the collective American ethos can permit us to believe that some inmates should be raped. *OZ* tests this notion with Adam Guenzel, the frat guy who raped and beat a young woman with a friend. We are reminded of his terrible crime by the other characters in *OZ* time and again. He brags about the rape, even relishing the experience. He attacks Beecher and is obnoxious and offensive in so many ways that I can't help but suspect that we're being set up to root for his rape. Even lovable Beecher feels this way. Unbelievably, Beecher makes a cruel deal with Schillinger. In exchange for Schillinger providing Beecher with the opportunity to see Keller, who has just returned to an adjacent unit after a long stint at another facility, Beecher agrees to facilitate Schillinger's access to Guenzel. As a result, Guenzel is gang-raped, forced to wear make-up, and otherwise made to service Schillinger and his Aryan gang. This kind of trade is reminiscent of real-life transactions in which prisoners' bodies are made available for as little as a few dollars or other favors.

Beecher himself comes across Guenzel, naked and battered, collapsed on the gym floor just after a brutal gang rape. As though this poignant moment isn't obvious enough to illustrate that what Beecher did was *wrong*, he later delivers a line certain to please anyone who bemoans postmodern amorality: "I was convinced that Adam deserved to be raped. You know, he raped that girl, attacked me. But when I saw him in the gym, I realized that no matter what Adam had done, no one deserves that." As a viewer, I felt that my intelligence had been insulted. As an advocate, I was impressed that *OZ* came out against the rape of a rapist, one of the biggest advocacy challenges the movement faces.

EDU-TAINMENT AND SOCIAL CHANGE

The important process of truth-telling about rape behind bars on HBO has helped pave the way for progress. *OZ*'s sixth and final season ran in 2003, the same year in which the first federal legislation to address prisoner rape, the *Prison Rape Elimination Act*,[5] was passed unanimously by both houses of Congress and signed into law by the president. While fictional characters faced rape in *OZ*, SPR arranged for seven survivors of prisoner rape and family members to speak on Capitol Hill in support of the bill. *OZ* was the first television show to deal repeatedly and seriously with this phenomenon – and our group of survivors was the first to describe publicly the abuses they were forced to endure.[6]

Survivors of rape in prison, long since freed and coping with their abuse on the outside, began to write to Stop Prison Rape in record numbers, sometimes citing *OZ* as the spark that inspired them to disclose their abuse. The show forced memories to the surface and accomplished the time-honored advocacy goal of "raising awareness." To further this goal, SPR often seeks celebrities and other prominent people who might lend their name to our cause. We sought Tom Fontana from the beginning, along with several of the leading actors, to no avail. If they were unwilling to lend their celebrity, perhaps Tom Fontana would flash the name and website address of Stop Prisoner Rape after an episode of *OZ*. I thought *OZ*'s edu-tainment messages about the pointlessness of incarcerating aged inmates and the like might signal an open door for a request like this. A first inquiry was sent, but received no response.

A second attempt included a packet of information about SPR, explaining that we are the only organization in the country solely devoted to the issue, imploring him to help us get the few resources that do exist into the hands of those who need them, informing him that the drama he created was triggering responses from prisoner rape survivors, some of whom had never disclosed their abuse before. This time a friend who works at HBO hand-delivered our request to Fontana's office. I followed up with calls, which were answered by his assistant. You're breaking new ground with this show, I explained, and you have the potential to direct people in need to the one group that might help them. Just "Stop Prisoner Rape – www.spr.org" for five seconds at the end of an episode is all we ask. Fontana's response came through his assistant: "Sorry, but if we let your organization do this, we'd have to let all other kinds of prisoner organizations do the same thing."

What a weenie reply. It reminded me of the ineffectual, cardigan-wearing director of OZ, Tim McManus. A more direct response, inmate-style, would have been easier to take: "Fuck you. Fontana don't take orders from nobody."

Despite this disappointment, other successes emerged. SPR convinced nearly one hundred other groups to join in our protest of a 7UP commercial that used jokes about prisoner rape to sell soft drinks.[7] In response to our protest, Cadbury Schweppes eventually pulled the multi-million dollar ad campaign, stating, "We are with them on human rights."[8] Prisoner rape jokes persisted in adult comedy programming (though even the most risqué programs would refuse to air equivalent jokes about the rape of women), but not all television treatments of the topic were bad. In 2003, SPR worked with a staff writer for the NBC drama *ER* to develop a sympathetic story of a prisoner rape victim who tried to hide his rape from doctors.[9]

Prominent groups like the ACLU National Prison Project, Human Rights Watch, and Amnesty International added this issue to their agendas early in the decade, and Christian groups like Prison Fellowship Ministries were instrumental in garnering the political support of the right, which was essential to the passage of the federal bill. SPR continued to release human rights reports, draft new state legislation, and press for widespread changes in the way corrections facilities respond to rape. Perhaps most notably, more than one hundred survivors of rape in prison agreed to join SPR's list of speakers willing to talk to journalists or policymakers about their rape experience. The silence was receding.

When the Abu Ghraib scandal broke in 2004, with its photographs of sexual humiliation of prisoners at the hands of U.S. military personnel, media attention to this kind of mistreatment came into living rooms across the nation and around the globe. In 2005 celebrity politician Governor Arnold Schwarzenegger signed the first-ever state bill, the Sexual Abuse in Detention Elimination Act, drafted by SPR.[10]

And as the Prison Rape Elimination Act continues to roll out, National Prison Rape Elimination Commission hearings about prisoner rape are being held across the country. At these hearings, the testimony from survivors about their experiences feature prominently,[11] illustrating that policymakers, too, need more than data; they want to hear the stories. And while *OZ* was an imperfect series, its stories of prisoner rape were told and not ignored, and sometimes told movingly, and our cultural understanding of rape behind bars is richer for it.

NOTES

1. These phrases appear in Sullivan, Crouch, Bianculli, Collins, and Hall, respectively.
2. Episode 32, "You Bet Your Life." For example, "prison industrial complex" is defined by the Prison Moratorium Project as "a marriage of public and private interests working together to institutionalize repressive policies, enforcement practices, activities, and culture that target, control and exploit poor communities of color and rural communities, youth of color, women, immigrants and the lesbian and transgendered communities, among others," www.alternet.org/wiretap/12810/ (accessed 23 September 2005).
3. A brother of two of the actors, Brad Winders, described the show as "the most brutal, vulgar show that's ever been on television" (Lieberman).
4. Stop Prisoner Rape, "Survivor Letters."
5. Prison Rape Elimination Act of 2003, Public Law 108–79, signed on 4 September 2003.
6. Stop Prisoner Rape, "Survivors of Prisoner Rape Speak at Capitol for First Time."
7. Qutb and Stemple.
8. Stop Prisoner Rape, "7UP To Pull TV Ad Under Pressure from Human Rights Groups."
9. Stop Prisoner Rape, "Prisoner Rape Survivor Testifies at New York City Hall."
10. California State Assembly Bill, No. 550.
11. Stop Prisoner Rape, "Survivors Tell of Horrors Behind Bars at Federal Hearing on Prisoner Rape in San Francisco."

REFERENCES

Bianculli, David. "'*OZ*' Finales: Dramatic Wizardry." *New York Daily News* 24 August 1998.

Blanco, Robert. "'*OZ*' Imprisoned by Ill-Advised Liberties." *USA Today* 10 July 1998: 11E.

Bordo, Susan. *Unbearable Weight: Feminism, Western Culture, and the Body.* Berkeley: University of California Press, 1995.

Brownmiller, Susan. *Against Our Will: Men, Women, and Rape.* New York: Simon & Schuster, 1975.

Collins, Monica. "Land of '*OZ.*'" *Boston Herald,* 9 July 1998.

Crouch, Stanley. "On *OZ.*" *New York Times Magazine,* 20 September 1998: 85.

Fagan, Jeffrey, Martin Forst and T. Scott Vivona. "Youth in Prisons and Training Schools: Perceptions and Consequences of the Treatment–Custody Dichotomy." *Juvenile and Family Court* 2 (1989): 1–14.

Hall, Steve. "Bleeding Slice of Prison Life in '*OZ.*'" *Indianapolis Star,* 9 July 1998.

Kupers, Terry. *Prison Madness: The Mental Health Crisis Behind Bars and What We Must Do About It.* San Francisco: Jossey-Bass, 1999.

Lieberman, Paul. "Power of the Pen." *Los Angeles Times,* 8 August 1999.

Martin, Keith L. "Reviewing the "Prison Rape Reduction Act." Corrections.com 18 November 2002.

Projanksy, Sarah. *Watching Rape: Film and Television in a Postfeminist Culture.* New York: New York University Press, 2001.

Qutb, Sabrina and Lara Stemple. "Selling a Soft Drink, Surviving Hard Time, Just What Part of Prison Rape Do You Find Amusing?" *San Francisco Chronicle,* 9 June 2002.

Sielke, Sabine. *Reading Rape: The Rhetoric of Sexual Violence in American Literature and Culture, 1790 to 1990.* Princeton: Princeton University Press, 2002.

Stop Prisoner Rape. "7UP to Pull TV Ad under Pressure from Human Rights Groups." 24 May 2002, www.spr.org/en/pressreleases/pr_02_0524027uppulls.html.

———. "Prisoner Rape Survivor Testifies at New York City Hall." 13 November 2003, www.spr.org/en/pressreleases/2003/1113.html.

———. "Survivor Letters," http://www.spr.org/en/survivorstories/main.html (accessed 17 December 2005).

———. "Survivors of Prisoner Rape Speak at Capitol for First Time." 24 June 2003, www.spr.org/en/pressreleases/2003/0624.html.

———. "Survivors Tell of Horrors Behind Bars at Federal Hearing on Prisoner Rape in San Francisco." 15 August 2005, www.spr.org/en/pressreleases/2005/0815.html.

Struckman-Johnson, Cindy and David Struckman-Johnson. "Sexual Coercion Rates in Seven Midwestern Prisons for Men." *Prison Journal* 80 (2000): 379–90.

———. "Sexual Coercion Reported by Women in Three Midwestern Prisons. *Journal of Sex Research* 39, no. 3 (2002): 217–27.

Struckman-Johnson, Cindy, et al. "Sexual Coercion Reported by Men and Women in Prison." *Journal of Sex Research* 33, no. 1 (1996): 67–76.

Sullivan, Jim. "Another Season in '*OZ.*'" *Boston Sunday Globe,* 11 July 1999.

7

"THE ROOM" AS "HETEROSEXUAL CLOSET": THE LIFE AND DEATH OF ALTERNATIVE RELATIONALITIES ON HBO'S *SIX FEET UNDER*

LESLIE HEYWOOD

"I don't want to be the one who denies you that. I want to be the one who helps you to have what you want."

David to Keith, "A Coat of White Primer" (5:1)

"When are you going to stop caring what I thought?"

Nate Sr. to Nate Jr., "The Room" (1:6)

"No matter how many white veils you put on, honey, you're just too fucked up for all that. Maybe you should just try to accept that instead of trying to be something that you're not."

Lisa's ghost to Brenda, "A Coat of White Primer" (5:1)

"The only way I get to get married in the long white gown is to have my dead baby leaking out of me all day."

Brenda to Nate, "A Coat of White Primer" (5:1)

(In)famously part of HBO's claim not to be TV – the network's claim to unique product – *Six Feet Under* catered to a large audience of subscribers that remained fairly consistent through its run. For a show with an audience that ranged from a high of 7 million viewers to a low of 2.5 million and that ran for five years, there is a surprising dearth of critical material.[1] Merri Lisa Johnson's "From Relationship Autopsy to Romantic Utopia: The Missing Discourse of Egalitarian Marriage on HBO's *Six Feet Under*," and Samuel A. Chambers, "Telepistemology of the Closet; Or, the Queer Politics of *Six Feet Under*" are at this writing the only full-length peer-reviewed academic articles devoted to the series, and *Reading Six Feet Under*, a collection of essays about the show, is the only book. Given this lack of critical conversation I necessarily frame my discussion not just in relation to this published material, but to the fields of third wave feminism, queer theory, and what Johnson, in her introduction to a special issue of *The Scholar and Feminist Online* devoted to third wave feminist television studies, terms "an emerging third wave feminist media theory." In fact, I specifically write this chapter as a contribution to that emerging field, a definitional project that helps to delineate and clarify its preoccupations and terms.

I will do so through a particular reading of *Six Feet Under* that investigates the following questions: (1) how the structure of straight white American middle-class masculinity is split between "the playboy/rebel" and "the breadwinner," in a model that often incorporates both; (2) how a queer perspective on heteronormativity can function to reveal the damage heteronormativity does not only to non-heterosexuals, but to heterosexuals as well; (3) the specific terms of that damage – the heterosexual closet in which one's life is lived in the service of social expectations and ideals – and the glimpsed possibilities of something else, what Calvin Thomas has called "queer heterosexuality." Thomas defines the term as "a generalized resistance to the normative interpretation of sexual difference as difference itself, a resistance in which straights could conceivably participate ... straights, who would be definitionally barred from the terms gay, lesbian, or bisexual, could not be excluded from the domain of the queer except by recourse to the very essentialist definitions queer theory is often at pains to repudiate" (14). In other words, the opposition between heterosexual and homosexual assumes fixed identities – assumes that heterosexuals conform to traditional patterns of masculinity and femininity and the identities associated with each. However, what the category "queer" reveals is that within heterosexual object choice there is no necessary correspondence between biologically male and female bodies and traditional gender identifications. "Queer heterosexuals" repudiate sexual difference. In order to show the way this concept is developed in *Six Feet Under*, I will examine what Chambers calls the "queer perspective" in *Six Feet Under* — a perspective that examines heteronormativity's dark side for heterosexuals. In that perspective, for heterosexuals who long for something other than traditional gender roles, living as a heterosexual can only be a process of "trying to be something you're not" (5:1, "A Coat of White Primer"), a process that makes characters like Nate Fisher "closeted," without a community to "come out" within.

My use of the term "heterosexual closet" differs from that in Bob Powers's *A Family and Friends' Guide to Sexual Orientation: Bridging the Line between Gay and Straight*. There, Powers defines the heterosexual closet as the process by which the family member or friend of someone who has come out hides their knowledge of their family member or friend's sexuality, and I am certainly not using it in the sense used by Henry Makow, who, from the perspective of the far Christian right, defines it as the process by which "generally speaking our [heterosexuals'] lifestyle and rituals are not celebrated. Instead they are portrayed in a jaundiced way." I also do not use it in the sense of someone straight who does not come out as straight to gays, as in an article about a female HIV/AIDS worker who worked primarily with a gay male population.[2] Instead, I am using it in the sense proposed by Calvin Thomas, the editor of *Straight with a Twist: Queer Theory and the Subject of Heterosexuality*, which claims to "proliferate the findings and insights of queer theory" by using queer theory to read the construction of heterosexuality as something other than the normative, and contribute to antihomophobic analysis that critically examines what it means to be straight (3). I will argue that, through the character of Nate and his heterosexual relationships, especially when compared to his brother David and his relationship with Keith, *Six Feet Under* shows the way heteronormativity literally and figuratively kills, and gestures toward, a "queer heterosexuality" that is similar to the "utopian realism" that Merri Lisa Johnson proposes, "a radical belief that marriage [and heterosexuality] might be otherwise" (29). *Six Feet Under* functions as one counter-narrative within the culture wars, offering a life-affirming vision of non-traditional families and relationships explicitly set against visions like those of Makow, who sees the straitjacket of heteronormativity with its strict gender roles and traditional nuclear family as the only option for a functional society. Both visions are related to the construction of institutions within a post-Fordist, globalized economy, and at stake is the question Roger Lancaster considers in *The Trouble with Nature*: "whether neoliberal capitalism requires at its base a network of total institutions or whether it recommends a laissez-faire approach to personal life. In play are two very different visions of social good: a locked down, chaste, sober society – random drug tests for everyone – versus a more open society committed to personal freedoms and free expression" (341). *Six Feet Under* works hard to contribute to the latter, while simultaneously showing the destructive effects of the former.

FRAMES: CHAMBERS, BUTLER, DERRIDA

In "Telepistemology of the Closet," Samuel A. Chambers writes that "*Six Feet Under* both promises and begins to provide its viewers with something never before seen on television: an illustration and illumination of the process of forming both gay and straight sexual identities in the face of societal heteronormativity" (24). Such processes are fraught with conflict of various kinds, and Chambers's discussion of David's ongoing process of "coming out" illuminates ways heteronormativity compromises and even violently destroys gay identity and lives, as in the episode that begins with the homophobic killing of a gay man ("A Private Life," 1:12), and all the countless daily incidents that proliferate across the series. Yet *Six Feet Under* is unique not only for showing, as Chambers argues, that the process of "coming out" is endless and identity is never consolidated across contexts, but also for showing what happens to those with straight sexual identities who do not fit into the norms prescribed by them.

As queer theory has established and *Six Feet Under* illustrates, the heterosexual/homosexual binary that structures heteronormativity – in Chambers's words, the idea that "heteronormativity is the norm in culture, in society, in politics" (25) – is a binary that excludes and leaves "remainders," ghosts, on both sides of the divide. The program's illustration of how heteronormativity excavates sexuality for some heterosexuals is only possible because it has what might be termed a "queer perspective" – a perspective that persistently questions the foundations of heteronormativity as a category. If, as Chambers writes, heteronormativity "means that everyone and everything is judged from the perspective of straight" (26), *Six Feet Under* judges everyone and everything from a particular queer perspective – "a different perspective on the presumption of heterosexuality." Itself a construction, this perspective does have a sometimes romanticized and totalizing take on gay communities and relationships since one of the program's major investments seems to be to present them as a positive alternative to straight, and takes a particular (family-oriented) view of what positive means, and many gays would not recognize themselves in this view. For instance, although the show makes everyone non-monogamous, gays and straights, these forays mostly seem to be constructed as problematic and something the couples need to "grow out of" – Keith's and David's three-ways, for instance, dropped away in favor of devotion only to each other, especially after they adopted kids. Despite these tendencies, however, *Six Feet Under* makes visible what no other program has revealed: the ways heteronormativity can make dissenting heterosexuals into the walking dead, who, with no community that would provide them with resources to articulate themselves differently, have few resources when they wake up and want something else.

Within the context of heteronormativity, "queer heterosexuals" are literally invisible, unthinkable, and unspeakable in their conjoining of opposites, the very undoing of that norm's categorical foundations. In the work of theorist Jacques Derrida, the concept of *le reste*, the remainder, is a figure for writing and representation, but also that which is left over, falls outside of any particular structure of meaning. It is related to the concept of the spectre or ghost that haunts the margins of signification, what signification banishes when it establishes its meanings. As social and political theorist Michael Hardt has said, contrary to being apolitical or "nihilistic" as Derrida was often accused of being, Derridean concepts such as *le reste* contain a "primary political insight": that in "even the most seemingly progressive identity, there is always some remainder, some people excluded, left out, abject" (quoted in McLeene). I will argue that Nate is "the remainder" in precisely these terms, someone whose subjectivity cannot be recognized because it isn't fully "straight" in the dominant senses of the term (the way straightness is associated not just with attraction to the supposedly "opposite sex," but also with very particular – and traditional – versions of masculinity and femininity, and a certain kind of romance narrative), but neither is his subjectivity gay. He is *le reste,* the remainder, what is left over when the opposition straight/gay has done its structural work. As Chambers writes, "the constant appearance of ghosts on *Six Feet Under* marks a queer space in the most general sense: the realm of the specter is a place where characters renegotiate boundaries, a place in which they can try to articulate to their ghosts (that is, to themselves), the very terms of their identities" (29).

In *Undoing Gender,* Judith Butler writes that "sometimes a normative conception of gender can undo one's personhood, undermining the capacity to persevere in a livable life" (1). *Six Feet Under* shows very clearly how gender "undoes" David's personhood, but it also shows how, on another level, it undoes Nate, whose life becomes anything but livable. "If I desire in certain ways," Butler writes, "will I be able to live?"

> Will there be a place for my life, and will it be recognizable to the others upon whom I depend for social existence? ... If my options are loathsome, if I have no desire to be recognized within a certain set of norms, then it follows that my sense of survival depends upon escaping the clutch of those norms by which recognition is conferred ... estrangement is preferable to gaining a sense of intel- ligibility by virtue of norms that will only do me in from another direction ... *the critical relation [to norms] depends on a capacity, invariably collective, to articulate an alternative, minority version of sustaining norms or ideals that enable me to act.* (2–3, my stress)

It is precisely this "collective" that David has in his life, while Nate doesn't. In its focus on their respective sexual relationships, *Six Feet Under* creates a structure in which David flourishes while Nate perishes, where David learns to "live as he wants" while Nate seems to live as everyone else wants: as Nate Sr. asks Nate in an early episode, "when are you going to stop caring what I thought?" ("The Room," 1:6). In the show's construction, hetero men like Nate who are, consciously or unconsciously, critical of the traditional terms of masculinity have no resources for forming this "collective alternative," and this is what "does him in" in the end, while David, who has exactly the kind of alternative structure that Butler describes here, survives and thrives. David's progressive gay communities give him a vibrant life outside the business of the funeral home, while Nate's world is narrowed to the confines of whatever antagonistic sexual relationship he is engaged in at the time. In this context, it might be said that Nate, who has no community precisely because he lives in the world of straights with its heterosexual privilege, is the "remainder" left outside of the normativity the definitions of "straight" impose upon him. He is not "other" in the sense of belonging to the marginalized identity, but he is marginalized within the dominant identity because he does not accept its terms. And while this might be said of all the characters in the show from Brenda to Ruth to Russell to Olivier to Claire, it is Nate who most keeps silent, "in the closet" regarding the terms of his dissent if he could articulate them at all.

Nate may have "heterosexual privilege," and there is no question that he does, but *Six Feet Under* is invested in showing the underside of that privilege. With no resources from which to create an alternative because he is not gay, the oppositional identity, that privilege is problematized. Men for whom their sexuality happens to be oriented toward "the opposite sex" but who simultaneously reject the terms of "masculine/feminine," and the social roles associated with that oppositional construction of sex, are left with few resources within the "modern categories" of gender identity which are created by the opposition heterosexual/homosexual. As Samuel A. Chambers writes of the character of Russell, Claire's sometime art school boyfriend, "the inadequacy of the modern, binary framework homosexual/ heterosexual makes his sexuality illegible, not the fact that he 'really is gay' but cannot accept it" (181). Russell, however, seems to be bisexual, both/and, not either/or, and although this confounds the opposition, this is, I would argue, a more legible form of sexuality than that of a heterosexual who nonetheless rejects the terms of heterosexuality if not its object choice. Similarly, *Six Feet Under* shows that the lack of resources from which to craft a collective alternative in some ways may be more difficult for dissenting heterosexual men than it is for dissenting heterosexual women, who at least have access to some version of feminism, and that this lack of an alternative can literally, as it is in Nate's case, be deadly. As Butler writes (albeit in the context of what happens to gays who do not have access to community), "if I am someone who cannot *be* without *doing*, then the conditions of my doing are, in part, the conditions of my existence. If my doing is dependent on what is done to me or, rather, the ways in which I am done by norms, then the possibility of my persistence as an 'I' depends on my being able to do something with what is done with me" (3). Nate, whose "abilities to do" are fatally compromised by his heterosexual status and the binary gay/straight that confers it, cannot then "persist as an I," or even, as the show repeatedly emphasizes, "exist as an I" in the first place. It is this inability that haunts him throughout the series. And the reason we are able to see or "read" this, a process that would normally be unintelligible or invisible because negated by the constitutive terms of the categories, is because *Six Feet Under* reverses the usual terms of heteronormativity and instead judges everything from the perspective of queer. The queer perspective is the condition of possibility for being able to see and articulate anything, like Nate's identity, that does not conform to binaristic terms of gender and sexuality.

But what, exactly, given his status of gender, race, class, and heterosexual privilege, makes Nate abject and trapped? It would be easy to dismiss such an argument with a reflexive "oh, poor white boy" gesture, but *Six Feet Under* is invested in meticulously showing, over the course of five years, how what looks like privilege from the perspective of those looking at a person can be experienced very differently by the person himself. The show takes for granted the fact that we live in a particular cultural moment, one in which the terms of heteronormativity have changed. As Roger N. Lancaster writes,

> [I]n so far as queer theory gives the same generic analyses of heteronormativity that described gender, sexuality, and family life in the mid-twentieth century, it ... draws a fixed, fast-frozen picture of sexual culture. In this sense, the prevailing variants of lesbigay studies, queer theory, and related forms of critical cultural studies are unable to account for the history in which they participate and ultimately remain locked in a past-tense politics: addicted to topics like gay visibility at a time of unprecedented visibility, enamored of questionable concepts like "abjection" in an era of increasing acceptance.... It is not my intention to say that the time has passed for the critique of heteronormativity.... Institutional heterosexism still affects everyone's life chances.... Still, it seems necessary to mark the distance traveled by queers everywhere. Gay liberation has affected even the lives of teens who live in trailer courts in rural North Carolina. (348)

It seems to me that *Six Feet Under* demonstrates both aspects of the argument Lancaster is making here, both the ways heterosexism persists and the ways it has changed, and thereby shows how Butler's analysis of being "undone by norms" can apply to heterosexuals – who may have none of the other identifications with traditional masculinity and femininity that go along with supposedly "opposite sex" attraction – albeit in a different way than it applies to gays. The show goes further, I am arguing, than a "generic analysis of heteronormativity" by showing not just David's struggle and eventual triumph, but also Nate's struggle, entrapment, and eventual demise. In order to articulate the not particularly visible terms of this entrapment that the show strives precisely to make visible, it will be necessary to examine the evolution of white male middle-class American masculinity, particularly in its shift from the "breadwinner ethic" to the "playboy/rebel" model to a configuration that incorporates both.

"THE ROOM": THE ECONOMICS OF HETERONORMATIVE AMERICAN MASCULINITY AND HETEROSEXUAL ROMANCE

In *The Hearts of Men: American Dreams and the Flight from Commitment*, Barbara Ehrenreich performs a historical analysis of masculinity, arguing that the "breadwinner ethic" that characterized the first half of the twentieth century "required men to grow up, marry, and support their wives. To do anything else was less than grown-up, and the man who willfully deviated was judged to be somehow 'less than a man'" (11). All the weight of cultural ideology, expressed through institutions such as medicine and psychology as well as religion, was thrown behind the idea of "maturity," which "required the predictable, sober ingredients of wisdom, responsibility, mature heterosexuality and … an acceptance of adult sex roles" (17). According to Ehrenreich, this ethic collapsed in the last thirty years of the century, however, and while that collapse is often taken to be the result of changes in women's roles from homemakers to workers, usually taken to be the result of feminism, she shows that this collapse actually had "begun well before the revival of feminism and stemmed from dissatisfactions every bit as deep, if not as idealistically expressed, as those that motivated our founding 'second wave' feminists" (12). So now, while "men still have the incentives to work and even to succeed at dreary and manifestly useless jobs," they are not necessarily supposed to "work for others" (12).

Ehrenreich furthermore argues that five factors other than feminism detached the idea of male maturity from the breadwinner ethic: (i) the medical rhetoric related to coronaries (heart attacks) that in the 1960s and 1970s began to attribute men's higher incidences of this disease to their gender roles (86); (ii) the human potential movement in psychology, which argued that anything that limited "personal growth" was unhealthy and that "growth" should be pursued for its own sake, even if it meant abandoning the wives and families that had earlier established one's "masculine maturity" (97); (iii) the counterculture, which questioned traditional gender roles and the confinement of sex to marriage, even as it maintained heterosexual privilege (116); (iv) the gay liberation movement, which, through the mechanism of "coming out," made who was and who was not gay visible for the first time, thereby removing the stigma of "latent homosexuality" that had functioned to police the behavior of all men, and allowed heterosexuals to not marry without the suspicion or stigma of homosexuality (129); and (v) the "rebel masculinity" associated with *Playboy* magazine, which made it acceptable for men to function as consumers for themselves and their own desires rather than as breadwinners whose salary must be spent on his family's needs. *Playboy's* real message, Ehrenreich argues, was not about sex: "*Playboy* was not the voice of the sexual revolution ... but of male rebellion. The real message was not eroticism, but escape – literal escape, from the bondage of breadwinning ... in every issue there was a Playmate to prove that a playboy didn't have to be a husband to be a man" (51).

For Ehrenreich, the contemporary definition of masculinity left middle-class heterosexual men free to consume women for sex much like they were free to spend their wages on consumer items such as expensive cars and stereo equipment. Heterosexual masculinity shed the provider function while it retained the consumer function. The two forms of straight American masculinity Ehrenreich delineates post-1950s, playboy and breadwinner, allowed men to be the former and still be a "man" – two options rather than one. However, as with most ideologies, when a dominant framework collapses and another emerges, the new dominant model nonetheless retains residues of that earlier model, something Ehrenreich's analysis does not allow for.[3] The "breadwinner ethic" persisted, but in much less monolithic terms. I would furthermore argue that these became incorporated into a developmental frame: playboy first, breadwinner/family man later. The latter is still seen as "growing up," but, corresponding to changes in the economy and labor market which made even a college degree no necessary guarantee of a "good job," the period in which one cannot be grown up was just extended much later. The consumer role of the playboy is similarly incorporated into consumption patterns once one has "grown up" – although a man might be responsible for at least half the wage-earning in the family, it is assumed he will still spend some of those wages on personally related consumption. As Douglas B. Holt and Craig J. Thompson argue in their analysis of the contemporary straight masculinity and consumption patterns, that consumption helps sustain a model of masculinity that doesn't use rebellion as an escape from the pressures of workers and husbands but rather is an integral part of it: "respectability and rebellion are dialectically entwined cultural models that together form the foundations of manhood in America." In other words, contemporary masculinity isn't so much structured as the either/or (either breadwinner or playboy) that Ehrenreich discusses, but rather both.

Six Feet Under seems to take each of the strands Ehrenreich analyzes as an object for critique, from the provider masculinity of Nate Sr. to the pop psychologizing and New Age sensibility of the Chenowiths to Nate Jr.'s supposed progression from playboy slacker to responsible family man at thirty-six. The absurdities of the world the characters inhabit – searingly codified by the series to the extent that Claire exclaims, "I wish just once people wouldn't act like the clichés they are!" ("The Foot," 1:3) – are all structured by these particular cultural strains: people treating each other as disposable commodities, pop-psych discourse about "soul twins" substituting for any honest discussion of relationships, and the constant conflict between personal development and larger responsibilities. This conflict between "responsibility" and "doing what you want" is dramatized in the pilot episode and throughout the series, as is the precariousness of the stable arrangements we do manage to craft against all odds:

the opening scene pictures Nathaniel Sr. driving the new hearse down sunny L.A. streets, singing along with the Christmas carol whose lyrics run "I'll be home for Christmas/ You can plan on me." His cellphone rings and it's Ruth, calling to ask him whether he's taken his blood pressure medicine and if he will pick some things up for her at the grocery store. In the midst of the conversation she hears him smoking, remonstrates with him about this, and he tells her he's "quitting right now" and throws his cigarette out the window. Then, in a motif that has been repeated throughout series creator Alan Ball's work, he hangs up the cellphone, looks down to light another, and is hit by an L.A. city bus.[4]

Nathaniel Sr.'s small, fatal gesture of rebellion serves as the frame for an episode in which the central conflict revolves around Nate Jr.'s supposed lack of responsibility to the family, and whether or not he will return to Seattle, where he has been working as "the Assistant Manager of Organic Produce at Seattle's highest-volume food co-op," a job that his brother David and others refer to as his being a "bag boy." After their father's funeral, at which Nate has helped their mother to grieve while David, who wants to deal through detachment, looks on, the brothers get into a fight that brings this conflict to the fore. According to David, "You had a responsibility to this family and you ran away from it and you left it all for me!" While Nate responds, "Don't blame me if you're not living the life you want. That is nobody's fault but your own," it was made clear in an earlier scene that Nate, who is continually read by the other characters as having "escaped," has not "been living the life he wants" either: "I live in a shitty apartment which was supposed to be temporary. I work at a job which was also supposed to be temporary until I figured out what I really wanted to do with my life, which apparently is nothing. I have lots of sex but I haven't had a relationship last more than a couple of months... I'm going to be one of those losers who ends up on his deathbed saying where'd my life go" ("Pilot," 1:1).

Here the two strains of Ehrenreich's model of straight masculinity emerge in direct contrast, and neither one of them looks good. Nate's playboy model has failed, and David's responsibility model has failed. While Holt and Thompson would argue that what is needed is a model that combines the two, or that at least this is what most contemporary men do, *Six Feet Under* has very different ideas about this. From the perspective of the show's queer sensibility, *no model* in the heterosexual paradigm works if you do not accept its terms. If you don't have what Butler terms the "capacity, invariably collective, to articulate an alternative, minority version of sustaining norms or ideals that enable me to act," collective resources through which one might "be able to do something with what is done with me," you will literally not be legible in the world. For Butler, being able to "do something" is a condition of existence since the "possibility of my persistence as an 'I' depends" on "being able to do something with what is done to me." One of the things that makes *Six Feet Under* original is the way it shows that while gays are "able to do something with what is done to me," straights, particularly men, are not. The show is a critique both of traditional straight masculinity and of its contemporary revisions.

As a white, heterosexual, middle-class man, Nate bounces from model to model. Brenda, Nate's first romantic/sexual relationship in the series, situates Nate's problematic social position in the first episode when she calls him on his cellphone in the grocery store immediately following the death of his father: "You think you're not easy to read? Coasting by on your looks and charm isn't working like it used to but you have no idea what else to do because you never had to learn. Any woman with half a brain looks at a guy like you and thinks 'good for a hot fuck but believe me, that's it'" ("Pilot," 1:1). The playboy model has started to fail. It bothers Nate that he hasn't had a relationship that has lasted more than a couple of months. It bothers him that he is still living in a "shitty apartment" that was "supposed to be temporary," working "at a job which was also supposed to be temporary until I figured out what I really wanted to do with my life, which apparently is nothing." What is a straight white middle-class man to do? Cut at least partially adrift from the provider role, facing an economy where the available jobs are mostly McJobs without benefits in the service sector, schooled in consumption for its own sake, struggling with an instrumental view of relationships that is part of the playboy/consumption paradigm and that nonetheless retains the residue of the earlier breadwinner paradigm in which, to use Ehrenreich's words, "what was at stake for women was … a claim on some man's wage" (2), Nate's prospects for something beyond that "temporary" status where his biggest source of cultural capital is his appearance and his status as a "hot fuck" look bleak. How is he to figure out what he really wants to do with his life if the available sources of meaning have been exhausted? With no larger community to call his own, thrown back on his individual resources, he is left with "apparently nothing."

Having exhausted the resources provided by the first model, Nate turns to the second, and decides to stay in L.A. to work in the family business. He is at least partially persuaded to do this through an exchange with his dead father (these exchanges function in the show as a projection of the character's inner conflicts) in which Nathaniel Senior asks him, "What are you doing? You have a gift. You can help people." When Nate responds negatively, his father says "Fine. What do I care? Go back to selling soymilk and bagging waitresses."

Nate then has an epiphany in which he proclaims, "My whole life I've been a tourist. Now's the chance to do something good instead of just sucking up air" ("The Foot," 1:3).

Due to a different exchange between Nathaniel Sr's ghost and Claire after his burial, the viewer knows, however, that working in the family business isn't going to be any better than "selling soymilk."

> *Claire*   No more bullshit.
> *Nathaniel Sr*   No more responsibility.
> *Claire*   No more having to care.
> *Nathaniel Sr*   No more boredom!!!!! (yells)
> *Claire*   No more waiting to die.
> *Nathaniel Sr*   Ha Ha Ha. (sardonic)

If work life brings only responsibility and boredom, Nate also turns to what is supposed to make work life bearable, and begins trying to craft a lasting relationship with Brenda despite the fact that he met her on a plane and fucked her in a supply closet at the airport right after. He trades the playboy model of gratuitous sex for the model of the "meaningful relationship," the one that is supposed to compensate for boring work life. "You're supposed to be my haven away from all that," he says to Brenda, who, pointing out the update on that traditional man-as-public-work/woman-as-private-haven model, replies "I'm not supposed to be anything" ("The Will," 1:2). Brenda behaves anything but conventionally in the first two seasons, even, in a classic "queer heterosexual" gesture, asking Nate to "be her wife" and giving him her grandfather's fraternity ring in a queer inversion of the usual grandmother's engagement ring ("The Invisible Woman," 2:5). Yet, as I will develop in more detail later, when in season five she has reached the age Nate was when the series began, her behavior will become so conventional it is clear that in Ball's vision heterosexuals eventually have no alternative but to conform.

By contrast – and it will remain a point of contrast throughout the series – David's relationship with Keith is figured as a site of genuine relation, support, and refuge from everyone else's craziness. Similarly, the scenes involving the gay community – David's participation in the gay men's chorus, and the day at the paintball range – also seem to offer refuge. In a scene in the pilot episode, David, stricken with grief after repressing it all day, appears at Keith's door crying and inarticulately mouthing the words "I need," and Keith draws him to his chest, and this is the one genuine, non-cynical scene of affection between couples in the episode. Although Keith and David have their problems, initially splitting up because of David's refusal to come out, and working through various conflicts when they reunite after he does, their relationship is meant as a direct contrast to the heterosexual relationships experienced by the other main characters, which tend to be characterized as polarities between partners who are never on the same page, desperate struggles where one partner (the woman) always wants the other partner (the man) more than the other wants them, or, as in the case of Lisa in the third season and Brenda in the final season, one partner so rigidly tries to conform to social expectations that the relationship itself, and the individuals involved in it, seem beside the point. In *Six Feet Under*, heterosexual relationships inevitably seem to take the form of what Merri Lisa Johnson calls "the inevitably disappointing expectations of romantic mythology or the disciplinary force of the traditional marriage contract" (22).

In fact, for the thinking man or woman anyway, heterosexual relationality seems to precisely involve effacement of the self, mythologies of "soul mates" and contractual obligations where one partner is supposed to fulfill the other's needs. The show explores this on the simplest level when Ruth nags Nathaniel to bring her home items from the store on the day of his death, and Lisa and Brenda – in a deliberate repetition – both nag Nate to bring them home items from Whole Foods: Lisa: "Oh God Nate, I love you so much that it terrifies me. Do you think you might be able to run by Whole Foods for me sometime tonight?" ("Nobody Sleeps," 3:4); Brenda, right after a fight: "On the way home, could you stop at Whole Foods and get some chocolate Silk for Maya?" ("Time Flies," 4:5). Similarly, when Claire tells Ruth "guys need a lot of space" and Ruth retorts that "he doesn't know how to take care of himself and he needs my help" ("The Liar and the Whore," 2:11), the structure of antagonism implicit in traditional gender roles is highlighted. Both deterministic ideas about gender (men can't stand too much emotional connection and "need space," or the idea that they can't "take care of themselves") end up causing problems.

While Nate initially seems to accept the terms of this model, sharing male bonding moments with Rico when a porn star dies and they go on and on about her movies, upsetting David ("An Open Book, 1:5), and joking with Brenda about whether she would "rather have an educated gasbag like Trevor [her former boyfriend] or a semi-literate fuck machine like me" ("The Invisible Woman," 2:5), it is clear that he longs to be something other than a "fuck machine," and has a hard time turning Lisa into the adored object which norms of heterosexual romance would dictate. On a camping trip Nate tells another newlywed, Todd, that Lisa "knows all that bullshit fairy-tale stuff isn't real anyway. Working through it, wanting to, it's probably the first adult relationship of my life." Todd looks at him skeptically: "Ours is more like we can't keep our hands off each other. She just loves to bang" ("Making Love Work," 3:6). Yet, as if it weren't clear enough to the viewer already that Lisa is full of "fairy tales" and that Nate is deluding himself, season 5 opens with Brenda, about to marry Nate, watching a videotape of his wedding to Lisa in which, when Claire asks Lisa how she feels, Lisa says "like every moment in my life has led up to this one, like all of it makes sense, like this is the destiny that's been waiting for me" ("A Coat of White Primer," 5:1) – at which point the viewer, at least this one, again thanks the writers for getting rid of her in the third season.

It is, in fact, Nate's relationship with Lisa – a relationship so determined by desires other than his own that she actually tells him "I'm proud in a weird way ... I'm having a child with the last person in the world who would want a child" ("The Secret," 2:10) – that best enables us to understand the importance of the first-season episode entitled "The Room," (1:6). In this episode, when he goes through the Fisher & Sons books, Nate discovers some strange transactions that turn out to reveal several surprising aspects of Nathaniel Sr. The first is that he had a pot dealer who provided him with a monthly supply as the balance on a funeral. It is this dealer who first tells Nate, "I know who you are. You're the one who took off. Your father really respected you for that. Said he wished he had the guts to do that when he was a kid."

And if that revelation isn't surprising enough, Nate also finds a transaction on the books that leads him to an Indian restaurant in Hollywood, where he asks the owner if he knew his father: "Your father buried my wife seven years ago. I had very little money for the funeral. He asked if he could have this room [above the restaurant] as his own and that would be his settlement."

Shocked, Nate asks, "What did he do here?," but the restaurant proprietor says only that he doesn't know, and tells Nate to stay as long as he likes. Nate walks in, and incredulously sorts through his father's vinyl LPs of groups like the Moody Blues, shuffles the playing cards left out on the table, picks up a glass with a lipstick print on it. He falls asleep on the couch, and, as so often happens, his father appears in a dream, and by way of explanation about the room says, "So I'm walking along one day and this asshole stops me and asks me if I'm alright. He says I've got a look. He'd seen a man with that same look once, and had ignored it, and that man had jumped out a nine-story window. Do you know the reconstruction involved in a death like that?"

Nate demands of his father, "What the hell is this place, this music? Since when do you listen to Classics IV? What the hell did you do here, who the hell are you?" Of course he doesn't get an answer, and he brings both David and Brenda to the room to ask the same question of them. While David says he doesn't care, that "people are allowed to have private lives," Brenda has a different interpretation: "I think your father wanted some place that was just his and nobody else's. Nate, if you didn't know him when he was alive, you never will." "I don't want to be somebody who when I die nobody knows who I was," Nate tells her. "So don't be," she says. Easier said than done.

What Brenda's comments and the existence of the room point to are the ways that traditional heterosexual lives involve a form of enclosure, the relegation of "who you are" to a secret room, hiding it from those around you. Nathaniel Sr.'s "some place just his and nobody else's" points to the way that the traditional heterosexual male role, despite appearances, is, like the female role, a form of being-for-others, an expectation that your time is spent in service of social expectations, your work and your family. So while Nate wants people to "know who he is" and never to have to hide this, the series insists throughout that this is precisely what he cannot have. He will always have to hide. In "Nobody Sleeps" (3:4), for instance, Nate withdraws from the birthday party Lisa is throwing for his mother and sleeps on a couch in a room below while they all dance.

As is usual in a context like this, he is visited by his father, who asks him, "Want a little time for yourself? I know this great little Indian restaurant in Hollywood…"

Nate   Yeah. I'm not quite there yet.

Nathaniel   Won't be long. You're a funeral director, which you never wanted to be, just like your old man. You married a woman that you knocked up because you thought it was the right thing to do, just like your old man. Want one? (offers Nate a cigarette, indirectly referencing the fact that, as has been shown earlier, Nate has to hide his smoking habit from Lisa)

Nate   No thanks.

Nathaniel   So when you wake up, are you going to throw out that pack you already have?

Nate   Probably. I'm not you.

Nathaniel   You just keep telling yourself that.

Nate (yells)   I'm not shut down. I'm not five hundred fucking million miles away. I haven't given up. I love my family!

Nathaniel   Buddy boy, you think I would have stuck around if I didn't love mine?

Of course, the irony of Nate's insistence here is that all season long he has seemed to be "five hundred fucking million miles away," going through the motions of his day robotically, nothing if not "shut down." It is made very clear that in order to function in relation to Lisa, Nate can only remain in the relationship by "shutting down," and that Lisa's expectations, which are traditionally heterosexual, are what is causing him to do so. She circles his "problem purchases" on the credit-card statement and remonstrates with him that he can't "keep spending as if he is single" ("The Trap," 3:5), and decides without letting him know that she is not going to try to find another job and instead stay home with Maya. She furthermore continually demands that he love her in a particular way (as the adored romantic object rather than as a partner or the mother of his child). In the face of this demand, Nate becomes like his father and emotionally shuts down.

Nate, like many of the other heterosexuals on the show, seems to think that he has only two choices: acceding to traditional demands or being alone. In fact, when he runs into Brenda right after this, he simultaneously tells her that Maya (his daughter) is "the best thing that ever happened to him," and that "relationships aren't easy … you just have to work at it every day, can't expect everything to be perfect all the time and if there's a moment when I feel like I'm in prison, I just have to think about all those moments when it feels safe, and remind myself that those moments outweigh the prison moments." Brenda's immediate response to this is that "Being alone is a prison, just thinking abut yourself, just being trapped in this fucking vortex, always watching yourself" ("The Trap," 3:5). Here it is as if heterosexuals have two choices, and each ends up conferring a sense of imprisonment. It's all self, being alone, or all relation, being for others. "Being alone" is a "prison." But so is being in a relation-ship, because a sense of being "in prison," living for others (not in the sense of *giving* to others, Nate never seems to have a problem with that, but rather in the sense of living up to their particular – traditional – expectations), is the price heterosexuals pay in *Six Feet Under* for their heterosexual privilege or "safety," the social sanction received for fulfilling the traditional roles of father/husband and wife/mother. Which is fine if you are happy with those particular roles and expectations, but if you are not – if you are interested in crisscrossing gender roles and heterosexual identity (i.e. the husband as mother or wife as breadwinner) – the only alternative, besides being alone, is to create a private "room" for yourself, some place of existence away from the gaze of, to use the name of episode 2:9, "Someone Else's Eyes."

The connection between heteronormativity and its "rooms" and homosexuality and its "closets" is developed in the series finale, "Everyone's Waiting" (5:12). In a dream of David's that takes place after Nate's death, Nathaniel Sr.'s "secret room" comes up one last time:

> *Nathaniel* So you're going to sell your birthright.
> *David* Yeah, good riddance.
> *Nathaniel* Well I can't say I'm surprised, you never had it in you.
> *David* Neither did you – the only way you could ever handle it was to have a secret room over a really bad Indian restaurant.
> *Nathaniel* Oh, and you think you don't have a secret room? What do you think being gay is, you fucking freak?

Here one of the show's central themes is articulated in the clearest terms. Like gays who are in the closet, "queer heterosexuals," for whom "being themselves" does not match with all the expectations of heteronormativity, have to have a "secret room" because they can't be themselves in public without compromising their "heterosexual privilege," their status as that which counts as "human." But gays who have come out *are* the "secret room" – they are, by definition, "being themselves" and don't have to have a secret apart from their public life since their life *is* the content (non-normative identifications and practices) that the "secret room" hides. And in order to force David to deal with the residual demons that have been haunting him throughout the series, Nathaniel continues: "You think you can just walk away from this? Are you really that stupid? It only gets closer, David." At this point, the hooded figure that has been David's hallucination of his attacker in season four (the controversial episode "That's My Dog," 4:5, in which David is kidnapped and tortured) becomes the jaws of the grim reaper, and leaps on David's chest, knocking him to the ground. For once he fights back, however, and just as he is about to stab the figure, it assumes his own face, and, flinging the knife down, he embraces it. The hooded monster is the last vestige of David's thinking, as he did in the beginning of the series, that his homosexuality is pathological, but this time David sees clearly that this thinking is in his own mind, and he is finally able to embrace his difference as fully part of himself. He wakes to see Nate's ghost smiling at him.

Perhaps Nate is smiling because David has just done what he was never himself able to do in life for lack of a community within which to do it. Instead, traditional heterosexual relationships are a trap that brings out the worst in people, which is reinforced in the camping episode when Nate overzealously kills a snake in a scene that mirrors David's final confrontation with himself. Nate, though, has no means for David's kind of self-acceptance, and, instead of symbolically accepting himself, he bludgeons the snake into a pile of bloody flesh with a baseball bat. Just as Nate's final relationship with Brenda is set up to mirror his relationship with Lisa, this snake scene is mirrored in season five when, at his fortieth birthday party where he fights viciously with Brenda, Nate beats the bird that flies into the house into a bloody mass of feathers ("Time Flies," 5:4). Although the scenes are certainly open to multiple interpretations, the context of each makes it tempting to read them – like David's almost-stabbing of himself – as a displacement of a wish to beat himself to a bloody pulp, as he is already shown to be doing figuratively in both cases.

This kind of self-murder or renunciation seems a dictate of the heterosexual relationship structure. The series argues that commitment for Nate is becoming what others want, while commitment for David and Keith is a becoming what each of them wants, so that, ironically, Nate's answer to David's question about whether relationships are always "a constant negotiation where you can never relax," that maybe they are "constantly doing things you have no absolutely no desire to do," is shown to be true of Nate's relationships, but not David's ("The Secret," 2:10). As if to reinforce this, Keith directly tells David in the series finale, "You can be whatever you want to be, David," and David replies, "So can you." ("Everyone's Waiting," 5:12). For Nate, however, because he is part of a dominant structure that doesn't recognize him, relationships are "doing what you have no desire to do." But because David is part of an alternative structure that *does* recognize him, his relationships are much more based on mutuality. Nathaniel Sr. comments on this problem for Nate in the same scene where Brenda calls Nate and asks him to stop at Whole Foods, in a gesture that completes the parallel drawn between Ruth, Lisa, and Brenda. Nate, looking at an old family album, says to Nathaniel, "Time flies when you're having fun, huh?", to which Nathaniel responds, "No. Time flies when you're pretending to have fun. Time flies when you're pretending to love Brenda and that baby she wants so much. Time flies when you're pretending to know what people mean when they say love. Let's face it buddy boy – there's you and there's everyone else, and never the twain shall meet" ("Time Flies," 5:4). "Pretending to love" the way he is supposed to, Nate never quite figures out what the problem is. He longs for an alternative heterosexuality but has no words for it, and certainly no role models. The idea that Nate simply isn't like everyone else – that is, isn't like the other heterosexual men his age with their drinking clubs and golf hobbies – is carefully marked throughout the series, perhaps most graphically in the contrast between Nate and his old high-school friend, with whom he is reunited when their other friend dies ("Dancing for Me," 5:2). And perhaps the reason why Nate spends the entirety of the series inarticulately longing, not understanding what is wrong and what he would like instead, is simply because as a "queer heterosexual," there is no terminology to describe him. Instead of being dehumanized by heteronormativity, as David often is (and to remind us of this, at the end of the series, Rico is still saying to David "I have a family to think about" as if David doesn't, to which David is finally forced to respond "So do I! I have a fucking husband. I have two children. When are you going to realize I'm a human being just like you? When? When?"), Nate is simply canceled out by it, made into a silent, non-signifying cipher.

Nate's problem is existential in that he seems to want something different from the instrumental relationality offered him, and that heterosexuality, in *Six Feet Under's* view, is precisely an instrumental relation, the means through which each partner is supposed to fulfill their own needs. The pancreatic cancer patient that Nate befriends in season two provides the most succinct description of this: "I suffer from that American thing big time, you know, always looking around for someone better, shopping…" ("I'll Take You," 2:12). By contrast, Keith and David's relationship seems much more based on relationality for its own sake. This contrast is perhaps best developed in three juxtaposed scenes in "A Coat of White Primer" (5:1). In this episode's "cold open," the initial framing scene in which we witness the death of someone who will be become a customer of Fisher & Sons later in the episode, a woman named Andrea Kuhn is talking to her therapist, who convinces her that she needs to overcome her fear of others' anger and to express her feelings to her family and husband. When she does so, her husband becomes so angry that he jerks the chair he has given her out from under her and she is flung violently to the side, landing on a pointed fireplace stanchion that kills her by putting out her eye. The camera then cuts to the scene of Nate and Lisa's wedding, where Claire, shooting the wedding video, is asking a robotic-looking Nate, "How do you feel?" When Nate says, "Alive, how about that?," it is clear that he, in not expressing his feelings, is alive, while the woman who did so is not. This "life," however, seems to be a kind of waking death – Nate moves like a dummy, all vibrancy drained from his face. And as if to reinforce why, the camera cuts to Ruth, who says upon being asked if she has any advice, "Don't give up when things get hard, and they always do eventually – never stop trying." The scene then shifts to Lisa in the passage already quoted where she says she feels as if the wedding fulfills her destiny, and this is then jumpcut with Nate, who at this point looks as if he is in pain and says, "Ok, let's do this thing!" The camera then pans out to Brenda, who, pregnant, is watching the video just before her wedding to Nate in order to make sure she doesn't do anything similar that will make people uncomfortable. Then, in a standard Alan Ball move, the scene shifts again to Andrea's (the woman whose eye was put out) sister, who tells Nate and David at the intake that she can't understand what happened because "they had such a good relationship I thought – they never fought." If we haven't gotten it before, it is impossible not to get it now: heterosexuals can't "be themselves" in relationships, because the burden of the structure itself with all its attendant expectations is so strong.

This theme is explicitly reinforced throughout the rest of the episode. Brenda miscarries the night before the wedding, but insists on going through with it anyway since not to do so would be to waste the "six months [she] spent planning [her] fucking dream wedding," and "because, she says, "when I think about not doing it I just want to throw myself under a bus … I would have to take every painkiller in the house just so I could pick up the phone and cancel the caterer." The rest of the episode makes it clear that Brenda, haunted by her unconventional past, is trying as hard as she can now to fulfill the traditional gender scripts despite the fact that Nate's attraction to her has to do with her unconventionality. The burden of social expectation proves heavier, however, and she is unable to see Nate himself and can only see the role he will fulfill in her life, giving her the social sanction of a husband and family. He reveals as much when, just prior to the ceremony, he tells David about the miscarriage and says "what Brenda needs is to get pregnant again, soon, because it's not like she's twenty ... I've already got Maya, so it's not for me... it's what Brenda wants more than anything in the world, and I can make that happen for her."

This is explicitly contrasted to David and Keith, who, in a scene right after the ceremony, continue the discussion about whether they should adopt or hire a surrogate so they can have their own biological child. David has been arguing against the latter, but, perhaps spurred on by the way his brother is ignoring his own desires to allow for Brenda's, he says to Keith: "I think we should hire a surrogate." Keith skeptically asks why, and David explains that having his own child is what Keith wants, and "I don't want to be the one who denies you that. I want to be the one who helps you to have what you want." His position is one of compromise, however. Rather than prioritizing Keith's desire over his own, he says that they should try for a child through both surrogacy and adoption, and take "whichever one comes first." Unlike Nate and Brenda's conflicted union in which Brenda is trying to live up to cultural expectations and is using Nate to fulfill them instead of being able to see and think about Nate and his own desires, David finds a way to satisfy both his and Keith's desires, insisting on a partnership that recognizes both – precisely because, the show suggests, there are no expectations that Keith and David, as a gay couple, have to fulfill in order to gain social acceptance. Living already outside that acceptance, they are freer to craft their own terms.

The episode reinforces this with a jumpcut to Brenda, hallucinating Lisa, who is voicing exactly those heteronormative social expectations and is chastising Brenda for not being able to live up to them: "You don't have to worry about this being like my wedding. I had a three-month-old baby when I got married, so it was a much happier event obviously, really joyful. It came very naturally to me, but I was always maternal, unlike you." The scene goes on for some time as they argue about whether or not Brenda is "natural" – that is, conventionally feminine – and Lisa concludes with the statement, "Every time you try to have a nice, normal life you fuck it up. You're never going to have your little happily-ever-after moment. No matter how many white veils you put on, honey, you're just too fucked up for all that. *Maybe you should just try to accept that instead of trying to be something that you're not*" (my emphasis). Brenda, however, is dead set on trying to be "something she's not." When Nate appears, she is distraught, and tells him that "the only way I get to get married in the long white gown is to have my dead baby leaking out of me all day ... you don't really fucking want me. Not that I blame you. Who would?" What Brenda fails to understand, and what makes their marriage a repetition of Nate and Lisa's, is that Nate does, in fact, really want *her* – that is, someone who is unconventional, someone who is "genderqueer." She thinks that he, like everyone else, wants a woman who is traditionally feminine, and doesn't believe that anyone can transgress traditional femininity and still be lovable to a man. And as much as Nate tries to convince her, she cannot hear it, confining them both to the same trap he and Lisa got caught in. When Nate dies of another ruptured AVM ("Ecotone," 5:9), a condition claimed by his doctors to be precipitated by stress, the rest of the season has made it indubitably clear what has symbolically killed him: his inability to craft what Butler calls "a livable life."

THIRD WAVE FEMINIST MEDIA THEORY: WHERE THE GENDER QUEERS ARE

So what does all this have to do with "third wave feminist media theory"? Although we were ignorant of the terms of queer theory at the time, in 1995 when Jennifer Drake and I were struggling to articulate the theoretical terms of third wave feminism in *Third Wave Agenda: Being Feminist, Doing Feminism*, we could only come up with a definition based on hybridity and contradiction, something that sounds a lot like what has become widely established as "queer":

> The lived messiness characteristic of the third wave is what defines it: girls who want to be boys, boys who want to be girls, boys and girls who insist they are both, ... people who are white *and* black, gay *and* straight, masculine *and* feminine, or who are finding ways

to be and name none of the above; successful individuals longing
for community and coalition, communities and coalitions longing
for success; tensions between striving for individual success and
subordinating the individual to the cause; identities formed within
a relentlessly consumer-oriented culture but informed by a politics
that has problems with consumption. (8)

[W]e are products of contradictory definitions and differences
within feminism, beasts of such a hybrid kind that perhaps we
need a different name altogether. (3)

As Rebecca Walker has written, third wave is queer at the core,
questioning binary oppositions in all their manifestations. She does
a "queer third wave" reading when, in an essay on bisexuality, she
writes, "instead of asking what gay and straight people should understand about being bisexual, I think we need to ask what gay, straight,
bisexual, and transgender people need to ask about permanent liberation from divisive thought itself.... Homophobia and heterophobia are
only symptoms of the problem. Let's get to the root. Can you stop
your mind from slicing the world into tiny, seemingly irreconcilable
pieces? Can I?" (486). Third wave is "queer" at its very roots, and
my queer, third wave reading of *Six Feet Under* demonstrates how
the show reveals queer heterosexuality as a kind of existence, but
also shows how, in the current normative structure, that existence
is confined to "a secret room." However, the developing conversations about "queer heterosexuality" would suggest that it may not
be confined to a secret room much longer.

So what is a "queer heterosexual," then, and what keeps people who
identify this way from being, as critics of this recently named identity
have said, "akin to upper-class whites who say they relate to the rap
music of Tupac Shakur or to celebrities like Madonna who practice
Jewish mysticism and sample trendy ethnic fashions" (Curiel) – in
other words, what makes a queer heterosexual something other than
a homosexual wannabe, or someone who is appropriating a discourse
not their own? Calvin Thomas, self-identified queer heterosexual
(married to a woman) and editor of *Straight With a Twist,* points to the
structural, classificatory problems that the heterosexual/homosexual
binary creates when he says "my partner and I are child-free, and want
to remain that way. There are gay couples who want to have kids.
When it comes to breeding and reproduction, where's the straightness

and where's the gayness?" Queer heterosexuality is about the fact that there are people who, while they retain an attraction the "opposite sex," do not then identify with the gender patterns usually associated with those "opposites." And while they may, unlike Thomas, still "want to have kids" or have kids, it does not then follow that the female takes the nurturing role and the male the world conqueror/protector role, or that the female does the emotional labor while the male does the manual labor. Instead, "queer heterosexuality" ends up being an awful lot like what Merri Lisa Johnson searches for in her article on *Six Feet Under*: a "utopian realism" that is "about believing things could be otherwise in this life" (35).

It also sounds a lot like what Helen Boyd describes on her website *(en)Gender*:

> going back to the childhood tomboy I was, the punk rocker who'd opted out of gender, the young adult who was 'sirred' regularly, the crew-cutted coed who got asked out more often by lesbians than by the boys I sought.... But at some point I learned to be more traditionally femme, just in order to date boys ... I wonder if there were guys who were attracted to me because I was kind of dyke-y and I just didn't recognize that because – well, maybe they were waiting for me to ask them out. Or maybe I was so intent that masculine boys were my only option that I didn't see them as potential romantic partners ... what I'm thinking these days is that heterosexuality stifles genderqueerness, while homosexual cultures – for whatever reasons – give people more room to express gender variance... And while it seems like I'm just going to point out again that gender identity and sexual orientation don't go together, what I'm really after is where the genderqueer heterosexuals are.

Since "queer" can allude to both the above as well as other combinations/patterns/identifications, where the genderqueer heterosexuals seem to be, according to *Six Feet Under*, is both everywhere and nowhere, invisible because, as the above quotation shows, they don't necessarily present in a cross-gender way because to do so takes them out of the hetero market.

Yet you can catch glimpses of them in whatever habitats "metrosexuals" frequent, and find them where Arnold Schwarzennegger's infamous "girly men" live: art schools, dance troupes, swim teams, yoga retreats, in jobs like elementary school teaching and nursing.

You can find them in the locker rooms of countless women's sports teams – and in the media's hysterical insistence that female athletes "stay feminine," which is about more than homophobia, as I discuss in more detail in *Bodymakers: A Cultural Anatomy of Women's Body Building*. While it is definitely about homophobia, it is also about "queer heterosexuals," those women who are attracted to men but not traditionally masculine men, who present physically as women but are in their personalities anything but traditionally feminine. You can find them at any workplace that is traditionally "man's work," such as the police department, the logging company, the contractor's site. And while I agree absolutely with Judith Halberstam's injunction in *Female Masculinity* that heterosexual female masculinity "represents an acceptable degree of female masculinity as compared to the excessive masculinity of the dyke," I would argue that we who identify this way also know that this "acceptance" is based on surface signifiers only, rather than our actual identification, which, if visible, would be similarly "unacceptable" (28). The same goes for feminine men who primarily present as masculine. So while there is definitely the functioning of "heterosexual privilege" to shield queer heterosexuals from social rejection, this acceptance is contingent upon our "passing" as traditionally heterosexual – a modified form of the closet.

Lest we go the way of Nate Fisher, I'd say it's time to come out: We're here. We're queer. We're heterosexual.

Get used to it.

NOTES

1. For the Nielsen Media Research numbers for each season, see *CNN Money* (August 2005): http://money.cnn.com/2005/08/26/news/fortune500/ hbo_showtime/; *Media Life Magazine* (June 2003): www.medialifemagazine. com/news2003/jun03/jun02/3_wed/news5wednesday.html; and *Eonline*, 10 January 2002, www.eonline.com/News/Items/0,1,9360,00.html
2. Gregory.
3. See Raymond Williams for this theory of dominant, emergent, and residual cultural forces.
4. As is well known, Ball was scriptwriter for the Academy Award-winning movie *American Beauty* (dir. Sam Mendes, 1999), which kills off its protagonist, Lester Burnham, as soon as he has decided to do what he wants with his life rather than what is expected. This happens to various characters on *Six Feet Under* throughout the series, suggesting that "doing what you want" is more complicated than pop psychology would have it.

REFERENCES

Butler, Judith. *Undoing Gender*. New York: Routledge, 2004.

Boyd, Helen. "Gender Queer Hets." *(en)Gender: Helen Boyd's Journal of Gender and Trans Issues*. http://myhusbandbetty.com/?p=477.

Chambers, Samuel A. "Telepistemology of the Closet; or, the Queer Politics of *Six Feet Under*." *Journal of American Culture* 26, no. 1 (2003): 24–41.

Curiel, Jonathan. "A Straight Embrace of Gay Culture – With a Twist." *San Francisco Chronicle*, 24 June 2001. www.sfgate.com/cgibin/article?file=chronicle/archive/2001.

———. "Revisiting the Closet: Reading Sexuality in *Six Feet Under*." In *Reading "Six Feet Under": TV to Die For*. Ed. Kim Akass and Janet McCabe. London: I.B. Tauris, 2005. 174–88.

Ehrenreich, Barbara. *The Hearts of Men: American Dreams and the Flight from Commitment*. New York: Anchor, 1983.

Gregory, Kia. "Safety in Numbers." www.philadelphiaweekly.com/view.php?id=9333.

Halberstam, Judith. *Female Masculinity*. Durham NC: Duke University Press, 1998.

Heywood, Leslie. *Bodymakers: A Cultural Anatomy of Women's Body Building*. New Brunswick: Rutgers University Press, 1998.

Heywood, Leslie and Jennifer Drake, eds. *Third Wave Agenda: Being Feminist, Doing Feminism*. Minneapolis: University of Minnesota Press, 1997.

Holt, Douglas B. and Craig Thompson. "Man of Action Heroes: How the American Ideology of Manhood Structures Men's Consumption." *Harvard Business School Marketing Research Papers* 3–4 (2002). Social Science Research Network Electronic Paper Collection, www.ssrn.com.

Johnson, Merri Lisa. "From Relationship Autopsy to Romantic Utopia: The Missing Discourse of Egalitarian Marriage on HBO's *Six Feet Under*." *Discourse* 26.3 (2004): 18–40.

——— "Way More Than a Tag Line: HBO, Feminism, and the Question of Difference in Popular Culture." *The Scholar and Feminist Online* 3, no. 1 (2004). www.barnard.edu/sfonline/hbo/intro.htm.

Lancaster, Roger N. *The Trouble with Nature: Sex in Science and Popular Culture*. Berkeley: University of California Press, 2003.

McLeeme, Scott. "Derrida, A Pioneer of Literary Theory Dies." *Chronicle of Higher Education* 51, no. 9 (2004). www.chronicle.com/free/v51/i09/09a00101.htm.

Makow, Hendry. "The Heterosexual Closet." http://savethemales.ca/000652.html.

Powers, Bob. *A Family and Friends' Guide to Sexual Orientation: Bridging the Line between Gay and Straight*. New York: Routledge, 1996.

Thomas, Calvin, ed. *Straight with a Twist: Queer Theory and the Subject of Heterosexuality*. Champaign: University of Illinois Press, 2000.

Walker, Rebecca. "Liberate Yourself From Labels: Bisexuality and Beyond." In *The Women's Movement Today: An Encyclopedia of Third Wave Feminism*, Vol. 2. Ed. Leslie Heywood. Westport, CT: Greenwood Press, 2005. 486.

Williams, Raymond. "Dominant, Residual, and Emergent." *Marxism and Literature*. Oxford: Oxford University Press, 1977. 121–2.

ABOUT THE CONTRIBUTORS

Katherine Frank is a cultural anthropologist, fiction writer, and former exotic dancer. She is the author of *G-Strings and Sympathy: Strip Club Regulars*, an exploration of the motivations and experiences of the heterosexual male customers of strip clubs, and a co-editor of *Flesh for Fantasy: Producing and Consuming Exotic Dance*. She is currently researching the ways that contemporary American couples negotiate sexual exclusivity in marriage, and she is writing an ethnography of contemporary "swinging" couples which explores the links between sexuality and leisure in addition to the cultural meanings of sex, love, and intimacy.

Rhonda Hammer is a Research Scholar with UCLA Center for the Study of Women for 1998–2000. She has taught courses in feminisms, communications, cultural studies, sociology, and video production at York University; University of Toronto; University of Windsor, Canada, Tampere School of Communications, Finland, and most recently USC and UCLA. Hammer is also an educational video producer as well as the author of several articles, chapters and books in the areas of feminism, communications and media literacy. Her book *Anti-feminism and Family Terrorism: A Critical Feminist Perspective* was published in 2003.

Leslie Heywood is a key figure in third wave feminism, having co-edited the landmark collection *Third Wave Agenda: Being Feminist, Doing Feminism*, the first book-length academic treatment of third wave feminism, co-edited with Jennifer Drake. She is also a shaping force in feminist sports studies, with her memoir *Pretty Good for a Girl*, and her sustained analysis of the athletic female body and media representations of female athletes in *Bodymakers: A Cultural Anatomy of Women's Body Building* and *Built to Win: The Female Athlete as Icon*. Heywood is co-editor of *The Women's Movement Today: An Encyclopedia of Third Wave Feminism* (with Jennifer Drake) and author of a recent volume of poetry, *The Proving Grounds*. She is a professor of English and Creative Writing at SUNY–Binghamton.

Merri Lisa Johnson's first book, *Jane Sexes It Up: True Confessions of Feminist Desire*, is a collection of essays by third wave feminists on sexual politics. Her most recent publication is *Flesh for Fantasy: Producing and Consuming Exotic Dance*, co-edited with Katherine Frank and Danielle Egan. She is Director of the Center for Women's Studies and Programs at the University of South Carolina Upstate.

Douglas Kellner is George Kneller Chair in the Philosophy of Education at UCLA and is author of many books on social theory, politics, history, and culture, including *Television and the Crisis of Democracy*, *The Persian Gulf TV War*, *Media Culture*, *Grand Theft 2000*, *Media Spectacle*, and *September 11, Terror War, and the Dangers of the Bush Legacy*. Kellner's website can be viewed at www.gseis.ucla.edu/faculty/kellner/kellner.html.

Candace Moore is a Ph.D. student in Critical Studies in Film, Television, and Digital Media at UCLA, where her work focuses on queer representation in television. She is film editor of the lesbian monthly *Girlfriends*, and writes regularly as a media critic for various print magazines and online sites, including *Curve*, *On Our Backs*, and AfterEllen.com. She co-edited the books *Resistance, Dignity, and Pride: African American Artists in Lost Angeles* and *Revolutions of the Mind: Cultural Studies in the African Diaspora Project 1996–2002*. An essay by Moore and sociologist Kristen Schilt, entitled "Is She Man Enough: Female Masculinities in *The L Word*," appears in *Reading "The L Word"*. Moore holds an MFA in Creative Writing.

Bobby Noble completed his doctorate at York University in 2000, and after teaching on the west coast at the University of Victoria, he has returned to York University to join the new Sexuality Studies program at York University, housed in the School of Women's Studies. His research focuses on sexuality, gender, anti-racist whiteness, and popular culture. In particular, Noble examines the intersections of masculinity, embodiment, and sexuality in the fields of transsexual/transgender studies, queer theory and cultural studies. Noble is the author of *Masculinities without Men?*, selected as a Choice Outstanding Title in 2004; co-editor of *The Drag King Anthology*, a 2004 Lambda Literary Finalist; and has just published a new monograph called *Sons of the Movement: FtMs Risking Incoherence in a Post-Queer Cultural Landscape*.

Carol Siegel, Professor of English and American Studies at Washington State University, Vancouver, is the author of *Lawrence among the Women*, *Male Masochism: Modern Revisions of the Story of Love*, *New Millennial Sexstyles*, and *Goth's Dark Empire*. She co-edits the interdisciplinary journals *Genders* and *Rhizomes* and has published essays on the representation of gender and sexuality in literature, popular music, and film. She lives with her partner in exile in Portland, Oregon, dreaming of their true home, San Francisco.

Lara Stemple is the Director of Graduate Studies at UCLA School of Law, where she directs the school's graduate degree programs and teaches a class on human rights and sexuality. Before working at UCLA, Stemple was the executive director of Stop Prisoner Rape, a national human rights organization whose mission is to end sexual violence in prisons, jails, and immigration detention. As an advocate, Stemple has drafted legislation, lobbied members of Congress and UN delegates, testified before legislative bodies, authored human rights reports, published op-eds, and appeared on national television and radio programs. She is a graduate of Mills College and Harvard Law School.

INDEX